Study Guide

for

Macroeconomics

Tenth Edition

David Colander
Middlebury College

Prepared by

David Colander

Jenifer Gamber

Mc
Graw
Hill
Education

Study Guide for
MACROECONOMICS, Tenth Edition
David Colander

Published by McGraw-Hill Education, 2 Penn Plaza, New York, NY 10121. Copyright © 2017 by McGraw-Hill Education. All rights reserved. Printed in the United States of America. Previous editions © 2013, 2010, and 2008. No part of this publication may be reproduced or distributed in any form or by any means, or stored in a database or retrieval system, without the prior written consent of McGraw-Hill Education, including, but not limited to, in any network or other electronic storage or transmission, or broadcast for distance learning.

Some ancillaries, including electronic and print components, may not be available to customers outside the United States.

This book is printed on acid-free paper.

1 2 3 4 5 6 7 8 9 0 PAT 21 20 19 18 17 16

ISBN 978-1-259-97263-8
MHID 1-259-97263-1

All credits appearing on page or at the end of the book are considered to be an extension of the copyright page.

The Internet addresses listed in the text were accurate at the time of publication. The inclusion of a website does not indicate an endorsement by the authors or McGraw-Hill Education, and McGraw-Hill Education does not guarantee the accuracy of the information presented at these sites.

mheducation.com/highered

Contents

Preface

We wrote this study guide to help you do well in your economics course. We know that even using a great book such as the Colander textbook, studying is not all fun. The reality is: most studying is hard work and a study guide won't change that. Your text and lectures will give you the foundation for doing well. So the first advice we will give you is:

1. Read the textbook.
2. Attend class.

We cannot emphasize that enough. Working through the study guide will not replace the text or lectures; this study guide is designed to help you retain the knowledge from the text and classroom by practicing the tools of economics. It is not an alternative to the book and class; it is **in addition to them**.

Having said that, we should point out that buying this guide isn't enough. You have to *use* it. Really, if it sits on your desk, or even under your pillow, it won't do you any good. Osmosis only works with plants. This study guide should be well worn by the end of the semester—dog-eared pages, scribbles beneath questions, some pages even torn out. It should look used.

WHAT CAN YOU EXPECT FROM THIS BOOK?

This study guide concentrates on the terminology and models in your text. It does not expand upon the material in the textbook; it reinforces it. It primarily serves to give you a good foundation to understanding principles of economics. Your professor has chosen this study guide for you, suggesting that your economics exams are going to focus on this kind of foundational understanding. You should be sure of this: if your professor is going to give you mainly essay exams, or complex questions about applying the foundations (such as the more difficult end-of-chapter questions in your textbook) this study guide will not be enough to ace that exam.

To get an idea of what your exams will be like, ask your professor to take a look at these questions and tell the class whether they are representative of the type of questions that will be on the exam. And if they will differ, how.

HOW SHOULD YOU USE THIS STUDY GUIDE?

As we stated above, this book works best if you have attended class and read the book. Ideally, you were awake during class and took notes, you have read the textbook chapters more than once, and have worked through some of the questions at the end of the chapter. (So, we're optimists.)

Just in case the material in the book isn't fresh in your mind, before turning to this study guide it is a good idea to refresh your memory about the material in the text. To do so:

1. Read through the margin comments in the text; they highlight the main concepts in each chapter.
2. Turn to the last few pages of the chapter and reread the chapter summary.
3. Look through the key terms, making sure they are familiar. (O.K., we're not only optimists, we're wild optimists.)

Even if you do not do the above, working through the questions in the study guide will help to tell you whether you really do know the material in the textbook chapters.

STRUCTURE OF THE STUDY GUIDE

This study guide has two main components: (1) a chapter-by-chapter review and (2) pretests based upon groups of chapters.

Chapter-by-chapter review
Each chapter has eight elements:

1. A chapter at a glance: A brief exposition and discussion of the learning objectives for the chapter.
2. Short-answer questions keyed to the learning objectives.
3. A test of matching the terms to their definitions.

4. Problems and applications.
5. Multiple choice questions.
6. Potential essay questions
7. Answers to all questions.

Each chapter presents the sections in the order that we believe is most beneficial to you. Here is how we suggest you use them:

Chapter at a Glance: These should jog your memory about the text and lecture. If you don't remember ever seeing the material before, you should go back and reread the textbook chapter. Remember, reading a chapter when you are thinking about a fantasy date is almost the same as not having read the chapter at all.

Short-Answer Questions: The short-answer questions will tell you if you are familiar with the learning objectives. Try to answer each within the space below each question. Don't just read the questions and assume you can write an answer. Actually writing an answer will reveal your weaknesses. If you can answer them all perfectly, great. But, quite honestly, we don't expect you to be able to answer them all perfectly. We only expect you to be able to sketch out an answer.

Of course, some other questions are important to know. For example, if there is a question about the economic decision rule and you don't remember that it excludes sunk costs and benefits, you need more studying. So the rule is: Know the central ideas of the chapter; be less concerned about the specific presentation of those central ideas.

After you have sketched out all your answers, check them with those at the end of the chapter and review those that you didn't get right. Since each question is based upon a specific learning objective in the text, for those you didn't get right, you may want to return to the textbook to review the material covering that learning objective.

Match the Terms and Concepts to Their Definitions: Since the definitions are listed, you should get most of these right. The best way to match these is to read the definition first, and then find the term on the left that it defines. If you are not sure of the matching term, circle that definition and move on to the next one. At the end, return to the remaining definitions and look at the remaining terms to complete the matches. After completing

this part, check your answers with those in the back of the chapter and figure out what percent you got right. If that percent is below the grade you want to get on your exam, try to see why you missed the ones you did and review those terms and concepts in the textbook.

Problems and Applications: Now it's time to take on the problems in the chapter. These problems are generally more difficult than the short-answer questions; they focus on numerical and graphical aspects of the chapter.

Working through problems is perhaps one of the best ways to practice your understanding of economic principles. Even if you are expecting a multiple choice exam, working through these problems will give you a good handle on using the concepts in each chapter.

If you expect a multiple choice exam with no problems, you can work through these fairly quickly, making sure you understand the concepts being tested. If you will have a test with problems and exercises, make sure you can answer each of these questions accurately.

Work out the answers to all the problems in the space provided before checking them against the answers in the back of the chapter. Where our answers differ from yours, check to find out why.

Most of the problems are objective and have only one answer. A few are interpretative and have many answers. We recognize that some questions can be answered in different ways than we did. If you cannot reconcile your answer with ours, check with your professor. Once you are at this stage—worrying about different interpretations—you're ahead of most students and, most likely, prepared for the exam.

Multiple Choice Questions: The next exercise in each chapter is the multiple choice test. It serves to test the breadth of your knowledge of the text material. Multiple choice questions are not the final arbiters of your understanding. They are, instead, a way of determining whether you have read the book and generally understood the material.

Take this test after having worked through the other questions. Give the answer that most closely corresponds to the answer presented in your text. If you can answer these questions you should be ready for the multiple choice part of your exam.

Work through all the questions in the test before grading yourself. Looking up the answer before you try to answer the questions is a poor way to study. For a multiple choice exam, the percent you answer correctly will be a good predictor of how well you will do on the test.

You can foul up on multiple choice questions in two ways—you can know too little and you can know too much. The answer to knowing too little is obvious: Study more—that is, read the chapters more carefully (and maybe more often). The answer to knowing too much is more complicated. Our suggestions for students who know too much is not to ask themselves "What is the answer?" but instead to ask "What is the answer the person writing the question wants?" Since, with these multiple choice questions, the writer of many of the questions is the textbook author, ask yourself: "What answer would the textbook author want me to give?" Answering the questions in this way will stop you from going too deeply into them and trying to see nuances that aren't supposed to be there.

For the most part questions in this study guide are meant to be straightforward. There may be deeper levels at which other answers could be relevant, but searching for those deeper answers will generally get you in trouble and not be worth the cost.

If you are having difficulty answering a multiple choice question, make your best guess. Once you are familiar with the material, even if you don't know the answer to a question you can generally make a reasonable guess. What point do you think the writer of the question wanted to make with the question? Figuring out that point and then thinking of incorrect answers may be a way for you to eliminate wrong answers and then choose among the remaining options.

Notice that the answers at the end of the chapter are not just the lettered answers. We have provided an explanation for each answer — why the right one is right and why some of the other choices are wrong. If you miss a question, read that rationale carefully. If you are not convinced, or do not follow the reasoning, go to the relevant material in the textbook . If you are still not convinced, see the caveat on the next page.

Potential Essay Questions: These questions provide yet another opportunity to test your understanding of what you have learned. Answer-ing these questions will be especially helpful if you expect these types of questions on the exams. We have only sketched the beginning of an answer to these. This beginning should give you a good sense of the direction to go in your answer, but be aware that on an exam a more complete answer will be required.

Questions on Appendixes: In the chapters we have included a number of questions on the text appendixes. To separate these questions from the others, the letter A precedes the question number. They are for students who have been assigned the appendixes. If you have not been assigned them (and you have not read them on your own out of your great interest in economics) you can skip these.

Answers to All Questions: The answers to all questions appear at the end of each chapter. They begin on a new page so that you can tear out the answers and more easily check your answers against ours. We cannot emphasize enough that the best way to study is to answer the questions yourself first, and then check out our answers. Just looking at the questions and our answers may tell you what the answers are but will not give you the chance to see where your knowledge of the material is weak.

Pretests

Most class exams cover more than one chapter. To prepare you for such an exam, we provide multiple choice pretests for groups of chapters. These pretests consist of 22-30 multiple choice questions from the selected group of chapters. These questions are identical to earlier questions so if you have done the work, you should do well on these. We suggest you complete the entire exam before grading yourself.

We also suggest taking these under test conditions. Specifically,

Use a set time period to complete the exam.
Sit at a hard chair at a desk with good lighting.

Each answer will tell you the chapter on which the question is based, so if you did not cover one of the chapters in the text for your class, don't worry if you get that question wrong. If you get a number of questions wrong from the chapters your class has covered, worry.

There is another way to use these pretests that we hesitate to mention, but we're realists so we will. That way is to forget doing the chapter-by-chapter work and simply take the pretests. Go back and review the material you get wrong.

However you use the pretests, if it turns out that you consistently miss questions from the same chapter, return to your notes from the lecture and reread your textbook chapters.

A FINAL WORD OF ADVICE

That's about it. If you use it, this study guide can help you do better on the exam by giving you the opportunity to use the terms and models of economics. However, we reiterate one last time: The best way to do well in a course is to attend every class and read every chapter in the text as well as work through the chapters in this study guide. Start early and work consistently. Do not do all your studying the night before the exam.

THANKS AND A CAVEAT

We and our friends went through this book more times than we want to remember. Pam Bodenhorn did an outstanding job typesetting the entire book and was patient with quirky programs and quirky authors. We also had some superb students who worked on the study guide, editing and proofing the questions. They include Jenna Danielle Marotta and Christian Alexander Schmitt. (Our sincere thanks go to them for doing so.) Despite our best efforts, there is always a chance that there's a correct answer other than the one the book tells you is the correct answer, or even that the answer the book gives is wrong. If you find a mistake, and it is a small problem about a number or an obvious mistake, assume the error is typographical. If that is not the case, and you still think another answer is the correct one, write up an alternative rationale and e-mail Professor Colander the question and the alternative rationale. Professor Colander's e-mail is:

colander@middlebury.edu.

When he gets your email he will send you a note either thanking you immensely for finding another example of his fallibility, or explaining why we disagree with you. If you're the first one to have pointed out an error he will also send you a copy of one of his latest books—just what you always wanted, right?

David Colander
Jenifer Gamber

ECONOMICS AND ECONOMIC REASONING

CHAPTER AT A GLANCE

1a. Economics is the study of how human beings coordinate their wants and desires, given the decision-making mechanisms, social customs, and political realities of the society.

1b. Three central coordination problems any economy must solve are:
- What, and how much, to produce.
- How to produce it.
- For whom to produce it.

Most economic coordination problems involve scarcity.

2. Microeconomics considers economic reasoning from the viewpoint of individuals and builds up; macroeconomics considers economic reasoning from the aggregate and builds down.

Microeconomics (micro) → concerned with some particular segment of the economy.
Macroeconomics (macro) → concerned with the entire economy.

3. If the marginal benefits of doing something exceed the marginal costs, do it. If the marginal costs of doing something exceed the marginal benefits, don't do it. This is known as the economic decision rule.

You really need to think in terms of the marginal, or "extra" benefits (MB) and marginal, or "extra" costs (MC) of a course of action. Also, ignore sunk costs.

Economic decision rule:
If MB>MC→<u>Do more of it</u> because "it's worth it."

If MB<MC→<u>Do less of it</u> because "it's not worth it."

NOTE: The symbol "→" means "implies" or "logically follows."

4. Opportunity cost is the basis of cost/benefit reasoning; it is the benefit forgone, or the cost

of the next-best alternative to the activity you've chosen. That cost should be less than the benefit of what you've chosen.

Opportunity cost → "What must be given up in order to get something else."

5. Economic reality is controlled by economic forces, social forces, and political forces.

What happens in a society can be seen as the reaction and interaction of these 3 forces.

- *Economic forces: Market forces.*

- *Social and cultural forces: Social and cultural forces can prevent economic forces from becoming market forces.*

- *Political and legal forces: Political and legal forces affect decisions too.*

6. Economic insights are based on generalizations about the workings of an abstract economy. These are called theories.

Precepts are based on theorems combined with knowledge of the real world and value judgments.

7a. <u>Positive economics</u> is the study of what is, and how the economy works.

Deals with "what is" (objective analysis).

7b. <u>Normative economics</u> is the study of what the goals of the economy should be.

Deals with "what ought to be" (subjective).

7c. The <u>art of economics</u> is the application of the knowledge learned in positive economics to the achievement of the goals determined in normative economics.

The art of economics is sometimes referred to as "policy economics."

SHORT-ANSWER QUESTIONS

1. How does microeconomics differ from macro-economics? Give an example of a macroeconomic issue and a microeconomic issue.

   Micro → Concerned with some particular segment of the economy (

   Macro → Concerned with the entire economy

2. What are the three central problems that every economy must solve?

   - What, and how much, to produce
   - How to produce it
   - From whom to produce it

3. What is scarcity? What are two elements that comprise scarcity? How do they affect relative scarcity?

   Scarcity - limited availability of a commodity

   lack of resources and demand

4. State the economic decision rule.

   $\int f\ MB > MC →$ Do more of it
   "worth it"

   $\int f\ MB > MC →$ Don't do it
   "Not worth it"

5. Define opportunity cost.

   "What must be given up in order to get something else"

6. What is the importance of opportunity cost to economic reasoning?

   The cost should be less than the benefit of what you've chosen

7. What is an economic force? What are the forces that can keep an economic force from becoming a market force?

   Factors that help to determine the competitiveness of the environment

   Social and cultural forces

8. Define positive economics, normative economics, and the art of economics. How do they relate to one another?

   Pos. economics - Study of what is and how the economy works

   Norm. economics - Study of what the goals of the economy should be.

   Cause and affect

MATCHING THE TERMS

Match the terms to their definitions

l	1.	art of economics	
c	2.	economic decision rule	
	3.	economic force	
	4.	economic model	
	5.	economic policy	
	6.	economic principle	
	7.	economics	
q	8.	efficiency	
	9.	experimental economics	
	10.	implicit cost	
	11.	invisible hand	
	12.	invisible hand theorem	
i	13.	macroeconomics	
c	14.	marginal benefit	
c	15.	marginal cost	
	16.	market force	
	17.	microeconomics	
s	18.	normative economics	
	19.	political forces	
f	20.	opportunity cost	
g	21.	positive economics	
	22.	precept	
	23.	social forces	
k	24.	scarcity	
t	25.	sunk cost	
w	26.	theorem	

a. Additional benefit above what you've already derived.

b. Additional cost above what you've already incurred.

c. If benefits exceed costs, do it. If costs exceed benefits, don't.

d. The study of individual choice, and how that choice is influenced by economic forces.

e. Necessary reactions to scarcity.

f. The benefit forgone, or the cost, of the next-best alternative to the activity you've chosen.

g. The study of what is, and how the economy works.

h. The insight that a market economy, through the price mechanism, will allocate resources efficiently.

i. The study of the economy as a whole.

j. The study of how human beings coordinate their wants.

k. Goods available are too few to satisfy individuals' desires.

l. The application of the knowledge learned in positive economics to the achievement of the goals determined in normative economics.

m. An economic force that is given relatively free rein by society to work through the market.

n. The price mechanism.

o. A framework that places the generalized insights of theory in a more specific contextual setting.

p. A commonly-held economic insight stated as a law or general assumption.

q. Achieving a goal as cheaply as possible.

r. Action taken by government to influence economic actions.

s. Study of what the goals of the economy should be.

t. Cost that has already been incurred and cannot be recovered.

u. A branch of economics that studies the economy through controlled laboratory experiments.

v. Rules that conclude that a particular course of action is preferable.

w. Propositions that are logically true based on the assumptions in a model.

x. Forces that guide individual actions even though those actions may not be in an individual's self interest.

y. Legal directives that direct individuals' actions.

z. costs associated with a decision that often aren't included in normal accounting costs.

PROBLEMS AND APPLICATIONS

1. State what happens to scarcity for each good in the following situations:

   a. New storage technology allows college dining services to keep peaches from rotting for a longer time. (Good: peaches).

   b. More students desire to live in single-sex dormitories. No new single-sex dormitories are established. (Good: single-sex dormitory rooms).

2. State as best you can:

   a. The opportunity cost of going out on a date tonight that was scheduled last Wednesday.

   b. The opportunity cost of breaking the date for tonight that you made last Wednesday.

   c. The opportunity cost of working through this study guide.

3. Assume you have purchased a $15,000 car. The salesperson has offered you a maintenance contract covering all major repairs for the next 3 years, with some exclusions, for $750.

   a. What is the sunk cost of purchasing the maintenance contract? Should this sunk cost be considered when deciding to purchase a maintenance contract?

   b. What is the opportunity cost of purchasing that maintenance contract?

   c. What information would you need to make a decision based on the economic decision rule?

   d. Based upon that information how would you make your decision?

4. State whether the following is a theorem or precept:

   a. The price mechanism tends to allocate resources efficiently.

   b. Because people find the selling of babies repugnant, government should ban their sale because the invisible hand will not be efficient.

5. State for each of the following whether it is an example of political forces, social forces, or economic forces at work:

   a. Warm weather arrives and more people take Sunday afternoon drives. As a result, the price of gasoline rises.

   b. In some states, liquor cannot be sold before noon on Sunday.

   c. Minors cannot purchase cigarettes.

● MULTIPLE CHOICE

Circle the one best answer for each of the following questions:

1. Economic reasoning:
   a. provides a framework with which to approach questions.
   b. provides correct answers to just about every question.
   c. is only used by economists.
   d. should only be applied to economic business matters.

2. Scarcity could be reduced if:
   a. individuals work less and want fewer consumption goods.
   b. individuals work more and want fewer consumption goods.
   c. world population grows and world production remains the same.
   d. innovation comes to a halt.

3. In the textbook, the author focuses on coordination rather than scarcity as the central point of the definition of economics because:
   a. economics is not really about scarcity.
   b. scarcity involves coercion, and the author doesn't like coercion.
   c. the author wants to emphasize that the quantity of goods and services depends upon human action and the ability to coordinate that human action.
   d. the concept "scarcity" does not fit within the institutional structure of the economy.

4. In the U.S. economy, who is in charge of organizing and coordinating overall economic activities?
   a. Government.
   b. Corporations.
   c. No one.
   d. Consumers.

5. You bought stock A for $10 and stock B for $50. The price of each is currently $20. Assuming no tax issues, which should you sell if you need money?
   a. Stock A.
   b. Stock B.
   c. There is not enough information to tell which to sell.
   d. You should sell an equal amount of both.

6. In deciding whether to go to lectures in the final weeks the semester, you should:
   a. include tuition as part of the cost of that decision.
   b. not include tuition as part of the cost of that decision.
   c. include a portion of tuition as part of the cost of that decision.
   d. only include tuition if you paid it rather than your parents.

7. In making economic decisions you should consider:
   a. marginal costs and marginal benefits.
   b. marginal costs and average benefits.
   c. average costs and average benefits.
   d. total costs and total benefits, including past costs and benefits.

8. According to the economic decision rule, if MB>MC, one should:
   a. do less.
   b. do more.
   c. do nothing
   d. exit the market.

9. In arriving at a decision, a good economist would say that:
   a. one should consider only total costs and total benefits.
   b. one should consider only marginal costs and marginal benefits.
   c. after one has considered marginal costs and benefits, one should integrate the social and moral implications and reconsider those costs and benefits.
   d. after considering the marginal costs and benefits, one should make the decision on social and moral grounds.

10. In making decisions economists primarily use:
    a. monetary costs.
    b. opportunity costs.
    c. benefit costs.
    d. dollar costs.

11. The opportunity cost of reading Chapter 1 of a 38-chapter text:
    a. is about 1/38 of the price you paid for the book because the chapter is about 1/38 of the book.

b. is zero since you have already paid for the book.

c. has nothing to do with the price you paid for the book.

d. is 1/38 the price of the book plus 1/38 the price of tuition for the course.

12. Rationing devices that our society uses include:
   a. the invisible hand only.
   b. the invisible hand and social forces only.
   c. the invisible hand and political forces only.
   d. the invisible hand, social forces, and political forces.

13. If at Female College there are significantly more females than males (and there are not a significant number of gays or off-campus dating opportunities), economic forces:
   a. will likely push for females to pay for dinners on dates.
   b. will likely push for males to pay for dinners on dates.
   c. will likely push for neither to pay for dinners on dates.
   d. are irrelevant to this issue. Everyone knows that the males always should pay.

14. Individuals are prohibited from practicing medicine without a license. The legal prohibition is a direct example of:
   a. the invisible hand.
   b. social forces.
   c. political forces.
   d. market forces.

15. Which of the following is most likely an example of a microeconomic topic?
   a. The effect of a flood in the Midwest on the price of bottled water.
   b. How a government policy will affect inflation.
   c. The relationship between unemployment and inflation.
   d. Why an economy goes into a recession.

16. Which of the following is most strongly an example of a macroeconomic topic?
   a. The effect of a frost on the Florida orange crop.
   b. Wages of cross-country truckers.

   c. How the unemployment and inflation rates are related.
   d. How income is distributed in the United States.

17. What best states the difference between theorems and precepts?
   a. Theorems are based on models while precepts add knowledge of real-world institutions and judgment.
   b. Theorems are based on models while precepts are not.
   c. Theorems lead to economic principles while precepts lead to economic insights.
   d. Theorems are not based on real-world observations while precepts are.

18. The statement, "The distribution of income should be left to the market," is:
   a. a positive statement.
   b. a normative statement.
   c. an art-of-economics statement.
   d. an objective statement.

19. "Given certain conditions, the market achieves efficient results" is an example of:
   a. a positive statement.
   b. a normative statement.
   c. an art-of-economics statement.
   d. a subjective statement.

● POTENTIAL ESSAY QUESTIONS

You may also see essay questions similar to the "Problems & Applications" exercises.

1. Respond to the following statement: "Theories are of no use to me because they are not very practical. All I need are the facts because they speak for themselves."

2. The United States is one of the wealthiest nations on earth, yet our fundamental economic problem is scarcity. How can this be?

3. Does economics help teach us how to approach problems, or does it give us a set of answers to problems?

━━━━ **ANSWERS** ━━━━

SHORT-ANSWER QUESTIONS

1. Microeconomics is the study of how individual choice is influenced by economic forces. Microeconomics focuses on a particular segment of the economy, like how a specific market price and quantity sold is determined. Macroeconomics is the study of the economy as a whole. It considers the problems of inflation, unemployment, business cycles, and growth.

2. The three central problems that every economy must solve are (1) what and how much to produce, (2) how to produce it, and (3) for whom to produce it.

3. Scarcity occurs when there are not enough goods available to satisfy individuals' desires. Scarcity has two elements: our wants and our means of fulfilling those wants. Since each of these two elements can change, relative scarcity can also change. If we can reduce our wants, relative scarcity will be reduced. Likewise if we can increase our efforts to produce more goods or if technological changes allow people to produce more using the same resources, relative scarcity will be reduced.

4. If the marginal benefits of doing something exceed the marginal costs, do it. If the marginal costs of doing something exceed the marginal benefits, don't do it.

5. Opportunity cost is the benefit forgone by undertaking an activity. That is, it is the benefit forgone of the next best alternative to the activity you have chosen. Otherwise stated, it is what must be given up in order to get something else.

6. Opportunity cost is the basis of cost/benefit economic reasoning. It takes into account benefits of all other options, and converts these alternative benefits into costs of the decision you're now making. In economic reasoning, opportunity cost will be less than the benefit of what you have chosen.

7. An economic force is the necessary reaction to scarcity. All scarce goods must be rationed in some way. If an economic force is allowed to work through the market, that economic force becomes a market force. Social and political forces can keep economic forces from becoming market forces.

8. Positive economics is the study of what is and how the economy works. Normative economics is the study of what the goals of the economy should be. The art of economics is the application of the knowledge learned in positive economics to the achievement of the goals determined in normative economics.

━━━━ **ANSWERS** ━━━━

MATCHING

1-l; 2-c; 3-e; 4-o; 5-r; 6-p; 7-j; 8-q; 9-u; 10-z; 11-n; 12-h; 13-i; 14-a; 15-b; 16-m; 17-d; 18-s; 19-y; 20-f; 21-g; 22-v; 23-x; 24-k; 25-t; 26-w.

━━━━ **ANSWERS** ━━━━

PROBLEMS AND APPLICATIONS

1. **a.** Scarcity will fall because fewer peaches will rot.

    b. Scarcity of single-sex dorm rooms will rise since the number of students desiring single-sex dorm rooms has risen, but the number available has not.

2. **a.** The opportunity cost of going out on a date tonight that was scheduled last Wednesday is the benefit forgone of the best alternative. If my best alternative was to study for an economics exam, it would be the increase in my exam grade that I would have otherwise gotten had I studied. Many answers are possible.

    b. The opportunity cost of breaking the date for tonight that I made last Wednesday is the benefit forgone of going out on that date. It would be all the fun I would have had on that date. Other answers are possible.

c. The opportunity cost of working through this study guide is the benefit forgone of the next-best alternative to studying. It could be the increase in the grade I would have received by studying for another exam, or the money I could have earned if I were working at the library. Many answers are possible.

3. a. The sunk cost of purchasing the maintenance contract is the $15,000 cost of the car because it is a cost that has already been incurred and cannot be recovered. Sunk costs should always be ignored when making a current decision because only marginal costs are relevant to the current decision.

b. The opportunity cost of purchasing the maintenance contract is the benefit I could receive by spending that $750 on something else, such as a moon roof.

c. I would need to know the benefit of the maintenance contract to assess whether the cost of $750 is worthwhile.

d. For me the benefit of the maintenance contract is the expected cost of future repairs that would be covered and the peace of mind of knowing that future repairs are covered by the contract. The cost is the opportunity cost of using the $750 in another way. Notice that the cost of a decision includes opportunity costs only; it does not include sunk costs because they are not relevant. If the benefit exceeds the cost, do it. If the cost exceeds the benefit, do not do it.

4. a. This is a theorem since it is the logical conclusion of a model.

b. This is a precept since it adds knowledge of social mores to the invisible hand theorem.

5. a. This is an example of an economic force.

b. This is an example of a political force. Some states have laws, called blue laws, against selling liquor on Sundays altogether or selling it before noon.

c. This is an example of a political force. This is a federal law.

━━━ ANSWERS ━━━

MULTIPLE CHOICE

1. a The textbook author clearly believes that economic reasoning applies to just about everything. This eliminates c and d. He also carefully points out that it is not the only reasoning that can be used; hence b does not fit. So the correct answer must be a.

2. b The author states that the problem of scarcity depends upon our wants and our means of fulfilling those wants. An implication of this is that scarcity could be reduced if individuals worked more and/or wanted less.

3. c The author emphasizes the human action reason for focusing on coordination. He explicitly points out that scarcity is important, but that the concept of coordination is broader.

4. c The invisible hand of the market coordinates the activities and is a composite of many individuals rather than just any one individual. If you were tempted to say b, corporations, your instincts are right, but the "overall" eliminated that as a possible answer.

5. c As discussed in the textbook, in making economic decisions you consider that only costs from this point on are relevant; historical costs are sunk costs and therefore have no relevance. Since the prices of the stocks are currently the same, it doesn't matter which you sell.

6. b As discussed in the text, in economic decisions, you only look at costs from this point on; sunk costs are sunk costs, so tuition can be forgotten. Economic decisions focus on forward-looking marginal costs and marginal benefits.

7. a The economic decision rule is "If marginal benefits exceed marginal costs, do it." The relevant benefits and relevant costs to be considered are *marginal* (additional) costs and *marginal* benefits. The answer d is definitely ruled out by the qualifying phrase referring to past benefits and costs. Thus, only a is correct.

8. b   The economic decision rule is "If marginal benefits exceed marginal costs, do it."

9. c   Economists use a framework of costs and benefits initially, but then later they add the social and moral implications to their conclusions. Adding these can change the estimates of costs and benefits, and in doing so can change the result of economic analysis, so there is an integration between the two. (This was a hard question that required careful reading of the text to answer correctly.)

10. b   Opportunity costs include measures of nonmonetary costs. The other answers either do not include all the costs that an economist would consider, or are simply two words put together. The opportunity costs include the benefit forgone by undertaking an activity and should always be included in measuring marginal costs.

11. c   The correct answer is that it has nothing to do with the price you paid since that is a sunk cost that has already been paid, so a and d are wrong. The opportunity cost is not zero, however, since there are costs of reading the book. The primary opportunity cost of reading the book is the value of the time you're spending on it, which is determined by what you could be doing with that time otherwise.

12. d   All of these are rationing devices. The invisible hand works through the market and thus is focused on in economics. However, the others also play a role in determining what people want, either through legal means or through social control.

13. a   if there are significantly more of one gender than another, dates with that group must be rationed out among the other group. Economic forces will be pushing for the group in excess quantity supplied (in this case women) to pay. Economic forces may be pushing in that direction even though historical forces may push in the opposite direction. Thus, even if males pay because of social forces, economic forces will be pushing for females to pay.

14. c   As discussed in the text, laws are political forces.

15. a   Macroeconomics is concerned with inflation, unemployment, business cycles and growth. Microeconomics is the study of individuals and individual markets.

16. c   Macroeconomics is concerned with inflation, unemployment, business cycles, and growth. Microeconomics is the study of individuals and individual markets. The distribution of income is a micro topic because it is concerned with the distribution of income among individuals.

17. a   See the definitions of both terms in the text. Since models are informed by real-world observations, d is not correct.

18. b   This could be either a normative or an art-of-economics statement, depending on whether there is an explicit "given the way the real-world economy operates." This qualifier is not there, so "normative" is the preferable answer. After all, normative economics deals with what *should* be.

19. a   As discussed in the text, this is a positive statement. It is a statement about *what is,* not about what should be.

ANSWERS

POTENTIAL ESSAY QUESTIONS

The following are annotated answers. They indicate the general idea behind the answer.

1. Theories are practical because they are generalizations based on real-world observations or facts. They enable us to predict and to explain real-world economic behavior. Because they are generalizations, they enable us to avoid unnecessary details or facts. The drawback, however, is that because they are generalizations, at times there will be exceptions to the prediction we would generally expect to observe.

    Facts, on the other hand, do not always speak for themselves. One can often be overwhelmed by a large set of data or facts. Not until one systematically arranges, interprets, and generalizes upon facts, tying them together, and distilling out a theory (general statement) related to those facts, do they take on any real meaning. In short, theory and facts are inseparable in the scientific process because theory gives meaning to facts and facts check the validity of theory.

2. The United States is still faced with scarcity because we are unable to have as much as we would like to have. Our resources (as vast as they are) are still scarce relative to the amount of goods and services we would like to have (indeed, our wants appear to be unlimited).

3. Economics is a methodology, or an approach to how we think about the world. It does not come to us equipped with a whole set of solutions to complex real-world problems. However, it may help shed some light on the complexities of real-world issues and thus help us to find solutions.

THE PRODUCTION POSSIBILITY MODEL, TRADE, AND GLOBALIZATION

CHAPTER AT A GLANCE

1. The production possibility curve shows the trade-off between two things.

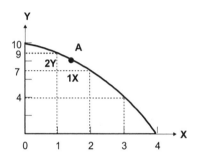

   The slope tells you the opportunity cost of good X in terms of good Y. In this particular graph you have to give up 2 Y to get 1 X when you're around point A.

2. In order to get more of something, generally one must give up ever-increasing quantities of something else.

   The production possibility curve shown in #1 demonstrates this principle.

3. The production possibility curve is bowed outward, meaning that in order to get more and more of something, we must give up ever-increasing quantities of something else.

   The outward bow of the production possibility curve reflects that when more and more of a good is produced, we must use resources whose comparative advantage is in the production of the other good.

4. Countries can consume more if they specialize in those goods for which they have a comparative advantage and then trade.

Country A can produce 30Y or 10X, or any combination thereof, while Country B can produce 20Y or 30X or any combination thereof. Since country A has a comparative advantage in Y, it should produce 30Y and Country B should produce 30X. If they divide the goods equally, each can consume 15 units of each good, or point C in the graph below. Each can consume beyond its individual production possibilities.

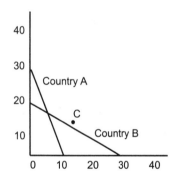

5. Globalization is a response to the forces of the law of one price.

   The law of one price states that wages of workers in one country will not differ significantly from the wages of equal workers in countries with similar institutions.

   Remember: all jobs cannot be outsourced. Every country has, by definition, a comparative advantage in the production of some good if the other country has a comparative advantage in the production of another good.

   See also, Appendix: "Graphish: The Language of Graphs."

● SHORT-ANSWER QUESTIONS

1. Design a grade production possibility curve for studying economics and English, and show how it demonstrates the concept of opportunity cost.

2. State the principle that is the basis of a production possibility curve that is bowed out.

3. What does the production possibility curve look like if opportunity cost is constant?

4. What happens to the production possibility curve when people specialize and trade? Why do specialization and trade make individuals better off?

5. What is the positive effect of globalization for firms? What is the negative effect?

6. State the law of one price. How is it related to globalization and U.S. companies moving production to foreign countries?

MATCHING THE TERMS
Match the terms to their definitions

___ 1. comparative advantage

___ 2. efficiency

___ 3. globalization

___ 4. inefficiency

___ 5. laissez-faire

___ 6. law of one price

___ 7. production possibility curve

___ 8. production possibility table

___ 9. productive efficiency

a. A curve measuring the maximum combination of outputs that can be obtained from a given number of inputs.

b. Achieving as much output as possible from a given amount of inputs.

c. An economic policy of leaving coordination of individuals' actions to the market.

d. Table that lists a choice's opportunity cost by summarizing alternative outputs that can be achieved with your inputs.

e. The advantage that attaches to a resource when that resource is better suited to the production of one good than to the production of another good.

f. Wages of (equal) workers in one country will not differ significantly from wages in another institutionally similar country.

g. Getting less output from inputs that, if devoted to some other activity, would produce more output.

h. Achieving a goal with as few inputs as possible.

i. The increasing integration of economies, cultures, and institutions across the world.

PROBLEMS AND APPLICATIONS

1. Suppose a restaurant has the following production possibility table:

Resources devoted to pizza in % of total	Output of pizza in pies per week	Resources devoted to spaghetti in % of total	Output of spaghetti in bowls per week
100	50	0	0
80	40	20	10
60	30	40	17
40	20	60	22
20	10	80	25
0	0	100	27

a. Plot the restaurant's production possibility curve. Put output of pizza in pies on the horizontal axis.

b. What happens to the trade-off between making spaghetti and pizzas as the number of bowls of spaghetti made increases?

c. What would happen to the production possibility curve if the restaurant found a way to toss and cook pizzas faster?

d. What would happen to the production possibility curve if the restaurant bought new stoves and ovens that cooked both pizzas and spaghetti faster?

2. Suppose Ecoland has the following production possibility table:

% resources devoted to production of guns	Number of guns	% resources devoted to production of butter	Pounds of butter
100	50	0	0
80	40	20	5
60	30	40	10
40	20	60	15
20	10	80	20
0	0	100	25

a. Plot the production possibility curve for the production of guns and butter. Put the number of guns on the horizontal axis.

b. What is the per unit opportunity cost of increasing the production of guns from 20 to 30? From 40 to 50?

c. What happens to the opportunity cost of producing guns as the production of guns increases?

d. What is the per unit opportunity cost of increasing the production of butter from 10 to 15? From 20 to 25?

e. What happens to the opportunity cost of producing butter as the production of butter increases?

f. Given this production possibility curve, is producing 26 guns and 13 pounds of butter possible?

g. Is producing 34 guns and 7 pounds of butter possible? Is it efficient?

3. Using the following production possibility tables and using production possibility curves, show how the United States and Japan would be better off specializing in the production of either food or machinery and then trading rather than producing both food and machinery themselves and not trading.

| United States Production per year | | Japan Production per year | |
Food (tons)	Machinery (1000 units)	Food (tons)	Machinery (1000 units)
10	0	12.5	0
8	5	10.0	1
6	10	7.5	2
4	15	5.0	3
2	20	2.5	4
0	25	0.0	5

4. Assume that France can produce wine for 25 euros per bottle and can produce butter for 5 euros per pound. Assume that Italy can produce wine for 16 euros per bottle and butter for 10 euros per pound.

a. In terms of pounds of butter, what is the opportunity cost of producing wine in each country?

b. Who has the comparative advantage in producing butter?

c. To obtain the greatest combined production possibilities, which country should specialize in wine and which should specialize in butter?

d. What is likely to happen to each country's consumption possibilities if each specializes in the good for which it has a comparative advantage and then trades?

⬤ MULTIPLE CHOICE

Circle the one best answer for each of the following questions:

1. If the opportunity cost of good X in terms of good Y is 2Y, so you'll have to give up 2Y to get one X, the production possibility curve would look like:

a. a.
b. b.
c. c.
d. a, b and c.

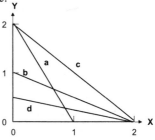

2. If the opportunity cost of good X in terms of good Y is 2Y, so you'll have to give up 2Y to get one X, the production possibility curve would look like:

a. a.
b. b.
c. c.
d. d.

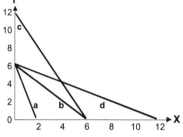

3. If the opportunity cost of good X in terms of good Y is 2Y, so you'll have to give up 2Y to get one X, the production possibility curve could look like:

a. A only.
b. B only.
c. C only.
d. A, B, or C.

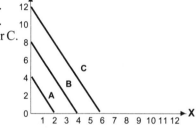

4. If the opportunity cost is constant for all combinations, the production possibility curve will look like:

a. a.
b. b.
c. c.
d. d.

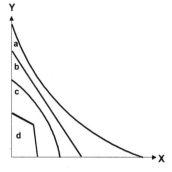

5. If the principle that in order to get more of something one must give up ever-increasing quantities of something else applies at all points, using the graph for Question #4, the production possibility curve looks like:

a. a.
b. b.
c. c.
d. d.

6. Given the accompanying production possibility curve, when you're moving from point C to point B the opportunity cost of butter in terms of guns is:

a. 1/3.
b. 1.
c. 2.
d. 3/2.

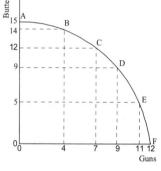

7. In the graph for question 6, in the range of points between A and B there is:

a. a high opportunity cost of guns in terms of butter.

b. a low opportunity cost of guns in terms of butter.

c. no opportunity cost of guns in terms of butter.

d. a high monetary cost of guns in terms of butter.

8. In the accompanying production possibility diagram, point A would be:

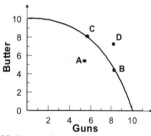

a. an efficient point.
b. a superefficient point.
c. an inefficient point.
d. a non-attainable point.

9. The efficiency of producing computers is increasing each year. In the graphs on the top of the next page, which of the four arrows would demonstrate the appropriate shifting of the production possibility curve?

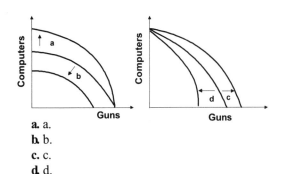

a. a.

b. b.

c. c.

d. d.

10. Say that methods of production are tied to particular income distributions, so that choosing one method will help some people but hurt others and that the society's income distribution is one of its goals. Say also that method A produces significantly more total output than method B. In this case:
    a. method A is more efficient than method B.
    b. method B is more efficient than method A.
    c. if method A produces more and gives more to the poor people, method A is more efficient.
    d. one can't say whether A or B is more efficient.

11. If the United States and Japan have production possibility curves as shown in the diagram below, at what point would their consumption possibilities most likely be after trade?
    a. A.
    b. B.
    c. C.
    d. D.

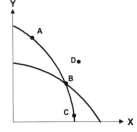

12. If countries A and B have production possibility curves A and B respectively, country A has a comparative advantage in the production of:
    a. no good.
    b. both goods.
    c. good X only.
    d. good Y only.

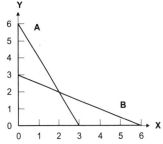

13. Suppose country A can produce either 100 cars or 50 tractors, or any combination thereof, while country B can produce either 200 cars or 50 tractors, or any combination thereof, and both countries consume both goods. Which of the following combination of goods can be produced only if the countries specialize and trade:
    a. 300 cars, 0 tractors.
    b. 0 cars, 100 tractors.
    c. 200 cars, 50 tractors.
    d. 300 cars, 100 tractors.

14. When trade is allowed between two countries, the slope of the combined production possibility curve is determined by the country with the:
    a. highest output.
    b. lowest output.
    c. highest opportunity cost.
    d. lowest opportunity cost.

15. According to the law of one price:
    a. wages will eventually be the same for every industry.
    b. wages will eventually be the same in every country.
    c. wage differences cannot continue unless they reflect differences in productivity.
    d. wage differences can continue as long as product prices can differ among countries.

16. Assuming productivity differentials diminish, the law of one price will likely result in:
    a. a decline in nominal U.S. wages.
    b. a rise in nominal U.S. wages.
    c. a decline in the value of the U.S. dollar.
    d. a rise in the value of the U.S. dollar.

17. Because of international competition and the ease with which technology is transferable among many nations with similar institutional structures, we can expect the wages for workers with similar skills to:
    a. increase in developing countries faster than they increase in developed nations.
    b. decrease in developing countries while they increase in developed nations.
    c. increase in developing countries while they decrease in developed nations.
    d. decrease in both developed and developing countries.

A1. In the graph below, point A represents:

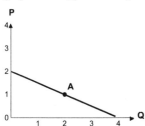

  a. a price of 1 and a quantity of 2.
  b. a price of 2 and a quantity of 2.
  c. a price of 2 and a quantity of 1.
  d. a price of 1 and a quantity of 1.

A2. The slope of the line in the graph below is:
  a. 1/2.
  b. 2.
  c. minus 1/2.
  d. minus 2.

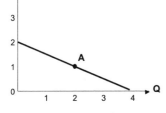

A3. At the maximum and minimum points of a nonlinear curve, the value of the slope is equal to
  a. 1.
  b. zero.
  c. minus 1.
  d. indeterminate.

A4. Which of the four lines in the graphs below has the largest slope?

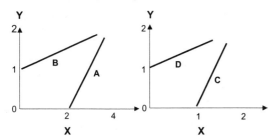

  a. A.
  b. B.
  c. C.
  d. A and C.

A5. Which of the following equations represents the line depicted in the graph to question A2?
  a. $P = 2 - .5Q$.
  b. $P = 2 - 2Q$.
  c. $Q = 4 - 2P$.
  d. $Q = 2 - .5P$.

A6. Suppose the demand curve is represented by $P = -2Q + 8$. Which of the following equations represents a *shift to the right* in that demand curve, with no change in slope?
  a. $P = -Q + 8$.
  b. $P = -2Q + 10$.
  c. $P = -2Q + 6$.
  d. $P = -4Q + 8$.

● POTENTIAL ESSAY QUESTIONS

You may also see essay questions similar to the "Problems & Applications" exercises.

1.   What did Adam Smith mean when he said, "It is not from the benevolence of the butcher, the brewer, or the baker, that we expect our dinner, but from their regard to their own interest" (*Wealth of Nations*, Book 1, Chapter 2)? How does this quotation relate to specialization?

2.   Your study partner tells you that because wages are higher in the United States than in many other countries, eventually all U.S. production will move abroad. How do you respond?

ANSWERS

SHORT-ANSWER QUESTIONS

1. The production possibility curve below shows the highest combination of grades you can get with 20 hours of studying economics and English. The grade received in economics is on the vertical axis and the grade received in English is on the horizontal axis. The graph tells us the opportunity cost of spending any combination of 20 hours on economics and English. For example, the opportunity cost of increasing your grade in economics by 6 points is decreasing your English grade by 4 points (a 2/3-point reduction in English grade for each one-point improvement in economics grade).

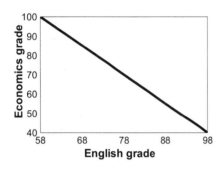

2. The principle that underlies a production possibility curve that is bowed out states that in order to get more of something, one must give up ever-increasing quantities of something else.

3. Such a production possibility curve would be a straight line connecting the maximum number of units of each product that could be produced if all inputs were devoted to one or the other good.

4. By concentrating on those activities for which one has a comparative advantage and trading those goods for goods for which others have a comparative advantage, individuals can end up with a combination of goods to consume that is greater than without trade.

5. The rewards for winning in a global market are bigger because the market is larger. The negative effect is that the firm faces more competitors, some of which may have lower costs.

6. The law of one price is that wages of workers in one country will not differ significantly from the wages of equal workers in another institutionally similar country. Globalization means that firms will seek low-cost areas for production throughout the world. Outsourcing is the result of differing wages among countries. As the high-wage country outsources some jobs to lower-wage countries, wages will tend to equalize. So, the fact that companies move production to foreign countries is the result of the law of one price in action.

ANSWERS

MATCHING

1-e; 2-h; 3-i; 4-g; 5-c; 6-f; 7-a; 8-d; 9-b.

ANSWERS

PROBLEMS AND APPLICATIONS

1. **a.** The restaurant's production possibility curve is shown below.

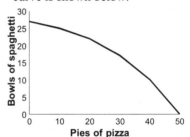

   b. The trade-off between spaghetti and pizza increases because the number of pizza pies that must be given up to make an additional bowl of spaghetti increases as the number of bowls of spaghetti produced increases.

   c. If the restaurant found a way to toss and cook pizzas faster, the production possibility curve would rotate out along the pizza axis as shown below.

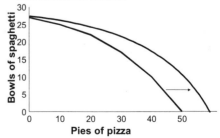

d. The production possibility curve would shift out to the right as shown in the figure below.

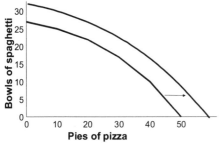

2. a. The production possibility curve is a straight line as shown below.

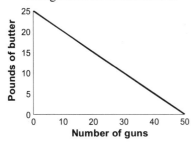

b. The opportunity cost of increasing the production of guns from 20 to 30 is 0.5 pounds of butter per gun (5/10). The opportunity cost of increasing the production of guns from 40 to 50 is also 0.5 pounds of butter per gun (5/10).

c. The opportunity cost of producing guns stays the same as the production of guns increases.

d. The per unit opportunity cost of increasing the production of butter from 10 to 15 is 2 guns per pound of butter. The opportunity cost of increasing the production of butter from 20 to 25 is also 2 guns per pound of butter.

e. The opportunity cost of producing butter stays the same as the production of butter increases.

f. Producing 26 guns and 13 lbs of butter is not attainable given this production possibility curve. We can produce 20 guns and 15 lbs of butter. To produce six more guns, Ecoland must give up 3 lbs of butter. Ecoland can produce only 26 guns and 12 lbs of butter.

g. Ecoland can produce 34 guns and 7 pounds of butter. To see this, begin at 30

guns and 10 pounds of butter. To produce 4 more guns, 2 pounds of butter must be given up. Ecoland can produce 34 guns and 8 pounds of butter, which is more than 34 guns and 7 pounds of butter. 34 guns and 7 pounds of butter is an inefficient point of production.

3. The production possibility of producing food and machinery for both Japan and the United States is shown in the graph below. The United States has a comparative advantage in the production of machinery. It must give up only 0.4 tons of food for each additional thousand units of machinery produced. Japan must give up 2.5 tons of food for each additional thousand units of machinery produced. If they specialize and trade, they could attain the combined production possibility curve shown below.

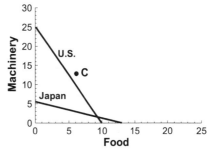

If each country specializes in their comparative advantage and equally divides that production they will each consume 6.25 units of food and 12.5 units of machinery (point C in the graph)—more than either could have consumed if they produced just for themselves.

4. a. In France, the opportunity cost of producing wine is 5 pounds of butter. In Italy, the opportunity cost of producing wine is 1.6 pounds of butter. Calculate this by finding how much butter must be forgone for each bottle of wine in each country.

b. France has the comparative advantage in producing butter because it can produce butter at a lower opportunity cost.

c. To obtain the greatest combined production possibilities Italy should specialize in producing only wine and France should specialize in producing only butter.

d. Each country's consumption possibilities increase.

ANSWERS

MULTIPLE CHOICE

1. a   The production possibility curve tells how much of one good you must give up to get more of the other good; here you must give up 2Y to get one X, making a the correct answer.

2. c   The production possibility curve tells how much of one good you must give up to get more of another good. Opportunity cost is a ratio; it determines the slope, not the position, of the production possibility curve. Thus, the correct answer is c because the 12 to 6 trade-off reduces to a 2 to 1 trade-off.

3. d   The production possibility curve tells how much of one good you must give up to get more of the other good. Opportunity cost is a ratio; it determines the slope, not the position, of the PPC curve. Since all have the same correct slope, all three are correct, so d is the right answer.

4. b   As discussed in the "Reminder" box in the text, if the opportunity costs are constant, the PPC is a straight line, so b must be the answer.

5. c   According to this principle, as you produce more and more of a good, you will have to give up more and more of the other good to do so. This means that the slope of the PPC must be bowed outward, so c is the correct answer. See Figure 2-2 for an in-depth discussion.

6. d   The slope of the PPC measures the trade-off of one good for the other. Since moving from point C to B means giving up 3 guns for 2 pounds of butter, the correct answer is 3/2 (d).

7. b   The flatter the slope, the higher the opportunity cost of the good measured on the vertical axis; alternatively, the flatter the slope the lower the opportunity cost of the good measured on the horizontal axis. In the AB range the slope is flat so guns have a low opportunity cost in terms of butter; one need give up only one pound of butter to get four guns.

8. c   Point A is an inefficient point because it is inside the PPC. See Figure 2-3.

9. a   Technological change that improves the efficiency of producing a good shifts the PPC out for that good, but not for the other good. So a is the correct answer. See Figure 2-3.

10. d   The answer is "You can't say." The term "efficiency" involves *achieving a goal as cheaply as possible.* Without specifying one's goal, one cannot say what method is more efficient. The concept of efficiency generally presumes that the goal includes preferring more to less, so if any method is more productive, it will be method A. But because there are distributional effects that involve making additional judgments, the correct answer is d. Some students may have been tempted to choose c because their goals involve more equity, but that is their particular judgment, and not all people may agree. Thus c would be incorrect, leaving d as the correct answer.

11. d   With trade, both countries can attain consumption possibilities outside their production possibility curves. The only point not already attainable by either country is D. See Figure 2-7.

12. d   Country A must give up 2Y to produce an additional X while Country B must give up only 1/2 Y to produce an additional X. Therefore, Country A has a comparative advantage in good Y and Country B has a comparative advantage in good X.

13. c   The greatest gains are when each country specializes in the good for which it has the lowest opportunity cost. If Country A specializes in tractors, producing 50 tractors, and Country B specializes in cars and produces 200 cars, production of 200 cars and 50 tractors is possible. The combination of 300 cars and 100 tractors is unattainable even with specialization and trade. The other combinations are possible without trade. See Figure 2-7.

14. d   This is the principle of lowest cost rules. It is by producing where costs are lowest that countries can achieve gains from trade.

15. c   According to the law of one price, wages of workers in one country will not differ substantially from wages of <u>equal</u> workers in another country with similar institutions. That is, there will be pressure for equally productive workers to receive similar wages.

16. c   The text suggests that it is unlikely that nominal wages will decline in the United States. It is more likely that the exchange value of the dollar will decline to offset wage differentials between the United States and other countries.

17. a   According to the law of one price, wages of (equal) workers in one country will not differ significantly from the wages of workers in another institutionally similar country. It is unlikely that wages will fall, but if the law of one price holds, then wages in developing countries will rise faster than wages in developed nations rise.

A1. a   Point A represents the corresponding numbers on the horizontal and vertical number lines.

A2. c   The slope of a line is defined as rise over run. Since the rise is -2 and the run is 4, the slope of the above line is minus 1/2.

A3. b   At the maximum and minimum points of a nonlinear curve the slope is zero.

A4. c   The slope is defined as rise over run. Line C has the largest rise for a given run so c is the answer. Even though, visually, line A seems to have the same slope as line C, it has a different coordinate system. Line A has a slope of 1 and line B has a slope of 1/4. Always be careful about checking coordinate systems when visually interpreting a graph.

A5. a   To construct the equation, use the form $y = mx + b$ where m is the slope and b is the y-axis intercept. The y-axis intercept is 2 and the slope is rise/run $= -2/4 = -.5$. Plugging in these values we get $y = -.5x + 2$. Since P is on the y-axis and Q is on the x axis, this can also be written as $P = 2 - .5Q$.

A6. b   A change in the intercept represents a shift in the curve. A higher intercept is a shift to the right.

ANSWERS

POTENTIAL ESSAY QUESTIONS

The following are annotated answers. They indicate the general idea behind the answer.

1.   Adam Smith was saying that it is not out of the kindness of producers that we are able to purchase what we want to consume, but the benefit that they will receive from selling their products. If each producer specializes in producing that good for which he receives the greatest benefit (produce at lowest cost) then the consumer will be able to consume the most goods at the lowest cost.

2.   I would remind my study partner that the U.S. does have a comparative advantage in creativity and innovation in industries such as advertising and marketing. In addition, I would remind my partner that the very definition of comparative advantage means that if one country has a comparative advantage in one good, the other country has a comparative advantage in another good.

ECONOMIC INSTITUTIONS

3

CHAPTER AT A GLANCE

1. A <u>market economy</u> is an economic system based on private property and the market. It gives private property rights to individuals, and relies on market forces to coordinate economic activity.

   A market economy's solutions to the central economic problems are:
   - *What to produce: what businesses believe people want and what is profitable.*
   - *How to produce: businesses decide how to produce efficiently, guided by their desire to make a profit.*
   - *For whom to produce: distribution according to individuals' ability and/or inherited wealth.*

2. <u>Capitalism</u> is an economic system based on the market in which the ownership of the means of production resides with a small group of individuals called capitalists.
   <u>Socialism</u> is, in theory, an economic system that tries to organize society in the same way that most families are organized—all people contribute what they can, and get what they need.

   A command, or centrally planned socialist economy's solutions to the three central economic problems are:
   - *What to produce: what central planners believe is socially beneficial.*
   - *How to produce: central planners decide, based on what they think is good for the country.*
   - *For whom to produce: central planners distribute goods based on what they determine are individuals' needs.*

   All economic systems are dynamic and evolve over time, so the meaning of terms referring to economic systems is evolving. Ours has evolved from feudalism, mercantilism, and capitalism.

3. Businesses, households, and government interact in a market economy.

   For a bird's-eye view of the U.S. economy, see Figure 3-1 (sometimes called the "circular flow of income model"). Be able to draw and explain it.

   Note: there are 3 basic economic institutions:

   - *Businesses:*
     a. Supply goods in a goods market.
     b. Demand factors in a factor market.
     c. Pay taxes and receive benefits from government.

   - *Households:*
     a. Supply factors.
     b. Demand goods.
     c. Pay taxes and receive benefits from government.

   - *Government:*
     a. Demands goods.
     b. Demands factors.
     c. Collects taxes and provides services.

   It will be important to remember who does the demanding and the supplying in goods and factor (resource) markets.

4. The advantages and disadvantages of the three forms of business are shown in the table in the text

    Know the advantages and disadvantages of the three forms of business:
    - *Sole Proprietorship*
    - *Partnership*
    - *Corporation*

    Flexible-purpose, or benefit, corporations are emerging as a new type of business.

5. Although, in principle, ultimate power resides with the people and households (consumer sovereignty), in practice the representatives of the people–firms and government–are sometimes removed from the people and, in the short run, are only indirectly monitored by the people.

    Also note: Economics focuses on households' role as the suppliers of labor.

    - *Do we control business and government, or do they control us?*
    - *The distribution of income (rich vs. poor) determines the "for whom" question. If you're rich you get more.*
    - *Social forces affect what business and government do or don't do.*

6. Six roles of government in a market economy are:

    - Provide a stable set of institutions and rules.
      The government specifies "the rules of the game."

    - Promote effective and workable competition.
      Know the different consequences associated with competition vs. monopoly power.

    - Correct for externalities.
      Government attempts to restrict the production and consumption of negative externalities, while promoting the production and consumption of positive externalities.

    - Ensure economic stability and growth.
      Government tries to ensure: full employment, low inflation, and economic growth (which increases the standard of living).

    - Provide public goods.
      A public good is a good that if supplied to one person must be supplied to all and whose consumption by one individual does not prevent its consumption by another individual.

    - Adjust for undesired market results.
      Sometimes the market result is not what society wants. For example, an unequal distribution of income may be undesirable. Government can adjust for these failures, but when doing so, it may make matters even worse. These are called "government failures."

7. It is impossible to talk about U.S. institutions apart from the world economy.

    Most large corporations are global.

    Countries have developed international institutions to oversee global business as well as promote economic relations among countries. These include the UN, the World Bank, the WTO, and the IMF. Regional trade organizations such as the EU and NAFTA work to reduce trade barriers among member countries.

    See also, Appendix: "The History of Economic Systems."

SHORT-ANSWER QUESTIONS

1. What is a market economy? How does it solve the three central economic problems?

2. What is socialism? In practice, how have socialist economies addressed the three central economic problems?

3. Draw a diagram showing the three groups that comprise the U.S. economy. What is the role of each group?

4. Your friend wants to buy a coin-operated laundromat. Her brother has offered to be a partner in the operation and put up half the money to buy the business. They have come to you for advice about what form of business to create. Of course you oblige, letting them know the three possibilities and the advantages and disadvantages of each.

5. What is consumer sovereignty? Why is much of the economic decision-making done by business and government even though households have the ultimate power?

6. Briefly distinguish between the two general roles of government.

7. What are the six roles of government?

8. Should government always intervene when markets fail?

9. Why are trade agreements important in the international market?

A1. Why did feudalism evolve into mercantilism?

A2. Why did mercantilism evolve into capitalism?

A3. Explain what is meant by the statement that capitalism has evolved into welfare capitalism.

MATCHING THE TERMS
Match the terms to their definitions

___ 1. business

___ 2. capitalism

___ 3. consumer sovereignty

___ 4. corporation

___ 5. demerit good or activity

___ 6. entrepreneurship

___ 7. externality

___ 8. global corporation

___ 9. government failure

___ 10. households

___ 11. institutions

___ 12. macroeconomic externalities

___ 13. market economy

___ 14. market failure

___ 15. merit good or activity

___ 16. partnership

___ 17. private good

___ 18. private property right

___ 19. profit

___ 20. public good

___ 21. socialism

___ 22. sole proprietorship

a. A business with two or more owners.

b. Principle that the consumer's wishes rule what's produced.

c. Corporation with substantial operations on both production and sales in more than one country.

d. A business that has only one owner.

e. Private producing units in our society.

f. What's left over from total revenue after all appropriate costs have been subtracted.

g. The ability to organize and get something done.

h. A business that is treated as a person, and is legally owned by its shareholders who are not liable for the actions of the corporate "person."

i. An economic system based on individuals' goodwill toward others, not on their own self-interest, in which society decides what, how, and for whom to produce.

j. An economic system based on private property and the market, in which individuals decide how, what, and for whom to produce.

k. A good that if supplied to one person must be supplied to all and whose consumption by one individual does not prevent its consumption by another individual.

l. A good or activity that government believes is good for you even though you may not choose to engage in the activity or consume the good.

m. A situation where the government intervenes and makes things worse.

n. A good or service that society believes is bad for people even though they choose to use the good or engage in the activity.

o. The effect of a decision on a third party not taken into account by the decision maker.

p. The formal and informal rules that constrain human economic behavior.

q. A good that, when consumed by one individual, cannot be consumed by another individual.

r. An economic system based on the market in which the ownership of the means of production resides with a small group of individuals called capitalists.

s. Externalities that affect the levels of unemployment, inflation, or growth in the economy as a whole.

t. Groups of individuals living together and making joint decisions.

u. Situations in which the market does not lead to a desired result.

v. The control a private individual or firm has over an asset.

● PROBLEMS AND APPLICATIONS

1. Fill in the blanks with the appropriate economic institution (households, businesses, or government).

    a. In the goods market, _____ and _____ buy goods and services from _____.

    b. In the goods market, _____ sell goods and services to _____ and _____.

    c. In the factor market, _____ and _____ buy (or employ) the resources owned by _____.

    d. In the factor market, _____ supply labor and other factors of production to _____ and _____.

    e. _____ redistributes income.

    f. _____ provides services to the public with tax revenue.

2. For each of the following, state for which of the three forms of business it is an advantage.

    a. Minimum bureaucratic hassle.

    b. Ability to share work and risks.

    c. Direct control by owner.

    d. Relatively easy (but not the easiest) to form.

    e. Limited individual liability.

    f. Greatest ability to get funds.

3. For each of the following, state for which form of business it is a disadvantage. (Some may have two answers.)

    a. Unlimited personal liability.

    b. Possible double taxation of income.

    c. Limited ability to get funds.

    d. Legal hassle to organize.

4. State some of the benefits global corporations offer countries. What is one problem that global corporations pose for governments?

● MULTIPLE CHOICE

Circle the one best answer for each of the following questions:

1. For a market to exist, you have to have:
    a. a capitalist economy.
    b. private property rights.
    c. no government intervention.
    d. externalities.

2. In theory, socialism is an economic system:
    a. that tries to organize society in the same ways as most families are organized, striving to see that individuals get what they need.
    b. based on central planning and government ownership of the means of production.
    c. based on private property rights.
    d. based on markets.

3. In practice, a command or socialist economy is an economic system:
    a. that tries to organize society in the same ways as most families organize, striving to see that individuals get what they need.
    b. based on central planning and government ownership of the means of production.
    c. based on private property rights.
    d based on markets.

4. In practice, in command or socialist economies, the "what to produce" decision is most often made by:
    a. consumers.
    b. the market.
    c. government.
    d. firms.

5. In a market economy, the "what to produce" decision in practice is most often made directly by:
    a. consumers.
    b. the market.
    c. government.
    d firms.

6. In the factor market:
    a. businesses supply goods and services to households and government.
    b. government provides income support to households unable to supply factors of production to businesses.
    c. households supply labor and other factors of production to businesses.
    d. households purchase goods and services from businesses.

7. The ability to organize and get something done generally goes under the term:
    a. the corporate approach.
    b. entrepreneurship.
    c. efficiency.
    d consumer sovereignty.

8. In terms of numbers, the largest percentage of businesses are:
    a. partnerships.
    b sole proprietorships.
    c. corporations.
    d nonprofit companies.

9. The largest percentage of business receipts are by:
    a. partnerships.
    b. sole proprietorships.
    c. corporations.
    d nonprofit companies.

10. A sole proprietorship has the advantage of:
    a. raising funds by selling stocks or bonds.
    b. limited personal liability.
    c. minimum bureaucratic hassle.
    d. sharing work and risks.

11. The largest percentage of state and local expenditures is on:
    a. education.
    b health.
    c. transporation.
    d income security.

12. The largest percentage of federal government expenditures is on:
    a. education.
    b national defense.
    c. infrastructure.
    d. income security.

13. All of the following are examples of government's role as referee *except*:
    a. setting limitations on when someone can be fired.
    b collecting Social Security taxes from workers' paychecks.
    c. setting minimum safety regulations for the workplace.
    d disallowing two competitors to meet to fix prices of their products.

14. When government attempts to adjust for the effect of decisions on third parties not taken into account by the decision makers, the government is attempting to:
    a. provide for a stable set of institutions and rules.
    b promote effective and workable competition.
    c. provide public goods and services.
    d correct for externalities.

15. The pressure for one firm to try to control the market is pressure to:
    a. take comparative advantage.
    b. fail the market.
    c. monopolize.
    d. externalize.

16. A good whose consumption by one individual does not prevent its consumption by another individual has a characteristic of:
a. a public good.
b. a private good.
c. a macroeconomic good.
d. a demerit good.

17. Global corporations:
a. offer enormous benefits to countries but rarely any problems.
b. are easy for governments to control.
c. reduce competition in countries.
d. have substantial operations on both the production and the sales sides in more than one country.

A1. In feudalism the most important force was:
a. the price mechanism.
b. cultural force.
c. government.
d. anarchy.

A2. In mercantilism, the guiding force is:
a. the price mechanism.
b. government.
c. cultural force.
d. anarchy.

A3. Mercantilism evolved into capitalism because:
a. government investments did not pan out.
b. the Industrial Revolution undermined the craft guilds' mercantilist method of production.
c. the guilds wanted more freedom.
d. serfs wanted more freedom.

A4. Marx saw the strongest tension between:
a. rich capitalists and poor capitalists.
b. capitalists and government.
c. capitalists and the proletariat.
d. government and the proletariat.

A5. State socialism is an economic system in which:
a. business sees to it that people work for their own good until the people can be relied upon to do that on their own.
b. business sees to it that people work for the common good until they can be relied upon to do that on their own.
c. government sees to it that people work for their own good until they can be relied upon to do so on their own.
d. government sees to it that people work for the common good until they can be relied upon to do so on their own.

POTENTIAL ESSAY QUESTIONS

You may also see essay questions similar to the "Problems & Applications" exercises.

1. Contrast the market economy and the command economy in addressing the three fundamental economic problems.

2. Uglies is a brand of boxer shorts sold on the Internet. Their claim to fame is that the front of the shorts doesn't match the back. Their marketing ploy is the boxer-short-of-the-month club. Suppose you were the one who came up with the idea for Uglies and wanted to start the business. What form of business would you select and why? (Thinking about where the funds to start the business will come from, who will make the shorts, and how the shorts will be sold will help you answer this question.)

3. How are global economic issues different from national economic issues? How have governments attempted to grapple with global economic issues? What is a major drawback associated with these attempts?

ANSWERS

SHORT-ANSWER QUESTIONS

1. A market economy is an economic system based on private property and the market. It gives private property rights to individuals and relies on market forces to coordinate economic activity. In a market economy, businesses produce what they believe people want and what they think can make a profit supplying. Businesses decide how to produce efficiently, guided by their desire to make a profit. Goods are distributed according to individuals' ability and/or inherited wealth.

2. In theory, socialism is an economic system that tries to organize society in the same way as most families are organized—all people contribute what they can and get what they need. In practice, socialism is an economic system based on government ownership of the means of production, with economic activity governed by central planning. So, central planners (not market forces) decide *what* is produced, *how* it is produced, and *for whom* it is produced.

3. As seen in the diagram below, the three groups that comprise the U.S. economy are households, businesses, and government. Households supply factors of production to businesses in exchange for money; businesses produce goods and services and sell them to households and government in exchange for money. The government taxes businesses and households, buys goods and services from businesses and labor services from households, and provides goods and services to each of them.

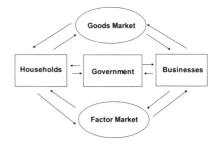

4. I would advise each of them to think hard about their situation. There are three main possibilities: sole proprietorship, partnership and a corporation. Each form of business has its disadvantages and advantages. If your friend wants to minimize bureaucratic hassle and be her own boss, the best form of business would be a sole proprietorship. However, she would be personally liable for all losses and might have difficulty obtaining additional funds should that be necessary. If her brother has some skills to offer the new business and is willing to share in the cost of purchasing the company, she might want to form a partnership with him. Beware though: Both partners are liable for any losses regardless of whose fault it is. I would ask her if she trusts her brother's decision-making abilities.

    As a partnership they still might have problems getting additional funds. What about becoming a corporation? Her liability would be limited to her initial investment, her ability to get funds is greater, and she can shed personal income and gain added expenses to limit taxation. However, a corporation is a legal hassle to organize, may involve possible double taxation of income, and if she plans to hire many employees she may face difficulty monitoring the business once she becomes less involved. I would tell her she needs to weigh the costs and benefits of each option and choose the one that best suits her needs.

5. Consumer sovereignty is the notion that the consumer's wishes rule what's produced. It means that if businesses wish to make a profit, they will need to produce what households want. That is not to say that businesses don't affect the desires of consumers through advertising. However, in practice, business and government do much of the economic decision-making even though households retain the ultimate power. This is because people have delegated much of that power to institutions and representatives—firms and the government–that are sometimes removed from the people. In the short run, households only indirectly control government and business.

6. Two general roles of government are as actor and as referee. As an actor, government collects taxes and spends money. As a referee, government sets the rules governing relations between households and businesses.

7. Six roles of government are (1) provide a stable set of institutions and rules, (2) promote effective and workable competition, (3) correct for externalities, (4) provide public goods, (5) ensure economic stability and growth, and (6) adjust for undesirable market results.

8. The fact that a market has failed does not mean that government intervention will improve the situation; it may make things worse.

9. Ongoing trade requires rules and methods of trade. The international market has no central government to set rules and methods for trade. Governments enter into voluntary trade agreements to fulfill some of these roles.

A1. Feudalism evolved into mercantilism as the development of money allowed trade to grow, undermining the traditional base of feudalism. Politics rather than social forces came to control the central economic decisions.

A2. Mercantilism evolved into capitalism because the Industrial Revolution shifted the economic power base away from craftsmen toward industrialists and toward an understanding that markets could coordinate the economy without the active involvement of the government.

A3. Capitalism has evolved into welfare capitalism. That is, the human abuses marked by early capitalist developments led to a criticism of the market economic system. Political forces have changed government's role in the market, making government a key player in determining distribution and in making the what, how, and for whom decisions. This characterizes the U.S. economy today.

ANSWERS

MATCHING

1-e; 2-r; 3-b; 4-h; 5-n; 6-g; 7-o; 8-c; 9-m; 10-t; 11-p; 12-s; 13-j; 14-u; 15-l; 16-a; 17-q; 18-v; 19-f; 20-k; 21-i; 22-d.

ANSWERS

PROBLEMS AND APPLICATIONS

1. a. In the goods market, **households** and **government** buy goods and services from **businesses**.
   b. In the goods market, **businesses** sell goods and services to **households** and **government**.
   c. In the factor market, **businesses** and **government** buy (or employ) the resources owned by **households**.
   d. In the factor market, **households** supply labor and other factors of production to **businesses** and **government**.
   e. **Government** redistributes income.
   f. **Government** provides services to the public with tax revenue.

2. a. Sole proprietorship. No special bureaucratic forms are required to start one.
   b. Partnership. The owners have each other to work with and risks are shared.
   c. Sole proprietorship. This is a firm of one person who controls the business.
   d. Partnership. This is easy to form relative to the easiest (sole proprietorship) and the hardest (corporation).
   e. Corporation. The individual liability is limited by individual investment.
   f. Corporation. Because it can issue stock and has limited liability, it has more access to financial capital.

3. a. Sole proprietorship and partnership.
   b. Corporation.
   c. Sole proprietorship and partnership.
   d. Corporation.

4. Global corporations can benefit countries by creating jobs, by bringing new ideas and new technologies to a country, and by providing competition to domestic companies, keeping them on their toes. But, global corporations, because they exist in many countries and there is no world government, may be difficult to regulate or to control. If they don't like one government's taxes, regulation, or other policies, they can shift operations to another country with more favorable policies.

ANSWERS

MULTIPLE CHOICE

1. b   Markets require private property rights because these give people the framework within which they can trade, and markets rely on trading. Markets also require government, but government and private property rights are not the same thing, which rules out a and c. And d is a throwaway answer.

2. a   a is the correct answer. If the question had said "In practice," b would have been an acceptable answer.

3. b   b is the correct answer. If the question had said "In theory, a socialist economy..." a would have been an acceptable answer.

4. c   In command economies, central planners decide what to produce based upon what they believe society needs.

5. d   Under a market economy, firms decide what to produce based on what they think will sell.

6. c.   In Figure 3-1 households supply labor and other factors of production while businesses demand these inputs used in the production process.

7. b   Entrepreneurship is the ability to organize and get something done.

8. b   Most businesses are sole proprietorships. See Figure 3-2.

9. c   Corporations account for most business receipts (revenues). See Figure 3-2.

10. c   Corporations have the advantages of options a and b. Partnerships have the advantage of option d.

11. a   The largest state and local government spending is on education. See Figure 3-3.

12. d   The largest component of federal government spending is income security. See Figure 3-4.

13. b   Collecting Social Security taxes to fund the Social Security system is government as an actor. Government as referee refers to laws regulating interaction between households and businesses.

14. d   Economists call the effect of a decision on a third party not taken into account by the decision maker an externality. Government sometimes attempts to adjust for these effects.

15. c   To monopolize is to try to be the only producer and control the market.

16. a   A public good is a good that if supplied to one person must be supplied to all and whose consumption by one individual does not prevent its consumption by another individual.

17. d   Option d is the definition of global corporations. They often create problems. Governments often find it difficult to control them and they increase competition, not decrease it.

A1. b   As discussed in the Appendix, in feudalism tradition reigned.

A2. b   As discussed in the Appendix, in mercantilism government directed the economy.

A3. b   Mercantilism evolved into capitalism because of the changes brought about by the Industrial Revolution.

A4. c   To the degree that government was controlled by capitalists, d would be a correct answer, but it is not as good an answer as c, which represents the primary conflict. Remember, you are choosing the answer that best reflects the discussion in the text.

A5. d   The author defines state socialism as option d. Socialists saw state socialism as a transition stage to pure socialism.

━━━ ANSWERS ━━━

POTENTIAL ESSAY QUESTIONS

The following are annotated answers. They indicate the general idea behind the answer.

1. Both economic systems have to address the three central economic problems. (1) What to produce? In a market economy, firms produce what they believe people want and what will make them a profit. In socialism, or a command economy, central planners decide what is produced. (2) How to produce? In a market economy, firms decide how to produce efficiently, guided by their desire to make a profit. In socialism, central planners decide how to produce. (3) For whom to produce? In a market economy, distribution is decided according to ability and inherited wealth. In socialism, distribution is according to individuals' needs (as determined by central planners).

2. The answer to this question will vary from person to person and will depend on personal finances, how much risk one is able and willing to undertake, how much responsibility one wants to take on, and whether or not you want to share any profits. Given limited financial resources, I'd find a partner I can trust who has the funds needed to launch a website, hire a firm to carry out transactions, and build inventory. With a partnership, I can share the work and the risks of the venture. Since the liability associated with selling boxer shorts is not too great, unlimited liability with a partnership is not a problem. I would not choose a corporation because establishing one is a legal hassle requiring even more money. I would not choose a sole proprietorship because I don't have the funds to start the company on my own.

3. Global economic issues differ from national economic issues because national economies have governments to referee disputes among players in the economy; global economies do not; no international government exists. Governments, however, have developed a variety of international institutions to promote negotiations and coordinate economic relations among countries. These include the UN, the World Bank, the World Court and the International Monetary Fund. Countries also have developed global and regional organizations whose jobs are to coordinate trade among countries and reduce trade barriers. Some are the WTO, the EU, and NAFTA. In addition to these formal institutions, there are informal meetings of various countries like the Group of Eight.

    A major drawback associated with governmental attempts to deal with global economic issues is that because government membership in international organizations is voluntary, the power of international organizations is limited. An individual government may simply choose to ignore an international ruling with little impunity.

SUPPLY AND DEMAND

CHAPTER AT A GLANCE

1. The <u>law of demand</u> states that the quantity of a good demanded is <u>inversely related</u> to the good's price. When price goes up, quantity demanded goes down. When price goes down, quantity demanded goes up.

   Law of Demand (Inverse Relationship):
   arrows move in $\uparrow P \rightarrow \downarrow Q_d$
   opposite directions $\downarrow P \rightarrow \uparrow Q_d$

   Law of Demand expressed as a <u>downward-sloping curve</u>:

   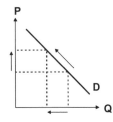

       To derive a demand curve from a demand table, plot each point on the demand table on a graph and connect the points.

   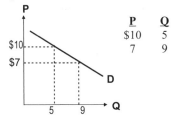

P	Q
$10	5
7	9

2a. The law of demand is based on opportunity cost and individuals' ability to substitute. If the price of a good rises, the opportunity cost of purchasing that good will also rise and consumers will substitute a good with a lower opportunity cost.

   As the P of beef ↑, we buy less beef and more chicken.

2b. The law of supply, like the law of demand, is based on opportunity cost and the individual firm's ability to substitute. Suppliers will substitute toward goods for which they receive higher relative prices.

If the P of wheat ↑, farmers grow more wheat and less corn.

3. Changes in quantity demanded are shown by movements along a demand curve. Shifts in demand are shown by a shift of the entire demand curve. *(Note: "Δ" means "change.")*

   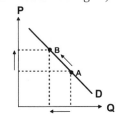

   $\uparrow P \rightarrow \downarrow Q_d$ *is a movement along a curve (e.g. from point A to point B).*

   ΔD is caused only by Δs in the shift factors of D (<u>not</u> a Δ in the P of the good itself!)
   <u>Δ in shift factors of D→ΔD→ shift of a D curve</u>

✔ *Know what can cause an increase and decrease in demand:*

4. The <u>law of supply</u> states that the quantity of a good supplied is <u>directly</u> <u>related</u> to the good's price. When price goes up, quantity supplied goes up. When price goes down, quantity supplied goes down.

   Law of Supply expressed as an <u>upward-sloping curve</u>:

   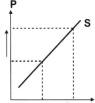

5. Just as with demand, it is important to distinguish between a change in supply (due to a change in shift factors and reflected as a shift of the entire supply curve) and a change in the quantity supplied (due to a change in price and reflected as a movement along a supply curve).
      Don't get this confused on the exam!

$\uparrow P \rightarrow \uparrow Q_s$: movement along a curve (e.g. from point A to point B).

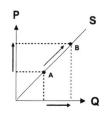

ΔS is caused only by Δs in the shift factors of S (<u>not</u> a Δ in the P of the good itself!)

<u>Δ in shift factors of S $\rightarrow \Delta S \rightarrow$ shift of a S curve</u>

✔ *Know what can cause an increase and decrease in supply:*

6. Equilibrium is where quantity supplied equals quantity demanded:

    • If quantity demanded is greater than quantity supplied (excess demand), prices tend to rise.
    • If quantity supplied is greater than quantity demanded (excess supply), prices tend to fall.
    • When quantity demanded equals quantity supplied, prices have no tendency to change.

Shortage	**Surplus**	**Equilibrium**
$(Q_d > Q_s)$	$(Q_s > Q_d)$	$(Q_s = Q_d)$
P is below equilibrium	P is above equilibrium	P is at equilibrium

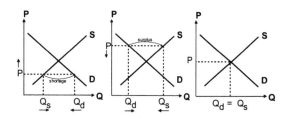

7. Demand and supply curves enable us to determine the equilibrium price and quantity. In addition, changes (shifts) in demand and supply curves enable us to predict the effect on the equilibrium price and quantity in a market.

    Anything other than price that affects demand or supply will shift the curves.

✔ *Know how a change in demand or supply affects the equilibrium price and quantity!*

$\uparrow D \rightarrow \uparrow P; \uparrow Q$ $\downarrow D \rightarrow \downarrow P; \downarrow Q$

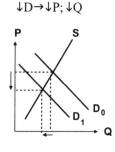

$\uparrow S \rightarrow \downarrow P; \uparrow Q$ $\downarrow S \rightarrow \uparrow P; \downarrow Q$

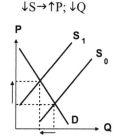

8. Simple supply and demand analysis holds other things constant. Sometimes supply and demand are interconnected, making it impossible to hold other things constant. When there is interdependence between supply and demand, a movement along one curve can cause the other curve to shift. This is especially prevalent when one analyzes goods that constitute a large percentage of the entire economy. Thus, supply and demand analysis used alone is not enough to determine where the equilibrium will be.

    When the "other things are constant" assumption is not realistic, feedback or ripple effects can become relevant. The degree of interdependence differs among various sets of issues. That is why there is a separate micro and macro analysis–microeconomics and macroeconomics.

    The fallacy of composition is the false assumption that what is true for a part will also be true for the whole. This means that what is true in microeconomics may not be true in macroeconomics.

● SHORT-ANSWER QUESTIONS

1. What is the law of demand?

2. Draw a demand curve from the following demand table.

   Demand Table

Q	P
50	1
40	2
30	3
20	4

3. Demonstrate graphically a shift in demand and on another graph demonstrate movement along the demand curve.

4. State the law of supply.

5. What does the law of supply say that most individuals would do with the quantity of labor they supply employers if their wage increased? Explain the importance of substitution in this decision.

6. Draw a supply curve from the following supply table.

   Supply Table

Q	P
20	1
30	2
40	3
50	4

7. Demonstrate graphically the effect of a new technology that reduces the cost of producing Adele CDs on the supply of Adele CDs.

8. Demonstrate graphically the effect of a rise in the price of Adele CDs on the quantity supplied.

9. What are three things to note about supply and demand that help to explain how they interact to bring about equilibrium in a market?

10. Demonstrate graphically what happens to the equilibrium price and quantity of M&Ms if they suddenly become more popular.

11. Demonstrate graphically what happens to the equilibrium price and quantity of oranges if a frost destroys 50 percent of the orange crop.

12. What is the fallacy of composition and how is it related to why economists separate micro from macro economics?

MATCHING THE TERMS
Match the terms to their definitions

___ **1.** demand

___ **2.** demand curve

___ **3.** equilibrium

___ **4.** equilibrium price

___ **5.** equilibrium quantity

___ **6.** excess demand

___ **7.** excess supply

___ **8.** fallacy of composition

___ **9.** law of demand

___ **10.** law of supply

___ **11.** market demand curve

___ **12.** market supply curve

___ **13.** movement along a demand curve

___ **14.** movement along a supply curve

___ **15.** quantity demanded

___ **16.** quantity supplied

___ **17.** shift in demand

___ **18.** shift in supply

___ **19.** supply

___ **20.** supply curve

a. A specific amount that will be demanded per unit of time at a specific price, other things constant.

b. Curve that tells how much of a good will be bought at various prices.

c. The effect of a change in a shift factor on the supply curve.

d. Curve that tells how much will be offered for sale at various prices.

e. The graphic representation of the effect of a change in price on the quantity supplied.

f. Quantity demanded rises as price falls, other things constant.

g. Quantity supplied rises as price rises, other things constant.

h. A schedule of quantities of a good that will be bought per unit of time at various prices, other things constant.

i. Quantity supplied is greater than quantity demanded.

j. A concept in which opposing dynamic forces cancel each other out.

k. The effect of a change in a shift factor on the demand curve.

l. The price toward which the invisible hand (economic forces) drives the market.

m. The horizontal sum of all individual demand curves.

n. Amount bought and sold at the equilibrium price.

o. Quantity demanded is greater than quantity supplied.

p. The graphic representation of the effect of a change in price on the quantity demanded.

q. A specific amount that will be offered for sale per unit of time at a specific price.

r. A schedule of quantities a seller is willing to sell per unit of time at various prices, other things constant.

s. The false assumption that what is true for a part will also be true for the whole.

t. The horizonal sum of all individual supply curves.

PROBLEMS AND APPLICATIONS

1. Draw two linear curves on the same graph from the following table, one relating P with Q_1 and the other relating P with Q_2.

P	Q_1	Q_2
$30	60	100
35	70	90
40	80	80
45	90	70

   a. Label the curve that is most likely a demand curve. Explain your choice.

   b. Label the curve that is most likely a supply curve. Explain your choice.

   c. What is the equilibrium price and quantity? Choose points above and below that price and explain why each is not the equilibrium price.

2. Correct the following statements, if needed, so that the terms "demand," "quantity demanded," "supply," and "quantity supplied" are used correctly.

   a. As the price of pizza increases, consumers demand less pizza.

   b. Whenever the price of bicycles increases, the supply of bicycles increases.

   c. The price of electricity is cheaper in the northwestern part of the United States and therefore the demand for electricity is greater in the northwest.

   d. An increase in the incomes of car buyers will increase the quantity demanded for cars.

   e. An increase in the quantity demanded of lobsters means consumers are willing and able to buy more lobsters at any given price.

   f. A decrease in the supply of frog legs means suppliers will provide fewer frog legs at any given price.

3. You are given the following individual demand tables for compact discs:

Price	Juan	Philippe	Ramone
$7	3	20	50
$10	2	10	40
$13	1	7	32
$16	0	5	26
$19	0	3	20
$22	0	0	14

   a. Determine the market demand table.

b. Graph the individual and market demand curves.

c. If the current market price is $13, what is the total market quantity demanded? What happens to total market quantity demanded if the price rises to $19 a disc?

d. Say that a new popular Usher compact disc hits the market that increases demand for compact discs by 25%. Show with a demand table what happens to the individual and market demand curves. Demonstrate graphically what happens to market demand.

4. The following table depicts the market supply and demand for oranges in the United States (in thousands of bushels):

Price per bushel	Quantity supplied	Quantity demanded
$15	7000	2000
$14	5500	3000
$13	4000	4000
$12	2500	5000
$11	1000	6000

a. Graph the market supply and demand for oranges.

b. What is the equilibrium price and quantity of oranges in the market? Why?

c. Suppose the price is $14. Would we observe a surplus (excess supply) or a shortage (excess demand)? If so, by how much? What could be expected to happen to the price over time? Why?

d. Suppose the price is $12. Would we observe a surplus or a shortage? If so, by how much? What could be expected to happen to the price over time? Why?

5. Draw a hypothetical demand and supply curve for Netflix movies streamed through the Internet. Show how demand or supply is affected by the following:

a. A technological breakthrough lowers the cost of streaming.

b. Consumers' income rises.

c. Movie producers charge Netflix higher prices to stream their movies.

d. The price of streaming videos using iTunes rises.

e. Possible suppliers expect streaming videos to become more popular.

6. Use supply and demand curves to help you determine the impact that each of the following events has on the market for surfboards in Southern California.

   a. Southern California experiences unusually high temperatures, sending an unusually large number of people to its beaches.

b. Large sharks are reported feeding near the beaches of Southern California.

c. Due to the large profits earned by surfboard producers there is a significant increase in the number of producers of surfboards.

d. There is a significant increase in the price of epoxy paint used to coat surfboards.

7. Use supply and demand curves to help you determine the impact that each of the following events has on the market for beef.

   a. New genetic engineering technology enables ranchers to raise healthier, heavier cattle, significantly reducing costs.

   b. The CBS program "60 Minutes" reports on the unsanitary conditions in poultry processing plants that may increase the chances of consumers getting sick by eating chicken.

c. In addition to developing new genetic engineering technology, highly credible new research results report that abundant consumption of fatty red meats actually prolongs average life expectancy.

d. Consumers expect the price of beef to fall in the near future.

● MULTIPLE CHOICE

Circle the one best answer for each of the following questions:

1. The law of demand states:
   a. quantity demanded increases as price falls, other things constant.
   b. more of a good will be demanded the higher its price, other things constant.
   c. people always want more.
   d. you can't always get what you want at the price you want.

2. There are many more substitutes for good A than for good B.
   a. The demand curve for good B will likely shift out further.
   b. The demand curve for good B will likely be flatter.
   c. You can't say anything about the likely relative flatness of the demand curves.
   d. The demand curve for good A will likely be flatter.

3. If the weather gets very hot, what will most likely happen?
   a. The supply of air conditioners will increase.
   b. Quantity of air conditioners demanded will increase.
   c. Demand for air conditioners will increase.
   d. The quality of air conditioners demanded will increase.

4. If the price of air conditioners falls, there will be:
   a. an increase in demand for air conditioners.
   b. an increase in the quantity of air conditioners demanded.
   c. an increase in the quantity of air conditioners supplied.
   d. a shift out of the supply curve for air conditioners.

5. An increase in demand:
   a. is reflected as a rightward (outward) shift of the demand curve.
   b. is caused by a decrease in price.
   c. means demanders are buying less at any price
   d. shifts the demand curve to the left (inward).

6. The demand curve will likely shift outward to the right if:
   a. society's income falls.
   b. the price of a substitute good falls.
   c. the price of the good is expected to rise in the near future.
   d. the good goes out of style.

7. The difference between the quantity demanded and demand is:
   a. the quantity demanded is associated with a whole set of prices, whereas demand is associated with a particular price.
   b. the quantity demanded is associated with a particular price, whereas demand is associated with a whole set of prices.
   c. the quantity demanded is the whole demand curve, whereas demand is a particular point along a demand curve.
   d. a change in the quantity demanded is reflected graphically as a shift of the demand curve, whereas a change in demand is reflected as movement along a given demand curve.

8. The movement in the graph below from point A to point B represents:

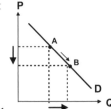

   a. an increase in demand.
   b. an increase in the quantity demanded.
   c. an increase in the quantity supplied.
   d. an increase in supply.

9. If there is a flood, what will most likely happen
    in the market for bottled water?
    a. Demand will increase.
    b. Demand will fall.
    c. Supply will increase.
    d. Supply will decrease.

10. Using the standard axes, the demand curve
    associated with the following demand table
    is:

 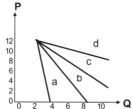

Demand Table	
P	**Q**
7	5
9	4
11	3

    a. a
    b. b
    c. c
    d. d

11. To derive a market demand curve from two
    individual demand curves:
    a. one adds the two demand curves horizon-
    tally.
    b. one adds the two demand curves vertically.
    c. one subtracts one demand curve from the
    other demand curve.
    d. one adds the demand curves both horizon-
    tally and vertically.

12. The market demand curve will always:
    a. be unrelated to the individual demand curves
    and slope.
    b. be steeper than the individual demand
    curves that make it up.
    c. have the same slope as the individual
    demand curves that make it up.
    d. be flatter than the individual demand curves
    that make it up.

13. The law of supply states that:
    a. quantity supplied increases as price in-
    creases, other things constant.
    b. quantity supplied decreases as price
    increases, other things constant.
    c. more of a good will be supplied the higher its
    price, other things changing proportionately.
    d. less of a good will be supplied the higher its
    price, other things changing proportionately.

14. In the graph below, the arrow refers to:

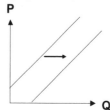

    a. a shift in demand.
    b. a shift in supply.
    c. a change in the quantity demanded.
    d. a change in the quantity supplied.

15. If there is an improvement in technology one
    would expect:
    a. a movement along the supply curve.
    b. a shift upward (or to the left) of the supply
    curve.
    c. a shift downward (or to the right) of the
    supply curve.
    d. a movement down along the supply curve.

16. You're the supplier of a good and suddenly a
    number of your long-lost friends call you to
    buy your product. Your good is most likely:
    a. in excess supply.
    b. in excess demand.
    c. in equilibrium.
    d. in both excess supply and demand.

17. At which point on the graph below will you
    expect the strongest downward pressure on
    prices?

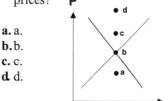

    a. a.
    b. b.
    c. c.
    d. d.

18. If at some price the quantity supplied exceeds
    the quantity demanded, then:
    a. a surplus (excess supply) exists and the
    price will fall over time as sellers competi-
    tively bid down the price.
    b. a shortage (excess demand) exists and the
    price will rise over time as buyers competi-
    tively bid up the price.
    c. the price is below equilibrium.
    d. equilibrium will be reestablished as the
    demand curve shifts to the left.

19. If the price of a good:
    a. rises, it is a response to a surplus (excess supply).
    b. falls, it is a response to a shortage (excess demand).
    c. is below equilibrium, then a shortage will be observed.
    d. is below equilibrium, then a surplus will be observed.

20. If the demand for a good increases, you will expect price to:
    a. fall and quantity to rise.
    b. rise and quantity to rise.
    c. fall and quantity to fall.
    d. rise and quantity to fall.

21. If the supply of a good decreases, you will expect price to:
    a. fall and quantity to rise.
    b. rise and quantity to rise.
    c. fall and quantity to fall.
    d. rise and quantity to fall.

22. Consider the market for bikinis. If bikinis suddenly become more fashionable, you will expect:
    a. a temporary shortage of bikinis that will be eliminated over time as the market price of bikinis rises and a greater quantity is bought and sold.
    b. a temporary shortage of bikinis that will be eliminated over time as the market price of bikinis rises and a smaller quantity is bought and sold.
    c. a temporary surplus of bikinis that will be eliminated over time as the market price of bikinis falls and a smaller quantity is bought and sold.
    d. a temporary surplus of bikinis that will be eliminated over time as the market price of bikinis rises and a greater quantity is bought and sold.

23. Compared to last year, fewer oranges are being purchased and the selling price has decreased. This could have been caused by:
    a. an increase in demand.
    b. an increase in supply.
    c. a decrease in demand.
    d. a decrease in supply.

24. If demand and supply both increase, this will cause:
    a. an increase in the equilibrium quantity, but an uncertain effect on the equilibrium price.
    b. an increase in the equilibrium price, but an uncertain effect on the equilibrium quantity.
    c. an increase in the equilibrium price and quantity.
    d. a decrease in the equilibrium price and quantity.

25. An increase in demand for a good will cause:
    a. excess demand (a shortage) until price changes.
    b. movement down along the demand curve as price changes.
    c. movement down along the supply curve as price changes.
    d. a higher price and a smaller quantity traded in the market.

26. The fallacy of composition is:
    a. the false assumption that what is false for a part will also be false for the whole.
    b. the false assumption that what is true for a part will also be true for the whole.
    c. the false assumption that what is false for a whole will also be false for the part.
    d. the false assumption that what is true for a whole will also be true for the part.

POTENTIAL ESSAY QUESTIONS

You may also see essay questions similar to the "Problems & Applications" exercises.

1. Many university campuses sell parking permits to their students allowing them to park on campus in designated areas. Although most students complain about the relatively high cost of these parking permits, what annoys many students even more is that after having paid for their permits, vacant parking spaces in the designated lots are very difficult to find during much of the day. Many end up having to park off campus anyway, where permits are not required. Assuming the university is unable to build new parking facilities on campus due to insufficient funds, what recommendation might you make to remedy the problem of students with permits being unable to find places to park on campus?

2. Discuss how changes in demand or supply impact a market equilibrium.

ANSWERS

SHORT-ANSWER QUESTIONS

1. The law of demand states that the quantity of a good demanded is inversely related to the good's price, other things constant.

2. To derive a demand curve from a demand table, plot each point of the demand table on a graph and connect the points. This is shown on the graph below.

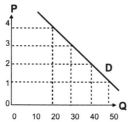

3. A shift in demand is shown by a shift of the entire demand curve resulting from a change in a shift factor of demand as shown in the graph below on the left (which illustrates an increase in demand because it is a rightward shift). A movement along a demand curve is shown on the right as a movement from point A to point B due to a price decrease. See Figure 4-2.

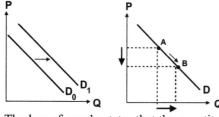

4. The law of supply states that the quantity supplied rises as price rises, other things constant. Or alternatively: quantity supplied falls as price falls.

5. The law of supply states that quantity supplied rises as price rises; quantity supplied falls as price falls. According to this law, most individuals would choose to supply a greater quantity of labor hours if their wage increased. They will substitute work for leisure. See Figure 4-5.

6. To derive a supply curve from a supply table, you plot each point on the supply table on a graph and connect the points. This is shown on the graph in the next column.

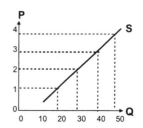

7. A new technology that reduces the cost of producing Adele CDs will shift the entire supply curve to the right from S_0 to S_1, as shown in the graph below.

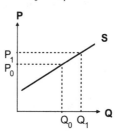

8. A rise in the price of Adele CDs from P_0 to P_1 results in a movement up along a supply curve and the quantity of Adele CDs supplied will rise from Q_0 to Q_1 as shown in the graph below.

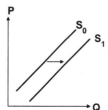

9. The first thing to note is that when quantity demanded is greater than quantity supplied, prices tend to rise and when quantity supplied is greater than quantity demanded, prices tend to fall. Each case is demonstrated in the graph below. Price tends away from P_1 and P_2 and toward P_0.

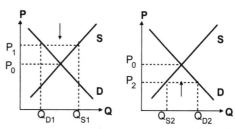

The second thing to note is that the larger the difference between quantity supplied and quantity demanded, the greater the pressure on prices to rise (if there is excess demand; a shortage) or fall (if there is excess supply; a surplus). This is demonstrated in the graph below. At P_2, the pressure for prices to fall toward P_0 is greater than the pressure at P_1 because excess supply (surplus) is greater at P_2 compared to excess supply at P_1.

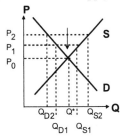

The third thing to note is that when quantity demanded equals quantity supplied, the market is in equilibrium. This is shown graphically at the point of intersection between the demand and supply curves.

10. Increasing popularity of M&Ms means that at every price, more M&Ms are demanded. The demand curve shifts out to the right from D_0 to D_1, and both equilibrium price and quantity rise to P_1 and Q_1 respectively.

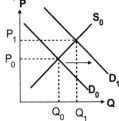

11. A frost damaging oranges means that at every price, suppliers will supply fewer oranges. The supply curve shifts in to the left from S_0 to S_1, and equilibrium price rises to P_1, and quantity traded falls to Q_1.

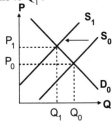

12. The fallacy of composition is the false assumption that what is true for a part will also be true for the whole. In micro, economists isolate an individual person's or firm's behavior and consider its effects, while the many side effects are kept in the background. In macro, those

side effects become too large and can no longer be held constant. These side effects are what account for the interdependence of supply and demand. Macro, thus, is not simply a summation of all micro results; it would be a fallacy of composition to take the sum of each individual's (micro) actions and say that this will be the aggregate (macro) result.

ANSWERS

MATCHING

1-h; 2-b; 3-j; 4-l; 5-n; 6-o; 7-i; 8-s; 9-f; 10-g; 11-m; 12-t; 13-p; 14-e; 15-a; 16-q; 17-k 18-c; 19-r; 20-d.

ANSWERS

PROBLEMS AND APPLICATIONS

1. The linear curves are shown on the right. See Figure 4-8.

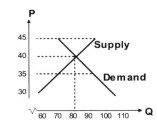

   a. As shown in the graph, the downward sloping curve is a demand curve. We deduce this from the law of demand: Quantity demanded rises (falls) as the price decreases (increases).

   b. As shown in the graph, the upward sloping curve is a supply curve. We deduce this from the law of supply: Quantity supplied rises (falls) as the price rises (falls).

   c. The equilibrium price and quantity are where the demand and supply curves intersect. This is at $P = \$40$, $Q = 80$. At a price above $40, such as $45, quantity supplied exceeds quantity demanded and there is pressure for price to fall. At a price below $40, such as $35, quantity demanded exceeds quantity supplied and there is pressure for price to rise.

2.   a. As the price of pizza increases, the *quantity demanded* of pizza decreases.

Note that a change in the price of an item will cause a change in the quantity demanded; not a change in demand! A change in something else other than the price may cause a change in demand–such as a change in one of the shift factors of demand discussed in the textbook.

b. Whenever the price of bicycles increases, the *quantity of bicycles supplied* also increases.

Note that a change in the price will cause a change in the quantity supplied; not supply! A change in something else other than the price–such as a change in one of the shift factors of supply discussed in the textbook–may cause a change in supply.

c. The price of electricity is cheaper in the NW part of the U. S. and therefore the *quantity demanded* of electricity is greater in the NW.

d. An increase in incomes of car buyers will increase the *demand* for cars.

Notice that a change in a shift factor of demand, such as income, will change demand; not the quantity demanded!

e. An increase in the *demand* for lobsters means consumers are willing and able to buy more lobsters at any given price (whatever the current price is).

In order for there to be an increase in the quantity demanded there would have to be a decrease in the price. Moreover, recall that an increase in demand is reflected as a rightward shift of the demand curve. Upon viewing a graph where the demand curve has shifted to the right you will see that more will be purchased at any given price.

f. This is a correct use of the term "supply." Notice that a decrease in supply is reflected graphically as a leftward shift of the curve and less will be provided in the market at any given price.

3. a. The market demand table is the summation of individual quantities demanded at each price as follows:

P	Q
$7	73
10	52
13	40
16	31
19	23
22	14

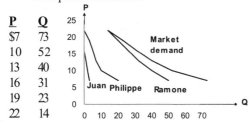

b. The individual and market demand curves are shown to the right of the demand table.

c. At $13 a disc, total market quantity demanded is 40 discs. Total market quantity demanded falls to 23 when the price of discs rises to $19 per disc.

d. Quantity demanded at each price rises by 25% for each individual and for the market as a whole. The new demand table is shown below. Graphically, both the individual and market demand curves shift to the right. The graph below shows the rightward shift in market demand.

Price	Juan	Philippe	Ramone	Market
$7	3.75	25	62.50	91.25
$10	2.50	12.5	50	65
$13	1.25	8.75	40	50
$16	0	6.25	32.5	38.75
$19	0	3.75	25	28.75
$21	0	0	17.5	17.5

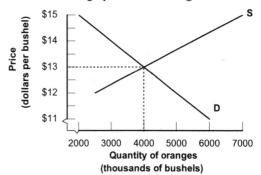

4. a. See the graph below. See Figure 4-8.

b. The equilibrium price is $13, the equilibrium quantity is 4000. This is an equilibrium because the quantity supplied equals the quantity demanded at this price. That is, there is neither a surplus (excess supply) nor a shortage (excess demand) and hence no tendency for the price to change.

c. Because the quantity supplied exceeds the quantity demanded when the price is $14 per bushel, we would observe a surplus of 2500 bushels (in thousands of bushels). We can expect the price of oranges per bushel to fall as sellers scramble to rid themselves of their excess supplies.

d Because the quantity demanded exceeds the quantity supplied at $12 per bushel, we would observe a shortage of 2500 bushels (in thousands of bushels). We can expect the price of oranges per bushel to rise as some buyers competitively bid up the price just to get some oranges.

5. A hypothetical market for Netflix streamed video shows an upward sloping supply curve, a downward sloping demand curve and an equilibrium price and quantity where the two curves intersect.

   a. A technological breakthrough that lowers the cost of streaming will shift the supply of streamed Netflix movies to the right as shown in the graph below.

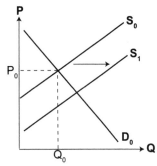

   b. A rise in consumers' income will shift the demand for streamed Netflix movies to the right as shown in the graph below.

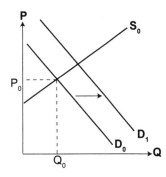

   c. Higher usage fees imposed by movie producers to Netflix will shift the supply of streamed movies to the left as shown in the graph on the top of the next column.

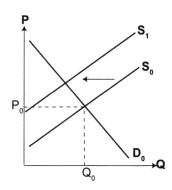

   d If the price of iTune movies rises, the demand for cyber cafes will shift to the right as shown in the graph for the answer to part *b*.

   e. If possible suppliers expect streamed movies to become more popular, the supply of streamed Netflix movies will shift to the right as shown in the graph for the answer to part *a*.

6. **a.** This will increase the demand for surf-boards shifting the demand curve to the right. At the original price a temporary shortage would be observed putting upward pressure on price. We end up with a higher equilibrium price and a greater equilibrium quantity as illustrated in the graph below. (*When dealing with a change in D or S curves, just remember to go from the initial point of intersection to the new point of intersection. The initial point of intersection will give you the initial equilibrium P and Q and the new point of intersection the new equilibrium P and Q. Then recall that if the price went up in the market, it was a response to a temporary shortage (excess demand). If the equilibrium price went down, then it was a response to a temporary surplus (excess supply).*)

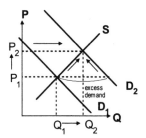

b. This would cause a decrease in the demand for surfboards shifting the demand curve to the left. At the original price a temporary surplus would be observed putting downward pressure on price. We end up with a lower equilibrium price and a lower equilibrium quantity, as illustrated in the graph below.

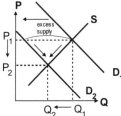

c. This would cause an increase in the supply of surfboards, shifting the supply curve to the right. At the original price a temporary surplus would be observed, putting downward pressure on price. We end up with a lower equilibrium price and a higher equilibrium quantity, as illustrated in the graph below.

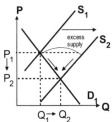

d. This would cause a decrease in the supply of surfboards, shifting the supply curve to the left. At the original price a temporary shortage would be observed, putting upward pressure on price. We end up with a higher equilibrium price and a lower equilibrium quantity, as illustrated in the graph below.

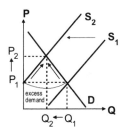

7. **a.** An increase in production technology will increase the supply of beef. The temporary surplus (excess supply) of beef at the

original price will cause the market price to fall. Eventually we get a lower equilibrium price of beef and a greater amount bought and sold in the market.

b. Chicken and beef are substitute goods– they can be used instead of each other. Therefore, this "60 Minutes" report will likely increase the demand for beef. The temporary shortage (excess demand) at the original price will cause the price to be competitively bid up. Eventually we observe a higher equilibrium price and a greater equilibrium quantity.

c. The new development would increase the supply of beef while the reports of the health benefits of beef would increase the demand for beef. Quantity of beef sold would definitely rise. The impact on equilibrium price, however, depends upon the relative sizes of the shifts.

d. Because people will postpone their purchases of beef until the price decreases, the demand for beef will fall today. A decrease in demand is reflected as a leftward shift of the demand curve. The temporary excess supply (surplus) that is created at the original price puts downward pressure on the market price of beef. Eventually we get a lower equilibrium price and quantity.

ANSWERS

MULTIPLE CHOICE

1. **a** The correct answer is a. A possible answer is d, which is a restatement of the law of demand, but since the actual law was among the choices, and is more precise, a is the correct answer.

2. **d** An equal rise in price will cause individuals to switch more to other goods when there are more substitutes.

3. **c** It is important to distinguish between a change in the quantity demanded and a change in demand. Weather is a shift factor of demand, so demand, not quantity demanded, will increase. Supply will not increase; the quantity supplied will, however. Who knows what will happen to the quality demanded? We don't.

4. b When the price falls there is a movement along the demand curve which is expressed by saying the quantity demanded increased. Moreover, as the price falls, the quantity supplied falls.

5. a An increase in demand is expressed as an outward (or rightward) shift of the demand curve. It is caused by something other than the price. It means people will buy more at any price or pay a higher price for a given quantity demanded.

6. c All of these are shift factors of demand. However, only c will increase demand and shift the demand curve to the right.

7. b As is discussed in the text, b is the only correct response.

8. b The curve slopes downward, so we can surmise that it is a demand curve; and the two points are on the demand curve, so the movement represents an increase in the quantity demanded, not an increase in demand. Moreover, as price falls, the quantity demanded rises. A shift in demand would be a shift of the entire curve. See the figure 4-2.

9. a A flood will likely bring about a significant increase in the demand for bottled water since a flood makes most other water undrinkable. A flood would be a shift factor of demand for bottled water.

10. b This demand curve is the only demand curve that goes through all the points in the table.

11. a Market demand curves are determined by adding individuals' demand curves horizontally. That is, you add the quantities demanded at each price. See Figure 4-4.

12. d Since the market demand curve is derived by adding the individual demand curves horizontally, it will always be flatter. See Figure 4-4.

13. a The law of supply is stated in a. The others either have the movement in the wrong direction or are not holding all other things constant.

14. b It is a shift in supply because the curve is upward sloping; and it's a shift of the entire curve, so it is not a movement along. See Figure 4-6.

15. c Technology is a shift factor of supply so it must be a shift of the supply curve. Since it is an improvement, it must be a shift rightward (or downward). See Figure 4-6.

16. b When there is excess demand, demanders start searching for new suppliers, as discussed in the text.

17. d The greater the extent to which the quantity supplied exceeds the quantity demanded, the greater the surplus (excess supply) and the greater the pressure for the price to fall.

18. a There is a surplus (excess supply) when the price is above equilibrium. A surplus will motivate sellers to reduce price to rid themselves of their excess supplies. As the price falls, the quantity demand rises and the quantity supplied falls; demand and supply curves do *not* shift.

19. c Whenever price is below equilibrium, a shortage is observed, and price rises.

20. b Since this statement says demand increases, then the demand curve shifts rightward. There is no change in the supply curve. Assuming an upward sloping supply curve, that means that price will rise and quantity will rise.

21. d Since this statement says supply decreases, then the supply curve shifts leftward. There is no change in the demand curve. Assuming a downward sloping demand curve, that means that price will rise and quantity will fall.

22. a The demand for bikinis would rise, shifting the demand curve to the right. The supply curve does not change. This creates a temporary shortage that is eliminated over time as the market moves to its new equilibrium at a higher price and a greater quantity traded.

23. c Only a decrease in demand will result in a decrease in quantity and a decrease in price.

24. a An increase in demand has a tendency to increase price and increase the quantity. An increase in supply has a tendency to *decrease* the price and increase the quantity. So, on balance, we are certain of an increase in the equilibrium quantity, but we are uncertain about the impact on the price in the market.

25. a An increase in demand causes the quantity demanded to exceed the quantity supplied, creating excess demand (a shortage). This increases the price causing movement *up* along the demand and supply curves resulting in a *greater* quantity traded in the market.

26. b The fallacy of composition is the false assumption that what is true for a part will also be true for the whole.

━━━━━━━ ANSWERS ━━━━━━━

POTENTIAL ESSAY QUESTIONS

The following are annotated answers. They indicate the general idea behind the answer.

1. The shortage of parking spaces implies that permit prices are below equilibrium. The price of a permit should be increased. At least with the purchase of a permit you could be reasonably certain that a space would be available.

2. Suppose there is an increase in demand. The demand curve shifts out to the right, creating a temporary shortage (excess demand) at the original price. As a result, buyers competitively bid up the price. As the price rises, the quantity demanded falls (movement up along the demand curve toward the new point of intersection) and the quantity supplied rises (movement up along the supply curve toward the new point of intersection). Eventually, the price rises enough until the quantity demanded is once again equal to the quantity supplied. Because there is neither a shortage nor a surplus at this new point of intersection, the new market equilibrium price and quantity is obtained. The market equilibrium price and quantity will both increase as a result of an increase in demand. *You should be able to illustrate this graphically as well.*

USING SUPPLY AND DEMAND

5

CHAPTER AT A GLANCE

1. Changes (shifts) in demand and supply are what cause changes in the price and the quantity traded in real-world markets.

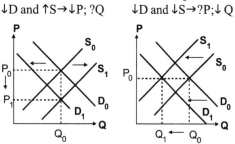

2. Price ceilings cause shortages; price floors cause surpluses.

   A price ceiling is a legal price set by government below equilibrium. An example is rent controls. A price floor is a legal price set by government above equilibrium. An example is the minimum wage.

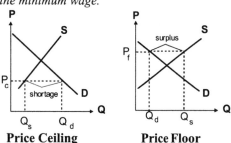

   Price Ceiling   **Price Floor**

3. Excise taxes and tariffs raise price and reduce quantity. Quantity restrictions also decrease supply (shift the supply curve up, to the left) raising the price and reducing the quantity.

Any excise tax imposed on suppliers shifts the supply curve up by the amount of the tax. Quantity restrictions also decrease supply.

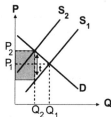

With tax t, price rises to P_2 and the government collects revenue shown by the shaded region. A quantity restriction of Q_2 has the same effect on price and quantity.

4. In a third-party payer system, the consumer and the one who pays the cost differ. In third-party payer systems quantity demanded, price, and total spending are greater than when the consumer pays.

   The graph below shows the effects of a third-party payer market. In a free market, given the supply and demand curve shown, equilibrium price is P_1 and equilibrium quantity is Q_1. If the co-payment, however, is P_0, the consumer purchases quantity Q_2. The supplier will only sell that quantity at price P_2, so the third party pays the difference ($P_2 - P_0$). Under a third-party payer system, total expenditures are larger—shown by the larger shaded square—than a free market—shown by the smaller and darker shaded square.

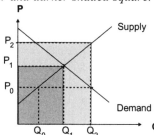

See also, Appendix: "Algebraic Representation of Supply, Demand, and Equilibrium."

● SHORT-ANSWER QUESTIONS

1. Demonstrate graphically what happens in the following situation: Income in the U.S. rose in the 1990s and more and more people began to buy luxury items such as caviar. However, about that same time, the dissolution of the Soviet Union threw suppliers of caviar from the Caspian Sea into a mire of bureaucracy, reducing their ability to export caviar. Market: Caviar sold in the United States.

2. What is a price ceiling? Demonstrate graphically the effect of a price ceiling on a market.

3. What is a price floor? Demonstrate graphically the effect of a price floor on a market.

4. Why are rent controls likely to worsen an existing shortage of housing?

5. Demonstrate graphically what happens to equilibrium price and quantity when a tariff is imposed on imports.

6. What is a third-party payer system? Name one example.

MATCHING THE TERMS
Match the terms to their definitions

___ 1. excise tax
___ 2. minimum wage law
___ 3. price ceiling
___ 4. price floor
___ 5. rent control
___ 6. tariff
___ 7. third-party payer market

a. The law that sets lowest wage a firm can legally pay an employee.
b. Tax on an imported good.
c. Tax that is levied on a specific good.
d. The person who decides how much of the good to buy differs from the person paying for the good.
e. A government-imposed limit on how high a price can be charged.
f. Price ceiling on rents set by government.
g. A government-imposed limit on how low a price can be charged.

PROBLEMS AND APPLICATIONS

1. Suppose you are told that the price of Cadillacs has increased from last year, as has the number bought and sold. Is this an exception to the law of demand, or has there been a change in demand or supply that could account for this?

2. The following table depicts the market supply and demand for milk in the United States.

Price in dollars per gal.	Quantity of gal. supplied in 1,000s	Quantity of gal. demanded in 1,000s
$1.50	600	800
$1.75	620	720
$2.00	640	640
$2.25	660	560
$2.50	680	480

    a. Graph the market supply and demand for milk.

    b. What is the equilibrium market price and quantity in the market?

    c. Show the effect of a government-imposed price floor of $2.25 on the quantity supplied and quantity demanded.

    d. Show the effect of a government-imposed price ceiling of $1.75 on the quantity supplied and quantity demanded.

    e. What would happen to equilibrium price and quantity if the government imposes a $1 per gallon tax on the sellers and as a result, at every price supply decreases by 100,000 gallons? What price would the sellers receive?

3. Suppose the U.S. government imposes stricter entry barriers on Japanese cars imported into the United States. This could be accomplished by the U.S. government either raising tariffs or imposing a quantity restriction (such as a quota).

    a. What impact would this have on the market for Japanese cars in the United States?

    b. What impact would this likely have on the market for American-made cars in the United States?

    c. What do you think could motivate the U.S. government to pursue these stricter entry barriers on Japanese cars coming into the U.S.?

    d. Would Japanese car manufacturers prefer a tariff or a quota? Why?

4. Describe what likely happens to market price and quantity for the particular goods in each of the following cases:

   a. A technological breakthrough lowers the costs of producing tractors in India while there is an increase in incomes of all citizens in India. Market: Tractors.

   b. The United States imposes a ban on the sale of oil by companies that do business with Libya and Iran. At the same time, fracking technology increases U.S. oil production. Market: Oil.

   c. In the summer of 2016, many people watched the Summer Olympics on television instead of going to the movies. At the same time, thinking that summer is the peak season for movies, Hollywood released a record number of movies. Market: Movie tickets.

   d. After a promotional visit by Michael Jordan to France, a craze for Nike Air shoes develops, while workers in Nike's manufacturing plants in China go on strike, decreasing the production of these shoes. Market: Nike shoes.

A1. The supply and demand equations for strawberries are given by $Q_s = -10 + 5P$ and $Q_d = 20 - 5P$ respectively, where P is price in dollars per quart, Q_s is millions of quarts of strawberries supplied, and Q_d is millions of quarts of strawberries demanded.

   a. What is the equilibrium market price and quantity for strawberries in the market?

   b. Suppose a new preservative is introduced that prevents more strawberries from rotting on their way from the farm to the store. As a result, the supply of strawberries increases by 20 million quarts at every price. What effect does this have on market price and quantity sold?

   c. Given the original supply, now suppose it has been found that the spray used on cherry trees has ill effects on those who eat the cherries. As a result, the demand for strawberries increases by 10 million quarts at every price. What effect does this have on market price for strawberries and quantity of strawberries sold?

A2. The supply and demand equations for roses are given by $Q_s = -10 + 3P$ and $Q_d = 20 - 2P$ respectively, where P is dollars per dozen roses and Q is dozens of roses in hundred thousands.

   a. What is the equilibrium market price and quantity of roses sold?

   b. Suppose the government decides to make it more affordable for individuals to give roses to their significant others, and sets a price ceiling for roses at $4 a dozen. What is the likely result?

c. Suppose the government decides to tax the suppliers of roses $1 per dozen roses sold. What is the equilibrium price and quantity in the market? How much do buyers pay for each dozen they buy for their significant others? How much do suppliers receive for each dozen they sell?

d. Suppose the government decides instead to impose a $1 tax on buyers for each dozen roses purchased. (Government has determined buying roses for love to be a demerit good.) What is the equilibrium price and quantity in the market? How much do the buyers pay and how much do the sellers receive?

● MULTIPLE CHOICE

Circle the one best answer for each of the following questions:

1. If a frost in Florida damages oranges, what will likely happen to the market for Florida oranges?
   a. Demand will increase.
   b. Demand will fall.
   c. Supply will increase.
   d. Supply will decrease.

2. Assume that the cost of shipping automobiles from the United States to Japan decreases. What will most likely happen to the selling price and quantity of cars made in the U.S. and sold in Japan?
   a. The price will rise, and quantity will fall.
   b. Both price and quantity will rise.
   c. The price will fall, and quantity will rise.
   d. The price will fall. What happens to quantity is not clear.

3. Assuming standard supply and demand curves, what will likely happen to the price and quantity of cricket bats in Trinidad as interest in cricket dwindles following the dismal performance of the national cricket team, while at the same time taxes are repealed on producing cricket bats?
   a. The price will decrease, but what happens to quantity is not clear.
   b. The price will decrease, and quantity will increase.
   c. The price will increase, but what happens to quantity is not clear.
   d. It is not clear what happens to either price or quantity.

4. A higher equilibrium price with no change in market equilibrium quantity could be caused by:
   a. supply shifting in and no change in demand.
   b. supply and demand both increasing.
   c. a decrease in supply and an increase in demand.
   d. demand and supply both shifting in.

5. Referring to the graph below, if there is a price ceiling imposed on this market of P_2, consumers will pay:

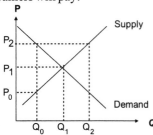

   a. P_1 and buy quantity Q_1.
   b. P_2 and buy quantity Q_2.
   c. P_0 and buy quantity Q_0.
   d. P_2 and buy quantity Q_0.

6. Referring to the graph below, if there is a price floor imposed on this market of P_2, consumers will pay:

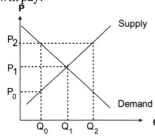

a. P_1 and buy quantity Q_1.
b. P_2 and buy quantity Q_2.
c. P_0 and buy quantity Q_0.
d. P_2 and buy quantity Q_0.

7. Effective rent controls:
    a. are examples of price floors.
    b. cause the quantity of rental occupied housing demanded to exceed the quantity supplied.
    c. create a greater amount of higher quality housing to be made available to renters.
    d. create a surplus of rental occupied housing.

8. An increase in the minimum wage can be expected to:
    a. cause unemployment for some workers.
    b. cause a shortage of workers.
    c. increase employment.
    d. help businesses by reducing their costs of production.

9. A tariff:
    a. is a tax imposed on an imported good.
    b. is a quantitative restriction on the amount that one country can export to another.
    c. imposed on a good will shift the supply of that good outward to the right.
    d. will reduce the price paid by the consumer of the good.

10. Quantity restrictions on supply imposed below equilibrium quantity on a market:
    a. increase price and reduce quantity traded.
    b. increase price and increase quantity traded.
    c. decrease price and reduce quantity traded.
    d. decrease price and increase quantity traded.

11. Referring to the graph below, suppose initial supply is represented by S_0. A tax T on suppliers will raise the price that:

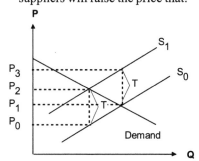

a. suppliers receive net of the tax to P_0.
b. suppliers receive net of the tax to P_1.
c. consumers pay to P_2.
d. consumers pay to P_3.

12. In a third-party payer system:
    a. the person who chooses the product pays the entire cost.
    b. the quantity demanded would be lower than it otherwise would be.
    c. the quantity demanded will be higher than it otherwise would be.
    d. consumers are hurt.

13. In the graph below that demonstrates a third-party payer market, suppose the consumer is required to make a co-payment of P_0. Which of the following areas represents the cost of the program to the third party?

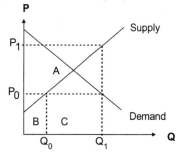

a. Rectangle A.
b. Rectangle B.
c. Rectangle C.
d. The sum of rectangles A, B, and C.

14. Third-party payer markets result in:
    a. a lower equilibrium price received by the supplier.
    b. a smaller quantity supplied.
    c. a smaller quantity demanded.
    d. increased total spending.

A1. The supply and demand equations for Nantucket Nectar's Kiwi-berry juice are given by $Q_s = -4 + 5P$ and $Q_d = 18 - 6P$ respectively, where price is dollars per quart and quantity is thousands of quarts. The equilibrium market price and quantity is:
    a. $P = \$2$, $Q = 6$ thousand quarts.
    b. $P = \$3$, $Q = 5$ thousand quarts.
    c. $P = \$14$, $Q = 66$ thousand quarts.
    d. $P = \$22$, $Q = 106$ thousand quarts.

A2. The supply and demand equations for sidewalk snow removal in a small town in Montana are given by $Q_s = -50 + 5P$ and $Q_d = 100 - 5P$ respectively, where price is in dollars per removal and quantity is numbers of removals per week. It snows so much that demand for sidewalk snow removals increases by 30 removals per week. The new equilibrium market price and quantity is:
   a. P = $15, Q = 6 sidewalk snow removals.
   b. P = $15, Q = 5 sidewalk snow removals.
   c. P = $18, Q = 66 sidewalk snow removals.
   d. P = $18, Q = 40 sidewalk snow removals.

A3. The supply and demand equations for Arizona Ice Tea in Arizona are given by $Q_s = -10 + 6P$ and $Q_d = 40 - 8P$; P is the price of each bottle in dollars; and quantity is in hundreds of thousands of bottles per month. Suppose the state government imposes a $1 per bottle tax on the suppliers. The market price the suppliers receive and the equilibrium quantity in the market are:
   a. $3 per bottle and 800 thousand bottles per month.
   b. $3 per bottle and 1,600 thousand bottles per month.
   c. $4 per bottle and 800 thousand bottles per month.
   d. $4 per bottle and 1,600 thousand bottles per month.

● POTENTIAL ESSAY QUESTIONS

You may also see essay questions similar to the "Problems & Applications" exercises.

1.   Who wins and who loses with a minimum wage? Explain your answer. How might it help those who had been unemployed without the minimum wage?

2.   Explain why a third-party payer system results in a greater quantity demanded and increases total spending.

ANSWERS

SHORT-ANSWER QUESTIONS

1. The demand curve for Russian caviar shifts
    out; supply shifts in; the price rises substan-
    tially. What happens to quantity depends
    upon the relative sizes of the shifts.

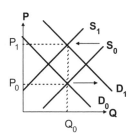

2. A price ceiling is a government-imposed limit
    on how high a price can be charged. An
    effective price ceiling below market equilibrium
    price will cause $Q_D > Q_S$ (a shortage) as shown
    in the graph below.

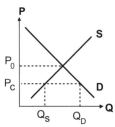

3. A price floor is a government-imposed limit on
    how low a price can be charged. An effective
    price floor above market equilibrium price will
    cause $Q_S > Q_D$ (a surplus) as shown in the
    graph below.

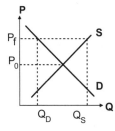

4. Rent controls are price ceilings and result in
    shortages in rental housing. As time passes
    and as the population rises, the demand for
    rental housing rises. On the supply side, other
    ventures become more lucrative relative to
    renting out housing. Owners have less
    incentive to repair existing buildings, let alone

build new ones, reducing the supply of rental
housing over time. As a result, the shortage
becomes more acute over time

5. A tariff is an excise tax paid by foreign produc-
    ers on an imported good. As a tariff of t is
    imposed, the supply curve shifts upward to S_1
    by the amount of the tariff. The equilibrium
    price goes up and quantity goes down.

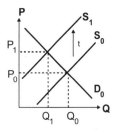

6. In a third-party payer system the person who
    decides how much of a good to buy differs
    from the person who pays for the good. One
    example is the health care system in the United
    States today.

ANSWERS

MATCHING

1-c; 2-a; 3-e; 4-g; 5-f; 6-b; 7-d.

ANSWERS

PROBLEMS AND APPLICATIONS

1. This is not an exception to the law of demand
    (there are very few exceptions). Instead, an
    increase in demand could account for a higher
    price and a greater amount bought and sold, as
    is illustrated in the figure below.

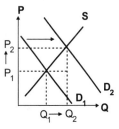

2. a. The market supply and demand for milk is graphed below.

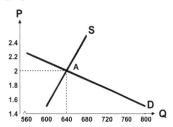

b. The equilibrium market price is $2 and equilibrium quantity in the market is 640 thousand gallons of milk because the quantity supplied equals the quantity demanded. This is point *A* on the graph above.

c. A government-imposed price floor of $2.25 is shown in the figure below. Since it is a price above market price, quantity supplied (660) exceeds quantity demanded (560) by 100 thousand gallons.

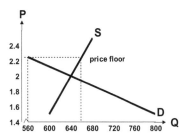

d. A government-imposed price ceiling of $1.75 is below market price. Quantity supplied (620 thousand gallons) will be less than quantity demanded (720 thousand gallons) by 100 thousand gallons, as shown below.

e. Because of the tax, the quantity supplied at every price level will decline by 100 thousand gallons. The supply and demand table will change as follows:

Price in dollars per gal.	Quantity of gal. supplied 1,000s	Quantity of gal. demanded 1,000s
$1.50	500	800
$1.75	520	720
$2.00	540	640
$2.25	560	560
$2.50	580	480

The market equilibrium price would be $2.25 and the equilibrium quantity would be 560 thousand gallons. Since the sellers will have to pay $1 tax on every gallon they sell, they will receive $1.25 per gallon of milk.

3. a. A higher tariff or a stricter quota imposed on Japanese cars would decrease the supply of Japanese cars in the United States. The upward (leftward) shift of the supply curve, such as from S_1 to S_2 shown in the figure below, creates a temporary shortage (excess demand) at the original price that puts upward pressure on the prices of Japanese cars. The result over time will be higher prices for Japanese cars, as well as a decrease in the amount bought and sold in the U.S. market, as shown below.

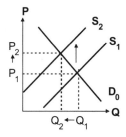

b. Because Japanese and American-made cars are substitutes for each other, some people will switch from buying the now relatively more expensive Japanese cars (law of demand in action) to buying more American-made cars. (Notice that "relative" prices are what are relevant.) This increases the demand for American-made cars, increasing their prices as well as the amount bought and sold. This is illustrated in the figure on the top of the following page.

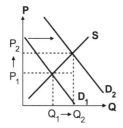

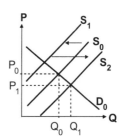

c. These trade barriers may be advocated by American car manufacturers. They could obviously benefit from the higher prices and greater sales. American automotive workers could also benefit from the greater job security that comes with more cars being produced and sold. These "special interest groups" may put political pressure on government, and the government may succumb to that pressure.

d. The Japanese would prefer a quota over a tariff. This is because a tariff would require them to pay taxes to the U.S. government, while a quota would not.

4. a. The supply curve will shift out from S_0 to S_1 as the new technology makes it cheaper to produce tractors. Increased incomes will shift the demand for tractors out from D_0 to D_1. Equilibrium price may go up, remain the same, or go down, depending on the relative shifts in the two curves. Equilibrium quantity, however, will definitely increase.

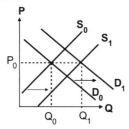

b. The ban on the companies doing business with Libya and Iran will shift the supply curve in from S_0 to S_1. The discovery of oil will, however, shift it back out to possibly S_2. Depending on the relative shifts, equilibrium price and quantity will change. In the case shown in the diagram, the shift resulting from the discovery of the new oil source dominates the shift resulting from the ban, and the equilibrium price falls and quantity goes up.

c. With more people watching the Olympics, the demand for movies shifts in from D_0 to D_1. At the same time the increased supply of movies will shift the supply curve out from S_0 to S_1. Equilibrium price will fall, while the change in equilibrium quantity will depend on the relative shifts in the curves.

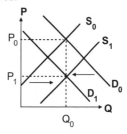

d. With more people demanding Nike Air shoes, the demand curve will shift out from D_0 to D_1. The worker strike will, however, reduce supply and shift it in from S_0 to S_1. The resulting equilibrium price will be higher, while the change in quantity depends on the relative shifts in the curves.

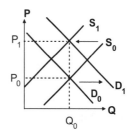

A1. a. Equating Q_s to Q_d and then solving for equilibrium price gives us $3 per quart. Substituting $3 into the demand and supply equations, we find that equilibrium quantity is 5 million quarts.

b. Since supply increases by 20 million quarts, the new supply equation is $Q_s = 10 + 5P$. Equating this with the demand equation, we find the new equilibrium price to be $1 per quart. Substituting into either the new supply equation or the demand equation we find that equilibrium quantity is 15 million quarts.

   c. With demand increasing, the new demand equation is $Q_d = 30 - 5P$. Setting Q_s equal to Q_d and solving for price we find equilibrium price to be $4 per quart. Substituting this into either the new demand or the supply equation we find equilibrium quantity to be 10 million quarts.

A2. a. Equating Q_s and Q_d, then solving gives equilibrium price $6 and quantity 8 hundred thousand dozen.

   b. If price ceiling is set at $4, $Q_s = 2$, and $Q_d = 12$, resulting in a shortage of ten hundred thousand dozen.

   c. If a $1 tax is imposed on suppliers, the new supply equation will be $Q_s = -10 + 3(P-1) = -13 + 3P$. Equating this with Q_d gives equilibrium price $6.60 and quantity 6.8 hundred thousand. Buyers pay $6.60 for each dozen they buy, and the sellers receive $1 less than that, or $5.60, for each dozen they sell.

   d. As a result of the tax, the new demand equation will be $Q_d = 20 - 2(P+1) = 18 - 2P$. Equating this with Q_s gives equilibrium price $5.60 and quantity 6.8 hundred thousand. Buyers pay $6.60 (P + 1) for each dozen they buy, and the sellers receive $5.60 for each dozen they sell.

ANSWERS

MULTIPLE CHOICE

1. d   A frost will reduce the quantity of oranges available for sale at every price. Supply will decrease.

2. c   The supply curve will shift out, market price will fall and the quantity will rise.

3. a   Demand for cricket bats will fall, shifting the demand curve in, while the tax repeal will shift the supply curve out. Price will fall, and quantity may change depending on the relative shifts of the supply and demand curves.

4. c   When the demand curve shifts out, while the supply curve shifts in, the price rises and the quantity can remain the same.

5. a   A price ceiling above equilibrium price will not affect the market price or quantity. Equilibrium price and quantity, in this case will be determined by the intersection of the supply and demand curves—at price P_1 and quantity Q_1.

6. d   At a price of P_2 the quantity demanded by consumers is Q_0. The quantity supplied by sellers would be Q_2 at price P_2. A surplus of $Q_2 - Q_0$ would put downward pressure on price. However, government does not allow a lower price. So, the equilibrium price and quantity of P_1 and Q_1 would not prevail when government intervenes with a price floor.

7. b   Rent controls are price ceilings and therefore cause the quantity demanded to exceed the quantity supplied. Indeed, the quantity demanded rises while the quantity supplied falls, creating a shortage.

8. a   Because the minimum wage is a price floor it increases the quantity supplied and decreases the quantity demanded (*decreasing* employment) and creating a *surplus* of workers (causing some unemployment). The higher minimum wage would *increase* costs of production to businesses.

9. a   The correct answer is a by definition. Also, a tariff will decrease supply, shifting the supply curve inward to the left. This causes the price consumers must pay to rise.

10. a   Quantity restrictions reduce supply and create a higher price and lower quantity traded in a market.

11. c   A tax shifts the supply curve up by the amount of the tax. The price consumers pay is determined by the price where the demand curve and the after-tax supply curve intersect. The after-tax price suppliers receive falls to P_0, the new equilibrium price less the tax $(P_2 - T)$.

12. c   In a third-party payer system the person who chooses the product pays some but not all of the cost. As a result of a lower effective price to the consumer, the quantity demanded will be higher than otherwise.

13. a   At a price of P_0, the consumer demands quantity Q_1. The supplier requires a price of P_1 for that quantity. Therefore, total expenditures are P_1 times Q_1 or areas A, B, and C. Of these, consumers pay areas B and C. The third party pays area A.

14. d   In third-party payer markets the quantity demanded, price, and total spending are greater than when the consumer pays.

A1. a   Equating the supply and demand equations gives equilibrium P = $2. Substituting this into either the supply or demand equation tells us that Q = 6 thousand quarts.

A2. d   The new demand becomes $Q_d = 130 - 5P$. Equating the supply and demand equations gives equilibrium P = $18. Substituting this into either the supply or demand equation tells us that Q = 40 sidewalk snow removals.

A3. a   A $1 per bottle tax on suppliers makes the supply equation $Q_s = -10 + 6(P - 1) = -16 + 6P$. Equating this with the demand equation gives equilibrium P = $4 and Q = 8 hundred thousand. The supplier receives $3 ($4 − $1).

━━━━━ ANSWERS ━━━━━

POTENTIAL ESSAY QUESTIONS

The following are annotated answers. They indicate the general idea behind the answer.

1. A minimum wage is a wage set by government that sets a floor in wages paid to employees. The effect is to reduce the quantity of employees firms demand and increase the quantity of people seeking work. Those who were previously employed but now are not are hurt. Firms are hurt because their costs rise. Because the limited supply must be rationed in some way, a person who had a job when price rationed jobs might not with non-price rationing.

2. Because part of the costs of obtaining a good or service in a third-party payer system is paid by someone other than the consumer, the effective price to the consumer is lower and the quantity demanded is greater. At this higher quantity demanded the price charged by sellers is greater. The result is greater consumption at a higher price and therefore greater total spending on the good or service. See Figure 5-6 for a graphic illustration of this.

Pretest
Chapters 1 - 5

Take this test in test conditions, giving yourself a limited amount of time to complete the questions. Ideally, check with your professor to see how much time he or she allows for an average multiple choice question and multiply this by 22. This is the time limit you should set for yourself for this pretest. If you do not know how much time your teacher would allow, we suggest 1 minute per question, or about 22 minutes.

1. You bought stock A for $10 and stock B for $50. The price of each is currently $20. Assuming no tax issues, which should you sell if you need money?
   a. Stock A.
   b. Stock B.
   c. There is not enough information to tell which to sell.
   d. You should sell an equal amount of both.

2. The opportunity cost of reading Chapter 1 of a 38-chapter text:
   a. is about 1/38 of the price you paid for the book because the chapter is about 1/38 of the book.
   b. is zero since you have already paid for the book.
   c. has nothing to do with the price you paid for the book.
   d. is 1/38 the price of the book plus 1/38 the price of tuition for the course.

3. If at Female College there are significantly more females than males (and there are not a significant number of gays or off-campus dating opportunities), economic forces:
   a. will likely push for females to pay for dinners on dates.
   b. will likely push for males to pay for dinners on dates.
   c. will likely push for neither to pay for dinners on dates.
   d. are irrelevant to this issue. Everyone knows that the males always should pay.

4. The statement, "The distribution of income should be left to the market," is:
   a. a positive statement.
   b. a normative statement.
   c. an art-of-economics statement.
   d. an objective statement.

5. If the opportunity cost of good X in terms of good Y is 2Y, so you'll have to give up 2Y to get one X, the production possibility curve could look like:
   a. A only.
   b. B only.
   c. C only.
   d. A, B, or C.

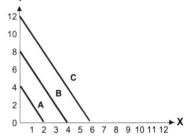

6. Given the accompanying production possibility curve, when you're moving from point C to point B the opportunity cost of butter in terms of guns is:
   a. 1/3.
   b. 1.
   c. 2.
   d. 3/2.

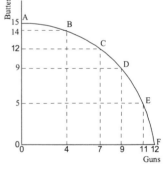

7. If countries A and B have production possibility curves A and B respectively, country A has a comparative advantage in the production of:
   a. no good.
   b. both goods.
   c. good X only.
   d. good Y only.

8. In theory, socialism is an economic system:
    a. that tries to organize society in the same ways as most families are organized, striving to see that individuals get what they need.
    b. based on central planning and government ownership of the means of production.
    c. based on private property rights.
    d. based on markets.

9. In practice, in command or socialist economies, the "what to produce" decision is most often made by:
    a. consumers.
    b. the market.
    c. government.
    d. firms.

10. In a market economy, the "what to produce" decision in practice is most often made directly by:
    a. consumers.
    b. the market.
    c. government.
    d. firms.

11. The largest percentage of business receipts are by:
    a. partnerships.
    b. sole proprietorships.
    c. corporations.
    d. nonprofit companies.

12. The largest percentage of state and local expenditures is on:
    a. education.
    b. health.
    c. transportation.
    d. income security.

13. When government attempts to adjust for the effect of decisions on third parties not taken into account by the decision makers, the government is attempting to:
    a. provide for a stable set of institutions and rules.
    b. promote effective and workable competition.
    c. provide public goods and services.
    d. correct for externalities.

14. There are many more substitutes for good A than for good B.
    a. The demand curve for good B will likely shift out further.
    b. The demand curve for good B will likely be flatter.
    c. You can't say anything about the likely relative flatness of the demand curves.
    d. The demand curve for good A will likely be flatter.

15. If the price of air conditioners falls, there will be:
    a. an increase in demand for air conditioners.
    b. an increase in the quantity of air conditioners demanded.
    c. an increase in the quantity of air conditioners supplied.
    d. a shift out of the supply curve for air conditioners.

16. The law of supply states that:
    a. quantity supplied increases as price increases, other things constant.
    b. quantity supplied decreases as price increases, other things constant.
    c. more of a good will be supplied the higher its price, other things changing proportionately.
    d. less of a good will be supplied the higher its price, other things changing proportionately.

17. If at some price the quantity supplied exceeds the quantity demanded, then:
    a. a surplus (excess supply) exists and the price will fall over time as sellers competitively bid down the price.
    b. a shortage (excess demand) exists and the price will rise over time as buyers competitively bid up the price.
    c. the price is below equilibrium.
    d. equilibrium will be reestablished as the demand curve shifts to the left.

18. An increase in demand for a good will cause:
    a. excess demand (a shortage) until price changes.
    b. movement down along the demand curve as price changes.
    c. movement down along the supply curve as price changes.
    d. a higher price and a smaller quantity traded in the market.

19. A higher equilibrium price with no change in market equilibrium quantity could be caused by:
   a. supply shifting in and no change in demand.
   b. supply and demand both increasing.
   c. a decrease in supply and an increase in demand.
   d. demand and supply both shifting in.

20. Effective rent controls:
   a. are examples of price floors.
   b. cause the quantity of rental occupied housing demanded to exceed the quantity supplied.
   c. create a greater amount of higher quality housing to be made available to renters.
   d. create a surplus of rental occupied housing.

21. Referring to the graph below, suppose initial supply is represented by S_0. A tax T on suppliers will raise the price that:

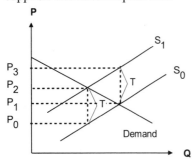

   a. suppliers receive net of the tax to P_1.
   b. suppliers receive net of the tax to P_2.
   c. consumers pay to P_2.
   d. consumers pay to P_3.

22. Third-party payer markets result in:
   a. a lower equilibrium price received by the supplier.
   b. a smaller quantity supplied.
   c. a smaller quantity demanded.
   d. increased total spending.

━━━━━ ANSWERS ━━━━━

1.	c	(1:5)	**12.**	a	(3:11)
2.	c	(1:11)	**13.**	d	(3:14)
3.	a	(1:13)	**14.**	d	(4:2)
4.	b	(1:18)	**15.**	b	(4:4)
5.	d	(2:3)	**16.**	a	(4:13)
6.	d	(2:6)	**17.**	a	(4:18)
7.	d	(2:12)	**18.**	a	(4:25)
8.	a	(3:2)	**19.**	c	(5:4)
9.	c	(3:4)	**20.**	b	(5:7)
10.	d	(3:5)	**21.**	c	(5:11)
11.	c	(3:9)	**22.**	d	(5:14)

Key: The figures in parentheses refer to multiple choice question and chapter numbers. For example (1:2) is multiple choice question 2 from chapter 1.

ECONOMIC GROWTH, BUSINESS CYCLES, AND UNEMPLOYMENT

CHAPTER AT A GLANCE

1. Keynesian economics developed as economists debated the cause of the Great Depression.

   In the 1930s, the economy was in a depression with 25 percent unemployment. Classical economists believed that wages would fall and eliminate the unemployment. Keynesian economists believed that the economy could remain in a depression unless government did something to increase spending.

2. As problems facing the economy changed, so did economic theory. By the 1980s, Keynesian and Classical economics merged into a new conventional economics. The policy agreement between Keynesians and Classicals started to unravel with the recent structural stagnation facing the economy.

   The short-run framework (Keynesian) focuses on demand. The long-run framework (Classical) focuses on supply.

   In the 1970s Keynesian and Classical policies were both used. This policy agreement unraveled when the economy experienced structural stagnation.

3a. Growth is usually measured by changes in total output and changes in per capita output. U.S. economic output has grown at an annual rate of 2.5 to 3.5 percent. It has recently slowed.

   Growth is desired because it increases standards of living.

3b. The range of growth rates among countries is wide.

Economies in Africa have consistently grown at below average rates. India and China have grown quickly over the past thirty years.

3c. Since 1945 the United States has had 11 recessions; the most recent was 2008-09.

   The 2008-09 recession was followed by slow growth and the economy not providing the type jobs society expects from it. This has given rise to the term structural stagnation.

4. The four phases of the business cycle are: the peak, the downturn, the trough, and the upturn.

   Structural stagnation is different from a business cycle. It is a period of protracted slow growth. Know the difference!

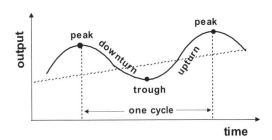

Note!
- *There is an overall upward secular growth trend of 2.5-3.5% shown by the dotted line.*
- *We want to smooth out fluctuations because of the problems associated with them.*

5. The unemployment rate is the percentage of people in the economy who are both able to and looking for work but who cannot find jobs.

Cyclical unemployment rises during a recession and falls during an expansion. Structural unemployment doesn't change over a business cycle. It is caused by restructuring in the economy.

The difference matters to policy. An economy can grow out of cyclical unemployment, but not structural unemployment. For structural unemployment to fall, the economy must go through structural changes. While the unemployment rate has fallen, many people cannot find the type of jobs they want. Others have dropped out of the labor force.

Some believe unemployment is an individual problem. Others believe it is a social problem.

SHORT-ANSWER QUESTIONS

1. How does the Keynesian explanation of the Great Depression differ from the Classical explanation?

2. What policies have Keynesians suggested to address structural stagnation? What policies have Classicals suggested?

3. What are the two frameworks economists use to analyze unemployment, inflation, growth, and business cycles? What distinguishes the two frameworks from one another?

4. How does the U.S. per capita growth rate today compare to its growth rate over the previous three decades?

5. How long has the average expansion since mid-1945 lasted?

6. What distinguishes a business cycle from a structural stagnation?

7. Label the four phases of the business cycle in the graph below.

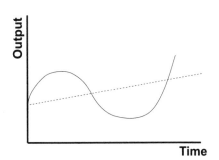

8. What distinguishes structural from cyclical unemployment? Who believes that more of the unemployment today is structural? Those who believe the structural stagnation view or the conventional business cycle view?

9. How is the unemployment rate calculated?

10. How might the offical unemployment rate overestimate the unemployment rate? How might it underestimate it?

MATCHING THE TERMS
Match the terms to their definitions

___ 1. business cycle
___ 2. Classical economists
___ 3. cyclical unemployment
___ 4. depression
___ 5. frictional unemployment
___ 6. Keynesian economists
___ 7. labor force
___ 8. macroeconomics
___ 9. per capita output
___ 10. potential output
___ 11. recession
___ 12. structural stagnation
___ 13. structural unemployment
___ 14. target rate of unemployment
___ 15. unemployment rate

a. The study of the problems such as lack of growth, recessions, unemployment, and inflation and what to do about them.

b. Economists who believe that business cycles (ups and downs of the economy) are temporary glitches, and who generally favor laissez-faire, or nonactivist, policies.

c. Economists who believe that business cycles reflect underlying problems that can be addressed with activist government policies.

d. A period of protracted slow growth with the economy not providing the type of jobs expected.

e. The highest amount of output an economy can sustainably produce and sell using existing production processes and resources.

f. A short-run, temporary upward or downward movement of economic activity, or real GDP, that occurs around the growth trend.

g. A decline in real output that persists for more than two consecutive quarters of a year.

h. Those in an economy who are willing and able to work.

i. The percentage of people in the economy who are both able to and looking for work but who cannot find jobs.

j. Unemployment resulting from fluctuations in economic activity.

k. Unemployment caused by the institutional structure of an economy or by economic restructuring making some skills obsolete.

l. Unemployment caused by people entering the job market and people quitting a job just long enough to look for and find another one.

m. The lowest sustainable rate of unemployment that policy makers believe is achievable given existing demographics and the economy's institutional structure.

n. Output divided by the total population.

o. A deep and prolonged recession.

PROBLEMS AND APPLICATIONS

1. State whether each of the following is likely to be opinions of a Classical economist, Keynesian economist, both, or neither.

    a. The current business cycle is a normal part of a market economy. The economy will return to its trend growth rate on its own.

    b. The current business cycle is a glitch in the workings of a market economy that can be addressed with government policies.

c. The current business cycle is not a business cycle at all. For the economy to return to its trend growth, it will have to undergo structural changes.

d. The decline in the growth trend of the economy can be addressed with a combination of demand- and supply-side policies.

2. Fill in the table below:

Output	Population	Per Capita Output
$100,000	200	
	150	$65,000
$1,250,000		$50,000

3. Economic growth differs among countries.

a. Rank the following according to growth over the past 10 years:

Africa

China

United States

b. What pressures will continued economic growth in other countries place on the United States?

4. For each, state whether the unemployment is structural or cyclical.

a. As the United States becomes a more high-tech producer, labor-intensive factories relocate to low-wage countries. Factory workers lose their jobs and the unemployment rate rises.

b. As it becomes more acceptable for mothers to work, more women enter the labor market looking for work. The unemployment rate rises.

c. Foreign economies slow and demand fewer U.S. exports. The unemployment rate rises.

5. Calculate the following given the information about the economy in the table:

Total population	290 million
Noninstitutional population	220 million
Incapable of working	70 million
Not in the labor force	75 million
Employed	135 million
Unemployed	10 million

a. Labor force.

b. Unemployment rate.

MULTIPLE CHOICE

Circle the one best answer for each of the following questions:

1. Classical economists are generally associated with:
   a. laissez faire.
   b. QWERTY.
   c. an activist policy.
   d. their support of low unemployment.

2. Keynesian economics focuses on:
   a. the long run.
   b. the short run.
   c. both the long run and the short run.
   d. neither the long run nor the short run.

3. Keynesians:
   a. generally favor activist government policies.
   b. generally favor laissez-faire policies.
   c. believe that frictional unemployment does not exist.
   d. believe that all unemployment is cyclical unemployment.

4. Classicals:
   a. generally favor activist government policies.
   b. generally favor laissez-faire policies.
   c. believe that frictional unemployment does not exist.
   d. believe that all unemployment is cyclical unemployment.

5. The two frameworks conventional economists generally use to analyze macroeconomic issues are:
   a. the inflation and the unemployment frameworks.
   b. the short-run and the long-run frameworks.
   c. the business cycle and the growth cycle frameworks.
   d. the stagnationist and the Post-Keynesian frameworks.

6. Classical and Keynesian economics merged into one conventional economics when the problem facing the economy was a period of:
   a. high growth.
   b. low unemployment.
   c. high inflation.
   d. high unemployment.

7. The combination of slow growth and not the type of jobs society expects is known as:
   a. structural stagnation.
   b. secular stagnation.
   c. a business cycle.
   d. a recession.

8. If a country of 300 million people has a total income of $12 trillion, its per capita income is:
   a. $36,000.
   b. $40,000.
   c. $360,000.
   d. $400,000.

9. The secular trend growth rate in the United States is approximately:
   a. 1 to 1.5 percent per year.
   b. 2.5 to 3.5 percent per year.
   c. 5 to 5.5 percent per year.
   d. 7 to 7.5 percent per year.

10. Which geographic area or country recently has the highest per capita growth rate?
    a. China.
    b. Western Europe.
    c. North America.
    d. Latin America.

11. The Great Depression occurred in the early:
    a. 1900s.
    b. 1930s.
    c. 1950s.
    d. 1960s.

12. Growth in the graph below is depicted by:

    a. A
    b. B
    c. C
    d. D

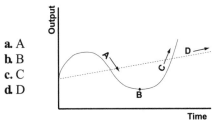

13. What turns a business cycle into a structural stagnation?
    a. A trough that is lower than the peak.
    b. Multiple business cycles in a short period of time.
    c. A slow expansion that keeps the economy below trend.
    d. A downturn that doesn't end.

14. Unemployment caused by people entering the job market and people quitting a job just long enough to look for and find another one:

a. is called structural unemployment.

b. is called frictional unemployment.

c. is called cyclical unemployment.

d. are not counted in the unemployment rate.

15. The total labor force is 100,000 out of a possible working age population of 160,000. The total number of unemployed is 8,000. What is the unemployment rate?

a. 5 percent.

b. 6 percent.

c. 7 percent.

d. 8 percent.

16. What effect will including discouraged workers have on the unemployment rate?

a. Lower it because it would reduce the number of unemployed.

b. Raise it because there are always discouraged workers.

c. Have no impact because discouraged workers are already included.

d. The measures are unrelated and therefore cannot be compared.

17. Keynesians are most likely to:

a. include discouraged workers in their calculation of the unemployment rate.

b. exclude discouraged workers in their calculation of the unemployment rate.

c. focus on the distinction between structural and cyclical unemployment.

d. focus on the distinction between voluntary and involuntary unemployment.

18. The highest amount of output an economy can sustainably produce and sell using existing production processes and resources is called:

a. nominal output.

b. actual output.

c. potential output.

d. utilized output.

POTENTIAL ESSAY QUESTIONS

You may also see essay questions similar to the "Problems & Applications" exercises.

1. What is the essence of the Classical explanation for the Great Depression? What is the essence of the Keynesian explanation? Why did the two views merge in the 1970s and 1980s? Why did the combination of the two views unravel?

2. What is potential output? Which is greater: Potential or actual output during a recession?

3. Why is the framework an economist uses to analyze problems in an economy important to their policy suggestions? Give examples of policies within the short-run framework and within the long-run framework.

ANSWERS

SHORT-ANSWER QUESTIONS

1. Classical economists focused on wages. They explained that unemployment would decline if wages were allowed to decline. Political and social forces were keeping wages too high. Keynesians focused on insufficient aggregate spending that resulted in a downward spiral. The economy was at a below-potential-income equilibrium.

2. Keynesians believed that government needed to increase spending. Classicals believed that the government needed to cut spending and cut taxes.

3. Economists use the long-run framework and the short-run framework to analyze macroeconomic problems. The long-run framework focuses on supply while the short-run framework focuses on demand.

4. Per capita output has grown about 1.5 percent a year in the past decade compared to about 2 percent in previous decades.

5. The average expansion since mid-1945 has lasted 59 months.

6. In a regular business cycle, the economy is expected to return to its long-term growth trend. In a structural stagnation, the economy does not grow enough after a recession to return to its long-term trend.

7. The four phases of the business cycle are: the peak, the downturn (recession), the trough, and the upturn. They are labeled in the graph below.

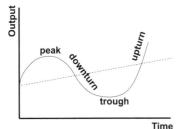

8. Structural unemployment is unemployment caused by the structure of an economy. An economy does not grow out of structural unemployment. Structural unemployment is lowered through structural change in an economy. Cyclical unemployment is unemployment caused by the ups and downs of the economy over the business cycle. Cyclical unemployment falls during an expansion. Structural stagnationists see more of the current unemployment rate as structural than do those who hold the conventional business cycle view.

9. The unemployment rate is equal to the total number of people able to, and looking for, work but who cannot find work (the unemployed) divided by the labor force times 100.

10. The official unemployment rate is an underestimate to the extent that those who are not employed and leave the labor force are discouraged and those working part time and who would prefer to be working full time are not counted among the unemployed. The official unemployment rate is an overestimate to the extent that those counted as unemployed are working off the books, are declining job offers because the wage is too low or the job doesn't utilize their skills and education, or are claiming to look for work, but are not really doing so.

ANSWERS

MATCHING

1-f; 2-b; 3-j; 4-o; 5-l; 6-c; 7-h; 8-a; 9-n; 10-e; 11-g; 12-d; 13-k; 14-m; 15-i.

ANSWERS

PROBLEMS AND APPLICATIONS

1. a. Classical.
    b. Keynesian.
    c. Neither.
    d. Keynesian and Classical.

2.

Output	Population	per capita output
$100,000	200	$500
$9,750,000	150	$65,000
$1,250,000	25	$50,000

3. a. 1. China, 2. United States, 3. Africa.
   b. Growth in China and India will put pressure on the United States to lower wages, improve efficiency, and move production abroad.

4. a. Structural because this is a structural change in the economy.
   b. Structural because this is a change in social structure.
   c. Cyclical because this is unemployment due to a change in economic activity.

5. a. Labor force = employed + unemployed = 145 million.
   b. Unemployment rate = (unemployed/labor force) $\times$ 100 = 6.9%.

━━━━ **ANSWERS** ━━━━

MULTIPLE CHOICE

1. a Laissez faire is the non-activist policy that Classical economists generally support.

2. b The essence of Keynesian economics is its focus on the short run.

3. a Keynesians generally favor activist government policies.

4. b Classicals generally favor laissez-faire policies.

5. b Stagnationist and Post-Keynesian frameworks are not conventional. The answers in a and c are not frameworks.

6. c Classical and Keynesian economics merged in the 1970s when inflation became a problem that fit neither the Keynesian nor Classical frameworks entirely.

7. a See the definition of structural stagnation in the text.

8. b Per capita income is calculated by dividing total income by total population as stated in the text.

9. b The secular trend is the long-term growth trend.

10. a China's economy has grown the fastest as can be seen in Figure 24-1.

11. b The Depression occurred in the 1930s.

12. d Growth is shown as the smooth upward line. It is the rise in output over the long run.

13. c A business cycle becomes a structural stagnation when the economy does not recover from a downturn fast enough to bring the economy back to its trend.

14. b See the definition of frictional unemployment in the text.

15. d The unemployment rate is the number of unemployed divided by the labor force times 100, in this case 8%. (8,000/100,000 x 100). Dividing by the non-institutional population is wrong.

16. b Because there are discouraged workers, adding them to the unemployed raises the unemployment rate.

17. a Keynesians believe that the economy ought to provide decent jobs at respectable wages and would therefore include people who have given up looking.

18. c See the definition of potential output in the text.

ANSWERS

POTENTIAL ESSAY QUESTIONS

The following are annotated answers. They indicate the general idea behind the answer.

1. The essence of the Classical explanation is that wages were too high. If labor unions would agree to lower wages and if government could institute policies that allowed wages to fall, the economy would get out of the Depression. The Keynesian view is that if wages adjusted (fell) in response to lower demand for goods, overall spending would fall, which would, in turn, lower demand for goods further. The economy could end up in a downward cycle from which it could not escape without government intervention.

   The Keynesian view dominated policy until the 1970s when the economy faced severe inflation. Because the Keynesian view held the price level constant, it had no explanation for the severe inflation and the Classical view gained influence. Policy makers still used Keynesian policies, but they also used Classical policies and the two views essentially merged—generally the economy would be fine without government intervention, but at times government would have to intervene.

   The combined Keynesian/Classical view unraveled when, in response to a large government stimulus, the economy didn't recover from the 2007/09 recession quickly enough to return to its trend as had been expected. Some Keynesians believed that an even larger stimulus was needed. Some Classical economists believed that the large debt precluded the use of such large stimulus measures. It was unclear which was right, but the different views meant that the consensus was lost.

2. Potential output is the highest amount of output an economy can sustainably produce and sell using existing production processes and resources. Potential output grows at the secular trend rate. When an economy is in a recession, actual output is below potential output.

3. Frameworks provide a lens through which one sees the economy—highlighting some things and downplaying others. Someone who sees the economy within a short-run framework will tend to view high unemployment as a demand-side problem. In this view government can solve the problem by spending money so that firms will hire unemployed workers. Once the workers are employed, the newly hired workers will spend money, raising output and lowering unemployment even more.

   Someone who sees the economy within a long-run framework will tend to see that same high unemployment as a supply-side problem—a lack of investment in productive capacity or insufficient quantity of labor available caused by too high wages, too-little education, or inflexible labor demands. Their policy advice would be to free up private investment by lowering government spending and taxes, for unions to be more flexible in labor negotiations, or for the educational system to train workers with the skills that match job vacancies.

MEASURING AND DESCRIBING
THE AGGREGATE ECONOMY

CHAPTER AT A GLANCE

1a. Gross domestic product (GDP): Aggregate final output of residents and businesses in an economy in a one-year period.

GDP is total market ($) value of all __final__ goods and services produced in a one-year period.

1b. GDP = C + I + G + (X − M) is an accounting identity because it is defined as true.

The above identity is really the expenditures approach, which states:

Total output = Total expenditures;
Total output = GDP;
Total expenditures=C+I+G+(X−M);
By substitution: GDP = C + I + G + (X−M).

✔ *Know what C, I, G, and X−M stand for!*

Also note:
(X − M) = Net exports.
If (X−M) is positive, then X>M→Trade surplus.
If (X−M) is negative, then X<M→Trade deficit.
If (X−M) is zero, then X=M→Trade balance.

2. To avoid double counting, you must eliminate intermediate goods, either by calculating only final output (expenditures approach), or by calculating only final income (income approach) by using the value-added approach.

✔ *Know what is and what is not included when calculating GDP.*
GDP does not include:
- *Intermediate goods (sold for resale or further processing);*
- *Second-hand sales;*
- *Government transfers, housespouse production, or any other non-market activity;*
- *Underground economic activity.*

3a. Net investment is gross investment less depreciation.

Depreciation is the wear and tear of machines that happens during production. Some production goes to replacing depreciated machinery and is therefore unavailable for consumption.

Net domestic product = GDP − Depreciation

3b. National output (GNP) is production by citizens of a country, whether the production happens within the geographic borders of a country or not. Domestic output (GDP) is production that occurs within the geographic borders of a country, whether it is done by citizens of the country or not.

GNP = GDP + Net foreign factor income where:

Net foreign factor income is the foreign income of a country's citizens less the income of residents who are not citizens.

4. Aggregate income is the sum of compensation of employees, rents, interest, and profit.

The largest component of aggregate income is compensation of employees.

5. Aggregate income≡Aggregate production ≡Aggregate outcome.

This relationship can be shown with a T-account with expenditures on one side and income on the other.

Profit is the key to the equality between aggregate output, production and output. It is what remains after all a firm's income is paid out.

6a. Real GDP is nominal GDP adjusted for inflation.

GDP is a price times quantity (P×Q) concept. GDP can rise due to an increase in P (price level) and/or an increase in Q (real quantity of output).

$$Real\ GDP = \frac{Nominal\ GDP}{GDP\ Deflator} \times 100$$

You can use this formula to calculate the GDP deflator too.

$$GDP\ deflator = \frac{Nominal\ GDP}{Real\ GDP} \times 100$$

The PCE deflator accounts for changes in buying habits

6b. Three measures of goods inflation are the CPI, PCE deflator and PPI.

The CPI measures inflation facing consumers assuming a fixed basket of goods. The PPI measures inflation facing producers. The PCE measures consumer inflation and each year accounts for changes in the composition of goods consumed.

7. The distinction between real and nominal concepts is central to economics.

Real equals nominal adjusted for inflation.

Output
Real output equals nominal output adjusted for inflation.

Interest rates
real interest rate
= nominal interest rate - inflation.

Wealth
Real wealth is nominal wealth adjusted for asset price inflation.

Economists have no actual measure for real wealth.

8. Limitations of national income accounting include:
- Comparison of GDP among countries has its problems;
- Measurement problems exist;
- Subcategories are often misinterpreted;
- GDP measures economic activity, not welfare.

GDP is not and was never intended to be a measure of social well-being.

GDP only measures market activity. In developing countries individuals often produce and trade outside the market.

Market prices often vary considerably among countries making income comparisons difficult. Purchasing power parity adjusts incomes to take into account differing relative prices among countries.

⬤ SHORT-ANSWER QUESTIONS

1. What are the four components of aggregate output?

2. Calculate the contribution of Chex cereal (from seeds to consumer) to GDP, using the following information:

Participants	Cost of Materials	Value of Sales
Farmer	0	200
Chex factory	200	500
Distributor	500	800
Grocery store	800	1000

3. What is GNP? How does it differ from GDP?

4. What is the difference between gross investment and net investment?

5. What are the four components of aggregate income?

6. Say the price level rises 10% from a deflator of 100 to a deflator of 110 and nominal GDP rises from $4 trillion to $4.6 trillion. What is nominal GDP in the second period? What is real GDP in the second period?

7. What distinguishes real from nominal interest rates?

8. What are two reasons the price of assets can rise?

9. As pointed out by the quotation that begins the chapter on measuring the aggregate economy, statistics can be misleading. In what way can aggregate economic statistics be misleading? Given your answer, why use them at all?

MATCHING THE TERMS
Match the terms to their definitions

___ **1.**	asset price inflation	**a.**	A balance sheet of an economy's stock of assets and liabilities
___ **2.**	consumer price inflation	**b.**	A continual rise in the price level.
___ **3.**	consumption	**c.**	A measure of the composite price of a specified group of goods.
___ **4.**	depreciation	**d.**	A method of comparing income that takes into account the
___ **5.**	final output		different relative prices among countries.
___ **6.**	GDP deflator	**e.**	A rise in the price of assets unrelated to increases in their
___ **7.**	government spending		productive capacity.
___ **8.**	gross domestic product (GDP)	**f.**	GDP less depreciation.
		g.	Goods and services purchased for their final use.
___ **9.**	gross national product (GNP)	**h.**	Goods and services that government buys.
		i.	Gross investment less depreciation.
___ **10.**	inflation	**j.**	Payments to individuals that do not involve production by
___ **11.**	intermediate products		those individuals.
___ **12.**	investment	**k.**	Products used as input in the production of some other product.
___ **13.**	net domestic product (NDP)	**l.**	Spending by households on goods and services.
		m.	Spending for the purpose of additional production.
___ **14.**	net exports	**n.**	Spending on goods and services produced in the United States
___ **15.**	net foreign factor income		that foreigners buy (exports) minus goods and services pro-
			duced abroad that U.S. citizens buy (imports).
___ **16.**	net investment	**o.**	The aggregate final output of citizens and businesses of an
___ **17.**	nominal GDP		economy in a one-year period.
___ **18.**	nominal interest rate	**p.**	The amount of goods and services produced measured at
___ **19.**	personal consumption expenditure deflator		current prices.
		q.	A price index that includes all goods and services in the
___ **20.**	price index		economy expressed relative to comparison year, or base year,
___ **21.**	producer price index		prices of 100.
___ **22.**	nominal wealth	**r.**	The decrease in an asset's value.
___ **23.**	purchasing power parity	**s.**	The income from foreign domestic factor sources minus foreign
___ **24.**	real GDP		factor income earned domestically.
___ **25.**	real wealth	**t.**	The increase in value that a firm contributes to a product or
___ **26.**	real interest rate		service.
___ **27.**	transfer payments	**u.**	The interest rate you pay or receive to borrow or lend money.
___ **28.**	value added	**v.**	The nominal interest rate adjusted for inflation.
___ **29.**	wealth accounts	**w.**	The value of productive capacity of assets of an economy
			measured by the goods and services it can produce now and in
			the future.
		x.	The value of assets measured at their current market prices.
		y.	The total amount of goods and services produced, adjusted for
			price-level changes.
		z.	The total market value of all final goods and services produced
			in an economy in a one-year period.
		aa.	A measure of prices of goods that consumers buy that allows
			yearly changes in the basket of goods that reflect actual
			consumer purchasing habits.
		bb.	An index of prices that measures average change in the selling
			prices received by domestic producers of goods and services
			over time.
		cc.	A measure of prices of goods that consumers buy that allows
			yearly changes in the basket of goods.

PROBLEMS AND APPLICATIONS

1. Using the value-added or final sales approach to calculate GDP, state how much the action described has added to GDP:

   a. A used car dealer buys a car for $3,000 and resells it for $3,300.

   b. A company sells 1,000 disks for $500 each. Of these, it sells 600 to other companies for production and 400 to individuals.

   c. A PC and software company sells 50 computers at a retail price of $1,000 apiece and 100 software packages at a retail price of $50 apiece to consumers. The same company sells 25 computers at $800 and 50 software packages at $30 apiece to retail companies. These companies then sell the 25 computers at $1,250 apiece and the 50 software packages at $75 apiece to consumers.

   d. Fred purchases 100 stock certificates valued at $5 apiece and pays a 10% commission. When the price declines to $4.50 apiece, Fred decides to sell all 100 certificates, again at a 10% commission.

   e. Your uncle George receives $600 Social Security income each month for one year.

2. Use the following table showing the production of 500 boxes of Wheaties cereal to calculate the contribution to GDP using the value-added approach.

Participants	Cost of Materials	Value of Sales
Farmer	$0	$150
Mill	$150	$250
Cereal maker	$250	$600
Wholesaler	$600	$800
Grocery store	$800	$1,000

   a. Calculate the value added at each stage of production.

   b. What is the total value of all sales?

   c. What is the total value added?

   d. What is the contribution to GDP of the production of those Wheaties?

3. There are three firms in an economy: X, Y, and Z. Firm X buys $200 worth of goods from firm Y and $300 worth of goods from firm Z, and produces 250 units of output at $4 per unit. Firm Y buys $150 worth of goods from firm X, and $250 worth of goods from firm Z, and produces 300 units of output at $6 per unit. Firm Z buys $75 worth of goods from firm X, and $50 worth of goods from firm Y, and produces 300 units at $2 per unit. All other products are sold to consumers. Answer the following:
   a. What is GDP?

   b. How much government revenue would a value-added tax of 10% generate?

c. How much government revenue would an income tax of 10% generate?

d. How much government revenue would a 10% sales tax on final output generate?

4. You have been hired as a research assistant and are given the following data about the economy:

Net exports	$10
Net foreign factor income	3
Gross investment	200
Government spending	190
Consumption	550
Depreciation	65

(All figures are in billions of dollars.)

You are asked to calculate the following:
a. GDP.

b. GNP.

c. NDP.

5. You have been hired as a research assistant and are given the following data about another economy (profits, wages, rents, and interest are measured nationally):

Profits	$505
Employee compensation	880
Rents	30
Interest	175

Calculate aggregate income.

6. Use the following table to answer the questions:

	Real output bils .of Year 1 $	Nominal output bils .of dollars	GDP deflator Year 1=100
Year 1	9,817.0	9,817	____
Year 2	9,890.7	10,128	____
Year 3	10,074.8	____	104.1
Year 4	____	____	106.0
Year 5	____	11,735	108.2

a. What is output for Year 5 in Year 1 dollars?

b. What is the output in nominal terms in Year 3?

c. What is the GDP deflator in Year 1?

d. Real output grew by 1.9% from Year 3 to Year 4. By how much did nominal output grow from Year 3 to Year 4?

7. Fill in the table below:

Inflation	Nominal Interest Rate	Real Interest Rate
2%		4%
1%	4%	
	1%	0%
5%	3%	

MULTIPLE CHOICE

Circle the one best answer for each of the following questions:

1. GDP is:
    a. the total market value of all final goods and services produced in an economy in a one-year period.
    b. the total market value of all goods and services produced in an economy in a one-year period.

c. the total market value of all final goods and services produced by a country's citizens in a one-year period.

d. the sum of all final goods and services produced in an economy in a one-year period.

2. To move from GDP to GNP, one must:
   a. add net foreign factor income.
   b. subtract inflation.
   c. add depreciation.
   d. subtract depreciation.

3. If a firm's cost of materials is $100 and its sales are $500, its value added is:
   a. $100.
   b. $400.
   c. $500.
   d. $600.

4. If you, the owner, sell your old car for $600, how much does GDP increase?
   a. By $600.
   b. By the amount you bought it for, minus the $600.
   c. By zero.
   d. By the $600 you received and the $600 the person you sold it to paid, or $1,200.

5. There are two firms in an economy, Firm A and Firm B. Firm A produces 100 widgets and sells them for $2 apiece. Firm B produces 200 gadgets and sells them for $3 apiece. Firm A sells 30 of its widgets to Firm B and the remainder to consumers. Firm B sells 50 of its gadgets to Firm A and the remainder to consumers. What is GDP in this economy?
   a. $210.
   b. $590.
   c. $600.
   d. $800.

6. If a woman divorces her husband (who has been cleaning the house) and hires him to continue cleaning her house for $20,000 per year, GDP will:
   a. remain constant.
   b. increase by $20,000 per year.
   c. decrease by $20,000 per year.
   d. remain unchanged.

7. The aggregate accounting identity shows that the value of:

a. aggregate income is equal to the value of final goods plus investment.

b. aggregate income is equal to the value of final goods plus savings.

c. aggregate income is equal to the value of final goods sold.

d. consumption goods is equal to the value of aggregate income.

8. Which of the following correctly lists the components of total expenditures?
   a. Consumption, investment, depreciation, exports minus imports.
   b. Consumption, investment, government spending, exports minus imports.
   c. Rent, profit, interest, wages.
   d. Consumption, net foreign factor income, investment, government spending.

9. The largest component of expenditures in GDP is:
   a. consumption.
   b. investment.
   c. net exports.
   d. government spending.

10. The largest component of aggregate income is:
    a. rents.
    b. net interest.
    c. profits.
    d. compensation to employees.

11. Gross investment differs from net investment by:
    a. net exports.
    b. net imports.
    c. depreciation.
    d. transfer payments.

12. While the size of the U.S. federal government budget is approximately $3.8 trillion, the federal government's contribution in the GDP accounts is approximately:
    a. $1.2 trillion.
    b. $2.7 trillion.
    c. $3.8 trillion.
    d. $5.0 trillion.

13. Which of the following factors serves to equate aggregate income and aggregate production?
    a. profit.
    b. depreciation.
    c. net foreign factor income.
    d. value added.

14. Switching from the exchange rate approach to the purchasing power parity approach for calculating GDP generally:
    a. does not make a significant difference for a developing country's GDP relative to a developed country's GDP.
    b. increases a developing country's GDP relative to a developed country's GDP.
    c. decreases a developing country's GDP relative to a developed country's GDP.
    d. changes the relative GDP of developing country's GDP, but not in a predictable fashion.

15. If inflation is 10 percent and nominal GDP goes up 20 percent, real GDP goes up approximately:
    a. 1 percent.
    b. 10 percent.
    c. 20 percent.
    d. 30 percent.

16. Asset inflation:
    a. is equal to goods inflation.
    b. is the rise in the physical increase in assets.
    c. is the rise in asset prices that exceed the rise in the real value of assets.
    d. does not occur when the economy faces globalization because prices are capped.

17. A one-time rise in the price level is:
    a. inflation if that rise is above 5 percent.
    b. inflation if that rise is above 10 percent.
    c. inflation if that rise is above 15 percent.
    d. not inflation.

18. Food and beverages make up about 15 percent of total expenditures. If food and beverage prices rise by 10 percent while the other components of the price index remain constant, by approximately how much will the price index rise?
    a. 1 percent.
    b. 1.5 percent.
    c. 15 percent.
    d. 25 percent.

19. If there are only two goods in an economy, one whose price rose 3% and one by 6%, which is a possible inflation rate for the economy?
    a. 3%.
    b. 5%.
    c. 6%.
    d. 9%.

20. If the real interest rate is 6% and inflation is 2%, what is the nominal interest rate?
    a. 2%
    b. 4%
    c. 6%
    d. 8%

21. Asset price inflation:
    a. is included in the GDP deflator.
    b. cannot be directly calculated.
    c. reflects an increase in the underlying value of an asset.
    d. is undesirable regardless of whether it is measurable.

22. Which of the following is the *preferable* measure available to compare changes in standards of living among countries over time?
    a. Changes in nominal income.
    b. Changes in nominal per capita income.
    c. Changes in real income.
    d. Changes in real per capita income.

23. If nominal GDP rises, welfare:
    a. has definitely increased.
    b. has definitely decreased.
    c. may have increased or decreased.
    d. most likely has increased.

24. Estimates of the importance of the underground economy in the United States indicate that it is:
    a. very small—under 1 percent of the total economy.
    b. somewhere between 1.5 percent all the way to 20 percent of the total economy.
    c. somewhere between 1.5 percent all the way to 60 percent of the total economy.
    d. as large as the non-underground economy.

● POTENTIAL ESSAY QUESTIONS

You may also see essay questions similar to the "Problems & Applications" exercises.

1. Using the circular flow model, explain why any dollar value of output must give rise to an identical amount of income.

2. How might an economy experience an increase in nominal GDP but experience negative growth at the same time?

ANSWERS

SHORT-ANSWER QUESTIONS

1. The four components of gross domestic product are consumption, investment, government spending, and net exports $(X - M)$.

2. $1,000. We could use either the value added approach or the final output approach. Summing the value-added at each stage of production — the difference between cost of materials and value of sales —we get $1,000.

Participants	Cost of Materials	Value of Sales	Value Added
Farmer	$0	$200	$200
Chex factory	200	500	300
Distributor	500	800	300
Grocery store	800	1000	200
Sum (total output)			1000

3. GNP is aggregate final output of *citizens* and businesses *of* an economy in a one-year period. GDP is output produced within a country's borders while GNP is output produced by a country's citizens anywhere in the world. Add net foreign factor income to GDP to get GNP.

4. Gross investment is expenditures on goods and services used for future production. Net investment is gross investment less expenditures used to replace worn out machinery, also called depreciation.

5. The four components that comprise aggregate income are compensation to employees, rents, interest, and profits.

6. A real value is a nominal value adjusted for inflation. So, nominal GDP in the second period is $4.6 trillion, but real GDP is $4.18 trillion ($4.6 divided by 110 times 100).

7. Nominal interest rates are the interest rates that you pay to borrow or the rates that you receive when you lend. The real interest rate is the nominal interest rate adjusted for inflation. That is, the real interest rate takes into account that with an inflation the dollars with which you pay back the loan (or the dollars you receive from the borrower if you are the lender)

are worth less than the dollars you borrowed (or lent).

8. Prices of assets can rise because the productive capacity of that asset has risen or because of asset price inflation (a rise in price for a reason unrelated to productive capacity).

9. Aggregate accounting statistics can be misleading. They are subject to measurement error; they are based on samples of data and assumptions about behavior. For example, GDP does not include non-market activities such as cleaning the house or gardening, which contribute to societal welfare. If you had to hire a cleaning person or gardener, your payment to the workers would be included, but not if you do the work yourself. Welfare comparisons across countries based on income can be misleading because relative prices often differ significantly and non-market activities are often more predominant in lesser-developed countries. These are just a few ways GDP can be a misleading measure. Nevertheless, aggregate accounting makes it possible to discuss the aggregate economy. It is important to be aware of the limitations of the data in those discussions.

ANSWERS

MATCHING

1-e; 2-aa; 3-l; 4-r; 5-g; 6-q; 7-h; 8-o; 9-z; 10-b; 11-k; 12-m; 13-f; 14-n; 15-s; 16-i; 17-p; 18-u; 19-cc; 20-c; 21-bb; 22-x; 23-d; 24-y; 25-w; 26-v; 27-j; 28-t; 29-a.

ANSWERS

PROBLEMS AND APPLICATIONS

1. **a.** $300. Only the value added by the sale would be added to GDP, which in this case is the difference between the purchase price and the sale price.
   b. $200,000. Total output produced is 1,000 × $500 = $500,000. The intermediate goods

are valued at $600 \times \$500 = \$300,000$. So, the company's contribution to GDP is $(\$500,000 - \$300,000) = \$200,000$.

c. Only the amount that is sold to the consumer is counted in GDP. This is $50 \times 1,000 + 100 \times 50 = \$55,000$ sold by the first company plus the sales of the retailer, which is $25 \times \$1250 + 50 \times \$75 = \$35,000$. Total contribution to GDP is $90,000$.

d. Only the commissions of $50 and $45 are counted in GDP. Together they contribute $95.

e. Nothing has been added to GDP. Government transfers are not included in GDP.

2.

Participants	Cost of Materials	Value of Sales	Value Added
Farmer	$0	$150	$150
Mill	$150	$250	$100
Cereal maker	$250	$600	$350
Wholesaler	$600	$800	$200
Grocery store	$800	$1,000	$200

a. The value added at each stage of production is shown in the table above.

b. The total value of sales is $2,800. Find this by adding the rows of the value of sales column.

c. The total value added is $1,000. Find this by adding the value added at each stage of production.

d. The contribution to GDP of the production of those Wheaties is $1,000. Value added at each stage of production is the contribution to GDP. This avoids double-counting.

3. a. $2,375: GDP is the sum of the value added by the three firms $= 500 + 1400 + 475$.

b. $237.50: A 10% value added tax would generate $(.10)(\$2,375) = \$237.50$ of revenue.

c. $237.50: A 10% income tax would generate the same revenue as a 10% value added tax because value added equals income.

d. $237.50: A 10% sales tax on final output would generate $237.50 of revenue: $(.10)(500+1400+475)$.

4. a. $950: $GDP = C + I + G + (X - M) = 550 + 200 + 190 + 10 = 950$.

b. $953: $GNP = GDP +$ net foreign factor income $= 953$.

c. $885: $NDP = GDP -$ depreciation $= 950 - 65 = 885$.

5. $1,590: Aggregate income $=$ Employee compensation $+$ rent $+$ interest $+$ profits$= 880 + 30 + 175 + 505$.

6. a. $10,845.7 billion in Year 1 dollars: Real output $=$ (Nominal output/deflator) $\times 100$ $= 11,735.0/108.2 \times 100$.

b. $10,487.9 billion: Nominal output $=$ (real output $\times$ deflator) $/ 100 = (10,074.8 \times 104.1)/100$.

c. 100: Deflator $=$ (Nominal output/real output) $\times 100 = (9,817/9,817) \times 100$.

d. Real output grew by 1.9% and inflation rose by 2.1%, so nominal output grew by 4.0%.

7.

Inflation	Nominal Interest Rate	Real Interest Rate
2%	6%	4%
1%	4%	3%
1%	1%	0%
5%	3%	-2%

ANSWERS

MULTIPLE CHOICE

1. a   As the text emphasizes, GDP is the total <u>market value</u> of all <u>final</u> goods and services produced <u>in</u> an economy in a one-year period.

2. a   Since GNP is a country's total market value of production of a country's citizens anywhere in the world, and GDP is total market value of production within a country, one must add net foreign factor income to GDP to get GNP.

3. b   Value added equals value of sales minus cost of materials.

4. c   As discussed in the text, sales of used goods do not contribute to GDP except to the degree that they are sold by a second-hand dealer. Then the dealer's profit would be the value added.

5. b   GDP doesn't include purchases made between businesses, only final sales to consumers. To calculate the answer, calculate total sales for Firms A and B ($600 + $200 = $800) and subtract those goods sold between the firms ($60 + $150 = $210) to get final sales ($800 − $210 = $590).

6. b   As discussed in the text, GDP measures market transactions. The divorce-and-hire changes the housecleaning activities from non-market to market and hence increases GDP.

7. c   The aggregate accounting identity shows that all income (value of aggregate income) equals all expenditures (value of goods sold to individuals).

8. b $GDP = C + I + G + (X - M)$.

9. a   Consumption makes up the majority of expenditures. See Table 25-1.

10. d   Compensation to employees is the largest percent of aggregate income.

11. c   Net investment equals gross investment less depreciation.

12. a   As discussed in the text, only federal government spending on goods and services is included as part of GDP. The federal government's entire budget also includes transfer payments.

13. a   Profit is what remains after all firms' other income is paid out. Thus, profit is the key to the income/production equality.

14. b   In developing countries, living expenses are generally lower than in developed countries. Thus moving towards a purchasing power parity approach generally increases GDP in a developing country.

15. b   Subtract inflation from nominal GDP growth to find real GDP growth as a first approximation.

16. c   Only goods prices in the tradable sector are capped by globalization.

17. d   Inflation is an ongoing rise in the price level.

18. b   The rise in the price level is the rise in the component price times its share of the entire index, in this case .10 × 15 = 1.5.

19. b   Inflation must be above the lowest and below the highest rates to reflect an economy with a composition of two goods.

20. d   The real interest rate=nominal rate-inflation. So, the nominal rate = real rate+inflation. In this case it is 8%.

21. b   Asset price inflation must be estimated because we do not have a good measure of real assets. The GDP deflator includes just goods and services. Whether it is desirable depends on the state of the economy. Accelerating asset price inflation is likely not good because eventually it will have to reverse, causing problems for the economy.

22. d   Nominal GDP must be adjusted for price level increases before comparisons over time can be made. Dividing total real income by the population is a good indication of relative standards of living.

23. c   Nominal GDP must be adjusted for inflation to arrive at real GDP before one can even start to make welfare comparisons. And even if real GDP increases, it is not clear that welfare has increased.

24. b   The text states that the underground economy in the United States is between 1.5 and 20 percent of the total economy.

![ANSWERS]

POTENTIAL ESSAY QUESTIONS

The following are annotated answers. They indicate the general idea behind the answer.

1. Whenever the business community produces some dollar value of output, that dollar value reflects costs of production that were incurred in producing that output level. Those costs of production are all paid out to the resource (input) owners as their income. Hence, any dollar output level (GDP) gives rise to an identical amount of aggregate income.

2. The price level could have increased by a greater percentage than the decrease in the real quantity of goods and services produced. This would result in an increase in nominal GDP but a decrease in real GDP (negative growth).

THE KEYNESIAN SHORT-RUN POLICY MODEL: DEMAND-SIDE POLICIES

26

CHAPTER AT A GLANCE

1. A key insight of the Keynesian AS/AD model is that in the short run, the economy can deviate from its potential output.

   If aggregate expenditures fall, firms will cut production and lay off workers. As people's incomes fall, they spend even less and a downward cycle begins. One cause of a downward cycle is the paradox of thrift that says an increase in saving, if not translated into investment, will reduce consumption for an economy as a whole.

2a. The slope of the AD curve is determined by the interest rate effect, the international effect, the money wealth effect, and repercussions of these effects.

   In principle we would expect the AD curve to be vertical because if all prices changed in the same way, behavior wouldn't change.

   As the price level falls:
   - *the value of money rises, inducing people to lend more money, which reduces the interest rate and increases investment expenditures (interest rate effect).*
   - *the price of U.S. goods relative to foreign goods goes down. Assuming the exchange rate doesn't change, U.S. exports increase and U.S. imports decrease (international effect).*
   - *the cash people hold is worth more, making people richer, so they buy more (money wealth effect).*

   Repercussions of these effects are called multiplier effects (and make the AD curve flatter than otherwise).

   Dynamic feedback effects can overwhelm these standard effects.

2b. Five important initial shift factors of the AD curve are:

   - Changes in foreign income.
     A rise in foreign income leads to an increase in U.S. exports and an increase (outward shift to the right) of the U.S. AD curve.
   - Changes in exchange rates.
     A decrease in the value of the dollar relative to other currencies shifts the AD curve outward to the right.
   - Changes in the distribution of income.
     Typically, as the real wage increases, the AD curve shifts out to the right.
   - Changes in government aggregate demand policy.
   - Changes in expectations.
     Positive (optimistic) expectations about the future state of the economy shift the AD curve outward to the right.
   - Changes in government aggregate demand policy.

   Expansionary macro policy (an increase in government spending and/or a decrease in taxes—fiscal policy; or an increase in the money supply—monetary policy) increases the AD curve, shifting it outward to the right.

   Note: Anything that affects the components of aggregate expenditures (AE) is a shift factor of AD (aggregate demand). (AE = C + I + G + X − M). Changes in these components are multiplied by the multiplier effect.

3a. In the short run, the SAS curve is upward sloping.

   The SAS curve is upward sloping for two reasons: (1) Some firms operate in auction markets where an increase in demand leads to higher prices immediately; (2) Firms tend to increase their markup when demand increases. Along an SAS curve, input prices are constant.

3b. The SAS curve shifts in response to changes in the prices of the factors of production (inputs).

Shift factors include changes in (1) input prices, (2) productivity, (3) import prices, and (4) excise and sales taxes.

The rule of thumb economists use to predict shifts in the SAS curve is:

% change in the price level = % change in wages − % change in productivity.

4. The *LAS* curve is vertical at potential output.

Resources are fully utilized at potential output. There is a range for potential output.

The LAS curve shifts when potential output rises or falls.

5a. Equilibrium in the short run is determined by the intersection of the SAS curve and the AD curve.

Increases (decreases) in aggregate demand lead to higher (lower) output and a higher (lower) price level.

To find the effect of a shift in aggregate demand, start where the AD curve and the SAS curve intersect. Given a shift of either the AD curve or SAS curve, simply find the new point of intersection. This is the new short-run equilibrium. Remember, initial shifts in the AD curve are magnified because of the multiplier effect.

5b. Equilibrium in the long run is determined by the intersection of the LAS curve and the AD curve.

If the economy begins at a long-run equilibrium, increases in aggregate demand will lead to changes in the price level only.

5c. A complete analysis integrates the short run and the long run with the AD, SAS, and, LAS curves.

If short-run equilibrium output is below long-run equilibrium output (point A in the figure

below), the economy is in a recessionary gap. The price level will fall and the SAS curve will shift down until output rises to potential (point B).

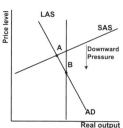

If short-run equilibrium output is above long-run equilibrium output (point B in the figure below), the economy is in an inflationary gap. The price level will rise and the SAS curve will shift up until output falls to potential (point A).

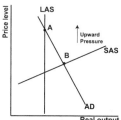

Aggregate demand policy tries to keep the economy at its potential by shifting the AD curve.

6. Dynamic feedback effects can destabilize the economy.

A decline in aggregate demand that leads to a drop in the price level may lead to an even larger decrease in aggregate demand, offsetting the effect of a declining price level in bringing the economy back to its potential income. See Figure 26-11 for how.

7. Macro policy is more complicated than the model makes it look.

Fiscal policy is a slow legislative process and is often determined for political, not economic, reasons.

We have no way of precisely determining potential output, making it difficult to know what is the right policy.

There are other interrelationships the model doesn't take into account.

SHORT-ANSWER QUESTIONS

1. What is the key insight of the Keynesian AS/AD model? How is it related to the paradox of thrift?

2. What effects determine the slope of the AD curve?

3. List five important shift factors of the AD curve.

4. What is the slope of the SAS curve? Why does it have this shape?

5. What will shift the SAS curve up or down?

6. What is the slope of the LAS curve? Why does it have this shape?

7. Show graphically the effect of increased government purchases on real output when (a) the economy is far below potential output and (b) the economy is at potential output.

8. How can declining prices destabilize an economy?

9. Why is the AS/AD model more complicated than it looks?

MATCHING THE TERMS
Match the terms to their definitions

___1.	aggregate demand curve	a.	As the price level falls the interest rate falls, which leads to greater investment expenditures.
___2.	countercyclical fiscal policy		
___3.	deflation	b.	A curve that shows the amount of goods and services an economy can produce when both labor and capital are fully employed.
___4.	equilibrium output		
___5.	fine tuning	c.	A curve that shows how a change in the price level will change aggregate quantity of goods demanded.
___6.	fiscal policy		
___7.	inflationary gap	d.	Markets in which firms modify their supply to bring about equilibrium instead of changing prices.
___8.	interest rate effect		
___9.	international effect	e.	A curve that tells us how changes in aggregate demand will be split between real output and the price level.
___10.	long-run aggregate supply curve	f.	Amount by which equilibrium output is below potential output.
___11.	monetary policy	g.	As the price level falls, people are richer, so they buy more.
___12.	money wealth effect	h.	As the price level in a country falls the quantity of that country's goods demanded by foreigners and by residents will increase.
___13.	multiplier effect	i.	Amplification of initial changes in expenditures.
___14.	paradox of thrift	j.	Amount by which equilibrium output is above potential output.
___15.	potential output	k.	Income toward which the economy gravitates in the short run.
___16.	quantity-adjusting markets	l.	Deliberate change in either government spending or taxes.
___17.	recessionary gap	m.	Government policy to offset the business cycle.
___18.	short-run aggregate supply curve	n.	An increase in savings can lead to a decrease in expenditures, decreasing output and causing a recession and lower savings.
		o.	A continual decline in the price level.
		p.	A policy of influencing the economy through changes in the money supply and interest rates.
		q.	Fiscal policy designed to keep the economy always at its target level of income.
		r.	The highest amount of output an economy can sustainably produce using existing production processes and resources.

● PROBLEMS AND APPLICATIONS

1. What will likely happen to the shape or position of the *AD* curve in the following circumstances?

   a. A rise in the price level does not make people feel poorer.

   b. Income is redistributed from poor people to rich people.

   c. The country's currency depreciates.

   d. The exchange rate changes from fixed to flexible.

   e. Expectations of future rises in the price level develop without any current change in the price level.

2. What will happen to the position of the *SAS* curve in the following circumstances?

    a. Productivity rises by 3 percent and wages rise by 3 percent.

    b. Productivity rises by 3 percent and wages rise by 5 percent.

    c. Productivity rises by 3 percent and wages rise by 1 percent.

3. Graphically demonstrate the effect of each of the following on either the *SAS* curve or the *LAS* curve. Be sure to label all axes.

    a. Businesses find that they are able to produce more output without having to pay more wages or increase their costs of capital.

    b. A severe snow storm paralyzes most of the United States.

    c. The country's currency appreciates dramatically.

4. The government of the UK wants to expand its economy through increased spending. Show the likely effects of an activist policy in the short run and in the long run in the following three cases.

    a. The economy is far below potential output.

    b. The economy is close to, but still below, potential output.

    c. The economy is at potential output.

5. Demonstrate the following two cases using the AS/AD model. What will happen in the long run if the government does nothing?

    a. Inflationary gap.

    b. Recessionary gap.

    c. What could government do with fiscal policy in parts *a* and *b* to keep the price level constant?

● MULTIPLE CHOICE

Circle the one best answer for each of the following questions:

1. In Keynesian economics equilibrium income:
   a. will be equal to potential income.
   b. will be below potential income.
   c. will be above potential income.
   d. may be different than potential income.

2. According the Keynesian model, deflation:
   a. leads to increasing asset prices that keep an economy from equilibrium.
   b. creates problems that keep an economy from equilibrium.
   c. is a good way to bring the economy back to equilibrium.
   d. has no effect on equilibrium output.

3. The paradox of thrift refers to the phenomenon that:
   a. a decline in the interest rate can cause a recession.
   b. a rise in saving can cause a recession.
   c. a declining price level can cause a downward cycle in output.
   d. an increase in foreign thriftiness will reduce exports.

4. In the AS/AD model, the:
   a. price of a good is on the horizontal axis.
   b. price level is on the horizontal axis.
   c. price of a good is on the vertical axis.
   d. price level is on the vertical axis.

5. Which of the following is *not* an explanation of the downward slope of the AD curve?
   a. The money wealth effect.
   b. The interest rate effect.
   c. The consumption effect.
   d. The multiplier effect.

6. If the exchange rate becomes flexible so that changes in the price level have little effect on exports and imports, the:
   a. AD curve will become steeper.
   b. AD curve will become flatter.
   c. AD curve will be unaffected.
   d. SAS curve will become steeper.

7. If the multiplier effect is 2 rather than 3, the:
   a. AD curve will be steeper.
   b. AD curve will be flatter.

   c. AD curve will be unaffected.
   d. SAS curve will be steeper.

8. If there is a rise in foreign income the AD curve will likely:
   a. shift in to the left.
   b. shift out to the right.
   c. become steeper.
   d. become flatter.

9. If there is a rise in a country's exchange rate, the AD curve will likely:
   a. shift in to the left.
   b. shift out to the right.
   c. become steeper.
   d. become flatter.

10. Expansionary monetary policy will likely:
    a. shift the AD curve in to the left.
    b. shift the AD curve out to the right.
    c. make the AD curve steeper.
    d. make the AD curve flatter.

11. If government spending increases by 40, the AD curve will shift to the:
    a. right by 40.
    b. left by 40.
    c. right by more than 40.
    d. right by less than 40.

12. The slope of the SAS curve is determined by:
    a. opportunity cost.
    b. the law of diminishing marginal returns.
    c. institutional realities.
    d. the money wealth effect, the international effect, and the interest rate effect.

13. If productivity rises by 2% and wages rise by 6%, the SAS curve will:
    a. likely shift up (to the left).
    b. likely shift down (to the right).
    c. become flatter.
    d. become steeper.

14. The LAS curve is:
    a. another name for the AD curve.
    b. another name for the SAS curve.
    c. a vertical line.
    d. a horizontal line.

15. Refer to the graph below. The graph demonstrates the expected short-run result if:

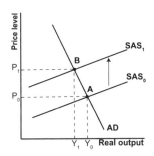

   a. productivity increases by less than wages.
   b. the government increases the money supply.
   c. the exchange rate value of a country's
      currency falls.
   d. there are suddenly expectations of a rising
      price level.

16. The graph below demonstrates the expected
short-run result if:

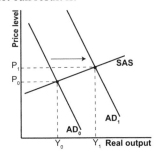

   a. productivity increases by less than wages.
   b. the government increases the money supply.
   c. a country's exchange rate appreciates (gains
      value).
   d. wages rise by less than the increase in
      productivity.

17. The graph below demonstrates the expected
short-run result if:

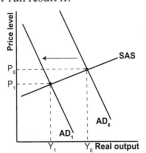

   a. productivity increases by less than wages.
   b. the government increases the money supply.

   c. a country's exchange rate appreciates (gains
      value).
   d. wages rise by less than the increase in
      productivity.

18. Assume the economy is initially at point B. The
graph below correctly demonstrates an
economy moving to point C if:

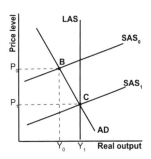

   a. productivity increases by less than the
      increase in wages.
   b. the government increases the money supply.
   c. the country's exchange rate appreciates
      (gains value).
   d. wages rise by less than the increase in
      productivity.

19. Assume the economy is initially at point B. The
graph below correctly demonstrates an
economy moving to point C if:

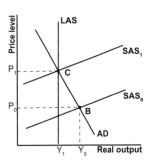

   a. productivity increases by less than the
      increase in wages.
   b. the government increases the money supply.
   c. a country's exchange rate appreciates (gains
      value).
   d. wages rise by less than the increase in
      productivity.

20. Which of the following distances in the graph below would represent an inflationary gap?

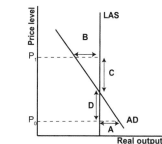

a. A.
b. B.
c. C.
d. D.

21. When the price level in an economy declines,
   a. an increase in the quantity of aggregate demand will bring the economy back to potential.
   b. a downward shift in the SAS curve will bring the economy back to potential.
   c. aggregate expenditures may decline, pushing the economy away from potential.
   d. potential output shifts out to the right.

22. If there are feedback effects in an economy, a decline in asset prices can lead to a decline in:
   a. aggregate demand followed by a decrease in the price level that brings the economy back to equilibrium.
   b. aggregate demand followed by a decrease in the price level, followed by further declines in aggregate demand.
   c. potential output that leads to a falling price level that brings the economy back to equilibrium at the new, lower potential output.
   d. potential output that leads to a falling price level that shifts the aggregate demand curve to the right, bringing the economy back to its original output.

23. Expansionary fiscal policy involves:
   a. increasing taxes.
   b. increasing the money supply.
   c. increasing government spending.
   d. changing the exchange rate.

24. If the economy has an inflationary gap that it wants to eliminate, the government should use fiscal policy to shift:
   a. the *LAS* curve out.
   b. the *SAS* curve down (to the right).
   c. the *AD* curve out to the right.
   d. the *AD* curve in to the left.

25. If an economy has an inflationary gap and the government does nothing, the macro policy model predicts that:
   a. the SAS curve will shift up (to the left) as input prices increase, and output will decline.
   b. the SAS curve will shift down (to the right) as input prices decline, and output will rise.
   c. the AD curve will shift out to the right as individuals collectively decide to increase expenditures, and output will rise.
   d. the AD curve will shift in to the left as individuals collectively decide to reduce expenditures, and output will decline.

26. During the 2008/09 recession, according to conventional economists:
   a. the prolonged high unemployment meant the need for continued expansionary policy.
   b. expansionary policy would not be effective because the economy needed to undergo structural adjustments.
   c. inflation would remain high even though unemployment remained high.
   d. expansionary policy would not bring output back to its potential because unemployment remained high.

27. If the target rate of unemployment falls, potential income will:
   a. first decrease, then increase.
   b. increase.
   c. decrease.
   d. first increase, then decrease.

POTENTIAL ESSAY QUESTIONS

You may also see essay questions similar to the "Problems & Applications" exercises.

1. Why is the AS/AD model more complicated than it looks?

2. Why doesn't the price level equilibrate aggregate supply and aggregate demand in the same way that it does in micro models?

3. What is the paradox of thrift and how does it relate to the AS/AD model?

ANSWERS

SHORT-ANSWER QUESTIONS

1. The key insight of the Keynesian AS/AD model is that in the short run, the economy can deviate from what it is capable of producing and that government can bring the economy back to its potential with demand-side policies. The paradox of thrift is that an increase in saving can lead to a decrease in expenditures, which leads to decreasing output, causing a recession and lowering total saving. This is how the economy can deviate from its potential.

2. The interest rate effect, the international effect, the money wealth effect, and the repercussions of these effects (the multiplier effect) determine the slope of the AD curve.

3. Five important initial shift factors of the AD curve are changes in: (1) foreign income, (2) exchange rates, (3) distribution of income, (4) expectations, and (5) government aggregate demand policy.

4. The SAS curve specifies how a shift in the aggregate demand curve affects the price level and real output. A standard SAS curve is upward sloping. That is, increases in aggregate demand lead to increases in output and the price level. Institutional realities about how firms set prices determine the shape of the SAS curve. Faced with an increase in demand, firms generally respond by increasing production. Some firms will take the opportunity to increase their markup over costs, which will also increase the price level.

5. The SAS curve will shift up or down when input prices rise or fall or if productivity rises or falls. Two other shift factors are import prices and excise and sales taxes. The shift in the SAS curve (and therefore the price level) is determined by the following: % change in price level = % change in wages − % change in productivity.

6. The LAS curve is vertical. It has this shape because at potential output, all inputs are fully employed. Changes in the price level do not affect potential output.

7. If the economy begins at point A, a well-planned increase in government expenditures (plus the multiplier effect) shifts the AD out to the right from AD_0 to AD_1. If the economy begins below potential output, the price level would rise slightly from P_0 to P_1 and real output would increase from Y_0 to Y_1. The graph is drawn so that the AD curve shifts out enough so that the economy is in both long-run and short-run equilibrium at potential output at point B.

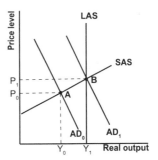

Now suppose the economy begins at point C (graph below) in both short-run and long-run equilibrium. In the short run, when the aggregate demand curve shifts from AD_0 to AD_1, real output rises from Y_0 to Y_1 and the price level rises from P_0 to P_1. Since the economy is now above potential output, however, input prices begin to rise and the SAS curve shifts up. The SAS curve continues to shift up to SAS_1 where the economy returns to a long-run equilibrium at a higher price level, P_2, but the same output level as before, Y_0. See Figures 26-8 and 26-9.

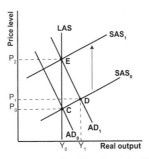

8. A declining price level can lead people to reduce expenditures, shifting the AD curve from AD_0 to AD_1 and pushing the economy to point B. This results in more pressure for the price level to fall. As the SAS curve shifts from SAS_0 to SAS_1 to return the economy to potential output at point C, the AD curve may

shift to the left enough to offset the effect of a declining price level on the quantity of aggregate demand. The economy ends up at point D. Further pressure for the price level to decline pushes the economy even further from potential.

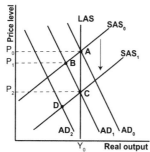

9. The AS/AD model is more complicated than it looks because fiscal policy is a slow legislative process and frequently determined by political, not economic, considerations. In addition, we do not know the level of potential output, which is the key to knowing whether contractionary or expansionary policy is needed. One method to estimate potential output is to estimate the unemployment rate where inflation begins to rise. Unfortunately, this is also difficult to predict. Lastly, there are many other possible relationships that the model doesn't take into account. One is that falling asset prices can destabilize the financial system and lead to a cycle of declining demand.

ANSWERS

MATCHING

1-c; 2-m; 3-o; 4-k; 5-q; 6-l; 7-j; 8-a; 9-h; 10-b; 11-p; 12-g; 13-i; 14-n; 15-r; 16-d; 17-f; 18-e.

ANSWERS

PROBLEMS AND APPLICATIONS

1. **a.** This would cause the money wealth effect to become inoperative and the AD curve will become steeper.
   b. Assuming rich people spend less of an increase in income compared to poor people, the AD curve will shift in to the left.

   c. As the exchange rate depreciates, exports will rise and imports will fall. This shifts the AD curve out to the right.
   d. If the exchange rate was originally fixed and became flexible, increases in the price level will be offset by changes in the exchange rate and the international effect becomes inoperative. The *AD* curve will be steeper.
   e. Expectations of future price increases without changes in the current price level will tend to cause the *AD* curve to shift out to the right.

2. **a.** The SAS doesn't shift at all because rises in input prices are completely offset by increases in productivity.
   b. The SAS curve shifts up because the rise in input prices exceeds the rise in productivity.
   c. The SAS curve shifts down because the rise in input prices is less than the rise in productivity.

3. **a.** The LAS curve shifts to the right as shown below because business people are finding that their productive capacity is larger than they had thought.

   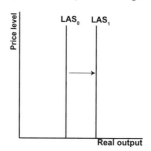

   b. The LAS curve shifts to the left as shown below because bad weather will hinder production. Because the storm is temporary, however, the shift in the LAS curve is also temporary.

   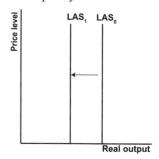

c. The short-run aggregate supply curve shown below shifts down from SAS_0 to SAS_1, because businesses will benefit from the declining import prices to the extent that imports are used in production. The fall in input prices is passed through to the goods market.

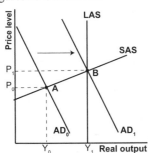

4. a. The economy is far below potential output at point A in the graph below. As the AD curve shifts out, the economy moves to point B—the price level rises slightly to P_1, and output increases to Y_1. As the graph is drawn the LAS curve, Y_1 is potential output, and point B is both a short-run and a long-run equilibrium. See Figures 26-8 and 26-9.

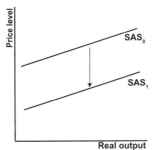

b. The economy is close to potential output at point A in the graph at the top of the next column. The AD curve shifts to AD_1. Real output rises to Y_1 and the price level rises to P_1. Because output is beyond potential, point B is a short-run equilibrium. Input prices begin to rise which shifts the SAS curve up. As the SAS curve shifts up, real output declines and the price level rises even further. The SAS curve will continue to shift up until the economy is at potential output Y_2 and a new price level P_2—point C. Expansionary fiscal policy will be less effective in increasing output when the economy is close to potential. Real output rises by less than in (a) and the economy experiences much more inflation. See Figures 26-8 and 26-9.

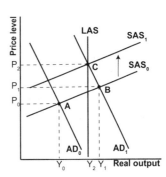

c. The economy is at potential output at point A in the graph below. As the AD curve shifts out, real output rises to Y_1 in the short run and the price level rises to P_1—point B. Since the economy is above potential however, eventually input prices will rise and the SAS curve will shift up. The SAS curve shifts up until real output falls back to potential output—Y_0—and the price level rises even further to P_2 (point C). In the long run, real output remains unchanged at Y_0 and only the price level increases from P_0 to P_2. When the economy is at or above potential, expansionary policy is ineffective in the long run. See Figures 26-8 and 26-9.

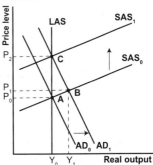

5. a. The graph below demonstrates an inflationary gap—short-run equilibrium output is above potential—at point A. If government does nothing, the price level will rise and real output will fall to potential—to point B.

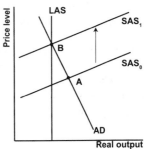

b. The graph below demonstrates a recessionary gap—short-run equilibrium output is below potential—at point A. Given the excess supply of resources, input prices will fall and the SAS curve will shift down to SAS$_1$. Real output will rise to potential and the price level will fall—to point B. Generally, government intervenes to increase expenditures (shifting the AD curve) before the price level declines.

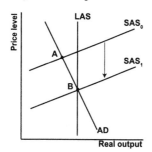

c. To avoid changes in the price level, if the economy is in an inflationary gap, the government can reduce government spending (or raise taxes) to shift the AD curve in to the left. If the economy is in a recessionary gap, it can increase government spending (or lower taxes) to shift the AD curve out to the right.

ANSWERS

MULTIPLE CHOICE

1. **d** Because of coordination problems equilibrium income could be different from potential income in Keynesian economics; it could be higher, lower, or equal to it.

2. **b** Deflation makes entrepreneurs hesitant to start businesses and is often accompanied by declining asset prices, which leads to lower consumption and investment. These effects keep the economy below potential.

3. **b** The paradox of thrift is the phenomenon where a rise in savings can cause a recession. Classical economists would predict that a rise in savings would lead to a rise in output through its effect on potential income. Option c appears to be a paradox also, but refers to dynamic feedback effects caused by price level declines.

4. **d** The AS/AD model is different than the micro supply/demand model. It has price *level* on the vertical axis and *total output* on the horizontal axis.

5. **c** The multiplier effect affects both the slope and the position of the AD curve. No consumption effect is discussed in the text.

6. **a** This question refers to the international effect; if the international effect is reduced, the change in the price level will have less effect on AD and the AD curve will be steeper.

7. **a** The multiplier effect increases the effect of the other effects and hence a smaller multiplier makes the AD curve steeper.

8. **b** The rise in foreign income will increase demand for exports, shifting the AD curve to the right. .

9. **a** The rise in the country's exchange rate will decrease demand for its exports, shifting the AD curve in to the left.

10. **b** Expansionary monetary policy will increase aggregate demand, shifting the AD curve out to the right.

11. **c** The multiplier effect would increase the effect, so the rightward shift would be more than 40.

12. **c** The SAS curve is not a derived curve; it is an empirical curve determined by institutional realities.

13. **a** Because wages are rising by more than productivity, the SAS curve will shift up.

14. **c** The LAS curve shows the amount of goods and services an economy can produce when both labor and capital are

fully employed. It is a vertical line since the price level does not affect potential output.

15. a The SAS curve shifts upward when wages rise by more than increases in productivity. Real output will decline and the price level will rise.

16. b An increase in the money supply will shift the AD curve to the right. In the short run, real output and the price level will rise.

17. c Demand for domestic goods will decline if one's currency appreciates because foreign goods will be less expensive compared to domestic goods. Real output will decline and the price level falls slightly.

18. d Since at point B, the economy is below potential, there will be downward pressure on wages, or at least wages will rise by less than the increase in productivity. The SAS curve will shift down until the economy reaches point C.

19. a Since at point B, the economy is above potential, there will be upward pressure on wages. Wages will rise by more than the increase in productivity. The SAS curve will shift up until the economy reaches point C.

20. a The inflationary gap occurs when the price level is such that the quantity of aggregate demand exceeds the quantity of potential income.

21. c Dynamic feedback effects from a declining price level to aggregate expenditures may create a vicious cycle in which declining prices lead to continual leftward shifts in the AD curve.

22. b An economy with feedback effects can end up in a vicious cycle in which a decline in aggregate demand that leads to a decline in the price level, leads people to believe that the price level will decline further. They will put off purchases, which further reduces aggregate demand.

23. c Expansionary fiscal policy is the deliberate increase in government expenditures or reduction in taxes.

24. d Aggregate demand management policies do not affect SAS, so a and b are out. With an inflationary gap you want to decrease output, so the answer is d. See Figure 26-8.

25. a Inflation results in higher input prices, which shift the SAS curve up.

26. a Unlike policies after World War II, expansionary policies in 2008 and beyond did not bring unemployment down as much as desired. Conventional economists called for continued expansionary policies. Others believed that because of globalization, that only structural adjustments would bring down unemployment and the economy back up to potential.

27. b Potential income varies inversely with unemployment.

ANSWERS

POTENTIAL ESSAY QUESTIONS

The following are annotated answers. They indicate the general idea behind the answer.

1. The macro model is more complicated than it appears because we do not know for sure where potential output is and because fiscal policy is more difficult to implement than is portrayed. Because we have no way of precisely determining how close the economy is to potential output, we don't know precisely by how much we should shift the AD curve. In addition, there are a number of other possible interrelationships the model does not take into account, which may destabilize the economy. One example is negative feedback effects of a declining price level on aggregate demand.

2. The price level doesn't always equilibrate aggregate supply and aggregate demand because it has side effects that keep the economy below its potential. One problem is that when product prices are declining entrepreneurs do not start businesses and existing business do not increase production because without a decline in costs, expected profits are low. In addition, deflation is often accompanied by a decline in asset prices. With lower asset prices consumers and businesses have less collateral against which to borrow, which lowers both consumer spending and investment. The economy can enter a downward spiral as declines in production lead to lower incomes, which lead to lower consumption, which once again leads to lower production.

3. The paradox of thrift is that when people collectively decide to save more and consume less, consumption expenditures fall. If that saving is not immediately transferred into investment, total expenditures fall. Faced with excess supply, firms cut production and income falls. As people's income falls, consumption and saving both fall. It is the paradox of thrift that leads to the multiplier effect. This multiplier effect makes the AD curve flatter than it otherwise would have been and accounts for the multiplied effect of shift factors of aggregate demand.

THE CLASSICAL LONG-RUN POLICY MODEL: GROWTH AND SUPPLY-SIDE POLICIES

CHAPTER AT A GLANCE

1. Growth is an increase in the amount of goods and services an economy produces.

   Growth can be measured either by increases in real output or increases in real output per person (per capita growth).

   Remember the Rule of 72: The number of years it takes for income to double equals 72 divided by the annual growth rate of income.

2. Classical economists focus on increasing potential output (growth) while Keynesians take potential output as given and focus on aggregate demand.

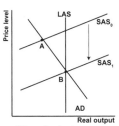
Classical view

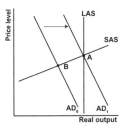
Keynesian view

   In the Classical view, the economy is always at potential. Classical economists focus on the LAS curve. If the economy is below potential output the SAS curve will shift down to bring the economy to its potential as shown in the left-hand figure above. Aggregate demand is not a concern because, based on Say's Law, supply creates its own demand.

   In the Keynesian view, the economy can deviate from potential. They focus on chang-ing aggregate demand to bring the economy to its potential—point A as shown in the right-hand figure above.

3. Markets create specialization and division of labor and have been empirically highly correlated with growth. The growth rate has increased as the importance of markets has increased.

4. Specialization and trade increase productivity and lead to growth. Per capita growth is real output divided by the population.

   Markets are often seen as unfair with regard to the distribution of income.

   % change in per capital output = % change in output / % change in population

5. Five important sources of growth are:

   ● Growth-compatible institutions;

   Government policy can help or hinder growth. Regulations have both costs and benefits, but too much regulation definitely hinders growth.

   ● Investment and accumulated capital;

   Can be: (1) Privately owned by business, (2) publicly owned and provided by government– infrastructure, (3) human capital–investment in people, and (4) social capital–institutions and conventions.

   Saving is translated into investment in the loanable funds market. The interest rate equilibrates the supply of loanable funds (saving) with the demand for loanable funds (investment).

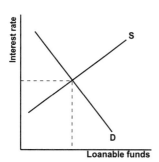

- Available resources;

Technological advances can help overcome any lack of resources.

- Technological development;

Technology changes not just how we produce goods, but also the goods we produce.

- Entrepreneurship.

This is the ability to get things done. It involves creativity, vision, and an ability to translate that vision into reality.

6. Classical economists emphasized saving and investment. The more an economy saves, the more it invests in productive capital, which leads to growth.

Early economists believed that eventually an economy would stop growing because of the law of diminishing marginal productivity

Growth didn't stop, instead technological development led to sustained growth.

7. New growth theory emphasizes technology. New technology leads to investment, which leads to more innovation, which leads to growth.

According to this view, economies continue to grow as positive externalities associated with technology create even more growth.

New growth economists focus on learning by doing.

It's possible that through lock-in, the economy doesn't always use the best technology.

8. Five policies that promote growth are:

a. Encourage saving and investment.
b. Formalize property rights and reduce corruption.
c. Provide appropriate education.
d. Encourage technological innovation.
e. Encourage taking advantage of specialization

The policy problem is translating these general policies into politically acceptable policies.

● SHORT-ANSWER QUESTIONS

1. What is the difference between the Keynesian model and the Classical model when it comes to potential output?

2. What are the two ways to measure growth?

3. What is the relationship between markets, specialization, and growth?

4. You've been called in by a political think tank to develop a strategy to improve growth in the U.S. What five things in reference to the sources of growth would you recommend they concentrate on to contribute positively to economic growth?

5. Why is a well-functioning financial market essential to growth?

6. Why did early Classical economists predict that an economy would eventually stop growing?

7. How does new growth theory explain ongoing economic growth of economies?

8. What is the role of positive externalities and learning by doing in technological innovation?

MATCHING THE TERMS
Match the terms to their definitions

____1.   Classical growth model

____2.   division of labor

____3.   human capital

____4.   law of diminishing marginal productivity

____5.   learn by doing

____6.   new growth theories

____7.   patents

____8.   per capita growth

____9.   positive externalities

____10. productivity

____11. Rule of 72

____12. Say's Law

____13. social capital

____14. specialization

____15. technology

a.   Producing more goods and services per person.

b.   Legal ownership of a technological innovation that gives the owner sole rights to its use and distribution for a limited time.

c.   The habitual way of doing things that guides how people approach production.

d.   Changes in the way we make goods and supply services and changes in the goods and services we buy.

e.   Model of growth that focuses on the role of capital in the growth process.

f.   Rule in which you divide 72 by the growth rate of income (or any variable) to get the number of years over which income (or any variable) will double.

g.   Positive effects on others not taken into account by the decision maker.

h.   The skills that are embodied in workers through experience, education, and on-the-job training.

i.   A theory that emphasize the role of technology rather than capital in the growth process.

j.   Increasing one input, keeping all others constant, will lead to smaller and smaller gains in output.

k.   The concentration of individuals on certain aspects of production.

l.   Supply creates its own demand.

m.   Improving the methods of production through experience.

n.   The splitting up of a task to allow for specialization of production.

o.   Output per unit of input.

PROBLEMS AND APPLICATIONS

1.   What is the difference between Keynesian and Classical views of the relationship between the economy and potential output? What are their views about the role of government in the economy?

2.   State the Rule of 72. Answer each of the following questions:

a.   How many years will it take for income to double if a country's total income grows at 2 percent? 4 percent? 6 percent?

b.   If a country's income doubles in 16 years, at what rate is its income growing?

c. In 2015 per capita output in the United States was about $57,000. If real income per capita is growing at a 2% annual rate, what will per capita output be in 36 years? In 72 years?

d. If real income is rising at an annual rate of 4% per year and the population is growing at a rate of 1% per year, how many years will it take for per capita income to double?

3. Calculate per capita income for each of the following countries:

	GDP (in mils. of $)	Population (in millions)
Brazil	773,400	164
Ghana	6,600	18
Croatia	20,700	4
France	1,526,000	59

5. What prediction did Thomas Malthus make about growth?

a. What law are those predictions based upon?

b. According to new growth theorists, why didn't his predictions come true?

MULTIPLE CHOICE

Circle the one best answer for each of the following questions:

1. The Classical model focuses primarily:
    a. on demand.
    b. on supply.
    c. on both supply and demand.
    d. on the distribution of output.

2. According to Say's Law:
    a. supply does not create demand.
    b. supply creates demand greater than supply.
    c. supply creates demand less than supply.
    d. supply creates demand equal to supply.

3. Refer to the graph below. According to Classical economists, if an economy is at point A what will bring the economy back to its potential?

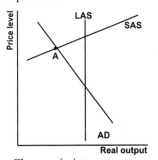

    a. Changes in interest rates.
    b. Capital accumulation.
    c. Government policy.
    d. Deflation.

4. If the growth rate is 6%, how many years will it take for output to double?
   a. 4.
   b. 8.
   c. 12.
   d. 16.

5. When earnings are adjusted for inflation, the average worker today earns:
   a. about the same as a worker in 1919.
   b. less than a worker in 1919.
   c. more than a worker in 1919.
   d. more than a worker in 1919 if he/she is unionized, but otherwise less.

6. Suppose output grew at 8% in China and 2% in the United States. Based on this information alone, we can know that:
   a. per capita income grew faster in China.
   b. per capita income grew faster in the U.S.
   c. per capita income could have grown faster in either country. We cannot tell which.
   d. per capita output grew faster in China.

7. Investment relates to capital in the following way:
   a. It is the same thing as capital stock.
   b. It causes a decrease in capital over time.
   c. It causes an increase in capital over time.
   d. It is unrelated to capital.

8. If saving increases from S_0 to S_1:

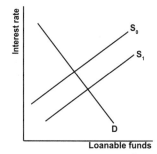

   a. the interest rate will rise, investment will rise, and the economy will grow.
   b. the interest rate will fall, investment will rise, and the economy will grow.
   c. the interest will rise, investment will fall, and the economy will contract.
   d. the interest rate will fall, investment will fall, and the economy will contract.

9. Types of capital discussed in the book do *not* include:
   a. human capital.
   b. social capital.
   c. physical capital.
   d. investment capital.

10. Available resources:
    a. must always decrease.
    b. are always constant because of the entropy law.
    c. must always increase.
    d. may increase or decrease.

11. The law of diminishing marginal productivity states that as:
    a. inputs increase by equal percentages, output will increase by less than that percentage.
    b. inputs increase by equal percentages, output will eventually increase by less than that percentage.
    c. one input increases by a certain percentage, output will increase by less than that percentage.
    d. time progresses, the output from additional input declines.

12. The Classical growth model focuses on:
    a. technology.
    b. saving and investment.
    c. entrepreneurship.
    d. available resources.

13. Early predictions of the Classical model of growth were that:
    a. the economy would grow without limit.
    b. the economy will end because of pollution.
    c. growth would eventually slow because of diminishing marginal productivity.
    d. growth would eventually slow because of decreasing returns to scale.

14. New growth theories are theories that emphasize:
    a. technology.
    b. human capital.
    c. physical capital.
    d. entrepreneurship.

15. Positive externalities:
a. cannot happen if a technology is patented.
b. are not taken into account by the decision maker.
c. do not contribute to technological innovation.
d. are not beneficial to society because they are unintended.

16. QWERTY is a metaphor for:
a. the invisible hand.
b. technological lock-in.
c. the law of diminishing marginal productivity.
d. the pollution caused by positive spillovers.

17. Which of the following policies will likely *slow* an economy's growth rate?
a. Increased trade restrictions.
b. Increasing the level of education.
c. Increasing saving.
d. Protecting property rights.

POTENTIAL ESSAY QUESTIONS

You may also see essay questions similar to the "Problems & Applications" exercises.

1. How does the early Classical model differ from new growth theory in its prediction about growth? What accounts for the difference?

2. Why is specialization an important part of learning by doing? What does this suggest about the impact of globalization on world economic growth?

---------- **ANSWERS** ----------

SHORT-ANSWER QUESTIONS

1. The Keynesian view is that the economy can deviate from its potential. It is government's role to manage aggregate expenditures to bring the economy to its potential. The Classical view focuses on potential output and assumes supply creates its own demand. The price level will adjust when potential output increases or decreases, bringing the economy back to potential on its own.

2. Growth can be measured either as increases in the amount of goods and services an economy produces (real GDP), or as increases in the amount of goods and services an economy produces per person (per capita real GDP). Increase in per capita output is a better measure of improvements in the standard of living because it tells you how much more income an average person has.

3. Markets allow the breaking up of the production process into smaller parts. This specialization has led to learning by doing, which is a type of technological innovation, which leads to growth.

4. I would tell them: (1) To promote institutions with incentives compatible with growth. Institutions that encourage hard work will lead to growth. (2) To invest in capital. This would include not only buildings and machines, but also human and social capital. (3) To be creative in recognizing available resources. Growth requires resources and although it may seem that the resources are limited, available resources depend upon existing technology. New technology is a way of overcoming lack of resources. (4) To promote institutions that foster creative thinking and lead to technological development; (5) To encourage entrepreneurship.

5. For saving to contribute to growth it must be translated into investment, which requires a well-functioning financial market.

6. Classical economists predicted that economies would stop growing based on the law of diminishing marginal productivity.

7. New growth theory focuses on technology in the growth process. According to this theory, innovations lead to more innovation, which leads to growth. In addition growth leads to more innovation, which in turn leads to even more growth.

8. Positive externalities mean that the benefits of one technology spills over into the development of new technologies. Learning by doing means that people learn to do things better on the job. This learning is technological innovation.

---------- **ANSWERS** ----------

MATCHING

1-e; 2-n; 3-h; 4-j; 5-m; 6-i; 7-b; 8-a; 9-g; 10-o; 11-f; 12-l; 13-c; 14-k; 15-d.

---------- **ANSWERS** ----------

PROBLEMS AND APPLICATIONS

1. Keynesians believed that the economy is not necessarily at potential, nor is it self-correcting. In the graph below on the left, if the economy is at point A, output is less than potential. It is the role of government to increase aggregate expenditures so that the economy is operating at potential—point B. In contrast, the Classical view is that the economy will be at its potential, and therefore focus on potential output. If the economy is operating below potential—at point A in the graph below on the right, the price level will decline, shifting the SAS curve down until the economy reaches point B.

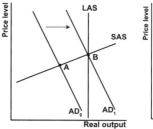 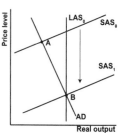

2. The Rule of 72 is, "the number of years that it takes income (or any variable) to double equals 72 divided by the annual growth rate of income (or that variable)."
   a. 36 years if income grows at 2 percent per year; 18 years if income grows at 4 percent per year; 12 years if income grows at 6 percent per year.
   b. Its income is growing at 4.5 percent per year. Divide 72 by 16 to find the answer.
   c. If real income per capita is growing at 2 percent per year, per capita output will double in 36 years. So, real per capita output will be $114,000 in 36 years and $228,000 in 72 years.
   d. Per capita real income is rising at an annual rate of 3% per year (4% - 1%). At 3% per year, real per capita income will double in 24 years (72/3 = 24).

3. Divide GDP by the population to find per capita income:
   a. Brazil $4,716
   b. Ghana $367
   c. Croatia $5,175
   d. France $25,864

4. Thomas Malthus predicted that since land was relatively fixed, as the population grew, diminishing marginal productivity would set in. The growth in output would not keep pace with the growth in the population and eventually people would starve.
   a. The predictions of Thomas Malthus are based upon the law of diminishing marginal productivity.
   b. According to new growth theorists, his predictions didn't come true because of technological innovation. As capital increases, even if land is fixed, output can also increase. The economy can still grow if capital increases at the same rate that labor increases.

ANSWERS

MULTIPLE CHOICE

1. b   The text states that in the short run the Keynesians focus on demand; the Classicals focus on supply.

2. d   Say's Law states that supply creates its own demand.

3. d   Because aggregate demand is less than potential, there will be pressure for the price level to decline, bringing the economy back to potential. While government policy might bring the economy back to potential, Classicals did not promote this policy. Keynesians promoted it.

4. c   According to the Rule of 72, divide 72 by the growth rate to determine the number of years in which output will double.

5. c   As discussed in the text, the average worker's wages buy many more goods now than in 1919. Whether that makes them better off is debatable, but they definitely earn more.

6. c   Per capita income (output) growth equals output growth less population growth. Without knowing population growth, we do not know for which country per capita income (output) growth is greater.

7. c   As defined in the text, investment is the increase in capital over time.

8. b   When saving increases from S_0 to S_1, there is downward pressure on the interest rate. This leads to higher investment (demand for loanable funds) and, according to the growth model, growth.

9. d   Investment is the change in capital; it is not a description of capital.

10. d   Available resources depend on technology. That is why they can increase or decrease.

11. c   The law of diminishing marginal productivity refers to one input, not all, and to what will happen to output as that input continually increases, keeping other inputs constant. It is likely that c is true but it is not the law of diminishing marginal productivity.

12. b   The Classical growth model focuses on increases in capital and hence on saving and investment.

13. c   In the early Classical model, fixed land and diminishing marginal productivity meant that eventually growth would slow.

14. a   New growth theories center their explanation of growth on technology.

15. b   Positive externalities, by definition, are not taken into account by the decision maker.

16. b   QWERTY stands for the upper left keys on a keyboard. Placing them there is not especially efficient, but once they were placed there, they were locked in.

17. a   Economists generally believe that trade increases growth, so increasing trade restrictions would decrease growth. It is unclear whether protecting patents would increase growth.

ANSWERS

POTENTIAL ESSAY QUESTIONS

The following are annotated answers. They indicate the general idea behind the answer.

1. Early Classical economists believed that growth was the result of increases in capital, and because the law of diminishing productivity said that increases in capital would lead to ever smaller increases in output, eventually the economy would cease to grow. New growth theory predicted that growth would continue because growth is the result of technological innovation. Their argument hinges on the belief that growth leads to more technological innovation.

2. Specialization is important to learning by doing because as a process is broken into smaller parts, a worker can become an expert through practice and by concentrating their focus on a specific job. Because globalization is leading to greater specialization, learning by doing will increase world growth.

Pretest
Chapters 24-27

Take this test in test conditions, giving yourself a limited amount of time to complete the questions. Ideally, check with your professor to see how much time he or she allows for an average multiple choice question and multiply this by 23. This is the time limit you should set for yourself for this pretest. If you do not know how much time your teacher would allow, we suggest 1 minute per question, or 23 minutes.

1. Keynesians:
   a. generally favor activist government policies.
   b. generally favor laissez-faire policies.
   c. believe that frictional unemployment does not exist.
   d. believe that all unemployment is cyclical unemployment.

2. The secular trend growth rate in the United States is approximately:
   a. 1 to 1.5 percent per year.
   b. 2.5 to 3.5 percent per year.
   c. 5 to 5.5 percent per year.
   d. 7 to 7.5 percent per year.

3. What turns a business cycle into a structural stagnation?
   a. A trough that is lower than the peak.
   b. Multiple business cycles in a short period of time.
   c. A slow expansion that keeps the economy below trend.
   d. A downturn that doesn't end.

4. Unemployment caused by people entering the job market and people quitting a job just long enough to look for and find another one:
   a. is called structural unemployment.
   b. is called frictional unemployment.
   c. is called cyclical unemployment.
   d. are not counted in the unemployment rate.

5. The total labor force is 100,000 out of a possible working age population of 160,000. The total number of unemployed is 8,000. What is the unemployment rate?
   a. 5 percent.
   b. 6 percent.
   c. 7 percent.
   d. 8 percent.

6. The highest amount of output an economy can sustainably produce and sell using existing production processes and resources is called:
   a. nominal output.
   b. actual output.
   c. potential output.
   d. utilized output.

7. To move from GDP to GNP, one must:
   a. add net foreign factor income.
   b. subtract inflation.
   c. add depreciation.
   d. subtract depreciation.

8. If you, the owner, sell your old car for $600, how much does GDP increase?
   a. By $600.
   b. By the amount you bought it for, minus the $600.
   c. By zero.
   d. By the $600 you received and the $600 the person you sold it to paid, or $1,200.

9. There are two firms in an economy, Firm A and Firm B. Firm A produces 100 widgets and sells them for $2 apiece. Firm B produces 200 gadgets and sells them for $3 apiece. Firm A sells 30 of its widgets to Firm B and the remainder to consumers. Firm B sells 50 of its gadgets to Firm A and the remainder to consumers. What is GDP in this economy?
   a. $210.
   b. $590.
   c. $600.
   d. $800.

10. Gross investment differs from net investment by:
   a. net exports.
   b. net imports.
   c. depreciation.
   d. transfer payments.

11. If inflation is 10 percent and nominal GDP goes up 20 percent, real GDP goes up approximately:
   a. 1 percent.
   b. 10 percent.
   c. 20 percent.
   d. 30 percent.

12. In Keynesian economics equilibrium income:
   a. will be equal to potential income.
   b. will be below potential income.
   c. will be above potential income.
   d. may be different than potential income.

13. According the Keynesian model, deflation:
   a. leads to increasing asset prices that keep an economy from equilibrium.
   b. creates problems that keep an economy from equilibrium.
   c. is a good way to bring the economy back to equilibrium.
   d. has no effect on equilibrium output.

14. If there is a rise in foreign income the AD curve will likely:
   a. shift in to the left.
   b. shift out to the right.
   c. become steeper.
   d. become flatter.

15. The slope of the SAS curve is determined by:
   a. opportunity cost.
   b. the law of diminishing marginal returns.
   c. institutional realities.
   d. the money wealth effect, the international effect, and the interest rate effect.

16. Refer to the graph below. The graph demonstrates the expected short-run result if:

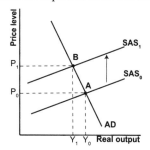

17. Assume the economy is initially at point B. The graph below correctly demonstrates an economy moving to point C if:

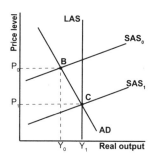

a. productivity increases by less than wages.
b. the government increases the money supply.
c. the exchange rate value of a country's currency falls.
d. there are suddenly expectations of a rising price level.

a. productivity increases by less than the increase in wages.
b. the government increases the money supply.
c. the country's exchange rate appreciates (gains value).
d. wages rise by less than the increase in productivity.

18. If there are feedback effects in an economy, a decline in asset prices can lead to a decline in:
   a. aggregate demand followed by a decrease in the price level that brings the economy back to equilibrium.
   b. aggregate demand followed by a decrease in the price level, followed by further declines in aggregate demand.
   c. potential output that leads to a falling price level that brings the economy back to equilibrium at the new, lower potential output.
   d. potential output that leads to a falling price level that shifts the aggregate demand curve to the right, bringing the economy back to its original output.

19. According to Say's Law:
   a. supply does not create demand.
   b. supply creates demand greater than supply.
   c. supply creates demand less than supply.
   d. supply creates demand equal to supply.

20. Suppose output grew at 8% in China and 2% in the United States. Based on this information alone, we can know that:
   a. per capita income grew faster in China.
   b. per capita income grew faster in the U.S.
   c. per capita income could have grown faster in either country. We cannot tell which.
   d. per capita output grew faster in China.

21. The law of diminishing marginal productivity states that as:
   a. inputs increase by equal percentages, output will increase by less than that percentage.
   b. inputs increase by equal percentages, output will eventually increase by less than that percentage.
   c. one input increases by a certain percentage, output will increase by less than that percentage.
   d. time progresses, the output from additional input declines.

22. New growth theories are theories that emphasize:
   a. technology.
   b. human capital.
   c. physical capital.
   d. entrepreneurship.

23. QWERTY is a metaphor for:
   a. the invisible hand.
   b. technological lock-in.
   c. the law of diminishing marginal productivity.
   d. the pollution caused by positive spillovers.

ANSWERS

1.	a	(24:3)	**13.**	b	(26:2)
2.	b	(24:9)	**14.**	b	(26:8)
3.	c	(24:13)	**15.**	c	(26:12)
4.	b	(24:14)	**16.**	a	(26:15)
5.	d	(24:15)	**17.**	d	(26:18)
6.	c	(24:18)	**18.**	b	(26:22)
7.	a	(25:2)	**19.**	d	(27:2)
8.	c	(25:4)	**20.**	c	(27:6)
9.	b	(25:5)	**21.**	c	(27:11)
10.	c	(25:11)	**22.**	a	(27:14)
11.	b	(25:15)	**23.**	b	(27:16)
12.	d	(26:1)			

Key: The figures in parentheses refer to multiple choice question and chapter numbers. For example (1:2) is multiple choice question 2 from chapter 1.

THE FINANCIAL SECTOR AND THE ECONOMY

28

CHAPTER AT A GLANCE

1. Money is a highly liquid, financial asset that (1) is generally accepted in exchange for goods and services, (2) is used as a reference in valuing other goods, and (3) can be stored as wealth.

   Money is any financial asset that serves these three functions.

2. The three functions of money are:

   - Medium of exchange;
     As long as people are confident that the purchasing power of the dollar will remain relatively stable over time (by the Fed controlling the money supply) then people will continue to swap real goods, services, and resources for money and vice versa.

   - Unit of account;
     Money acts as a measuring stick of the relative value (relative prices) of things. Therefore, the value of money itself must remain relatively stable over time.

   - Store of wealth.
     Money's usefulness as a store of wealth also depends upon how well it maintains its value. The key is for the Fed to keep the purchasing power of money (and therefore prices) relatively stable over time. Inflation can be a problem!

3a. M1 is the component of the money supply that consists of cash in the hands of the public plus checking account balances.

   M1 is the narrowest measure of the money supply. It is also the most liquid.

3b. M2 is the component of the money supply that consists of M1 plus savings and money market accounts, small-denomination time deposits, and retail money funds.

   M2 is the measure of the money supply most used by the Fed to measure the money supply in circulation. This is because M2 is most closely correlated with the price level and economic activity.

   Anything that changes M2 changes the money supply!

4. Banks "create" money because a bank's liabilities are defined as money. So when a bank incurs liabilities it creates money.

   Banks "create" money (increase the money supply) whenever they make loans. Whenever a person borrows from a bank he/she is swapping a promissory note to repay the loan (the loan is really an IOU; and an individual's IOU is not money because it doesn't meet the criteria of serving the functions of money) in exchange for cash or funds put in his/her checking account. Cash and checking account balances are money! Therefore, the money supply increases. Also note: When a loan is repaid, the money supply (M2) decreases.

5. The money multiplier is the measure of the amount of money ultimately created by the banking system per dollar deposited. It equals $1/r$, where r is the reserve ratio.

   A single bank is limited in the amount of money it may create. The limit is equal to its excess reserves–the maximum amount of funds that it can legally loan out. However, when considering an entire banking system, where any bank's loans, when spent, may end up being deposited back into that bank or another bank, then the entire banking system ends up being able to increase the money supply by a multiple of its initial excess reserves (the initial maximum amount of funds that can legally be loaned out) because of the money multiplier.

money multiplier = 1/r.

Change in the money supply = (initial change in money supply)×(money multiplier.)

6. The financial sector is central to almost all macroeconomic debates because behind every real transaction, there is a financial transaction that mirrors it.

    When you buy an apple for 50 cents, the financial transaction is the 50 cents; the real transaction is the transfer of the apple.

7. People demand money for three reasons: (1) transactions motive, (2) precautionary motive, and (3) speculative motive.

    The transactions motive is the need to carry money to buy things. The precautionary motive is the need to carry money in the event of an emergency. The speculative motive is the desire to hold money instead of another financial asset whose price is falling.

    These motives mean people will hold money even if it means forgoing interest payments from holding bonds instead. But, as the interest rate rises, the cost of holding money in terms of lost interest rises, so you hold less money.

8. Interest rates play a crucial role in channeling savings back into the economy.

    Dramatically higher interest rates for particular assets compared to other financial assets can cause bubbles that can cause problems for an economy.

    See also, Appendix: "A Closer Look at Financial Assets and Liabilities"

SHORT-ANSWER QUESTIONS

1. You are having another stimulating lunchtime conversation, this time about money. Your friend says, "I know what money is; it's cash, the dollar bills I carry around." What is your response?

2. You continue the conversation and begin to discuss why we have money. Your friend states that the function of money is to buy things like the lunch he has just bought. Another friend says that because she has money she is able to compare the cost of two types of slacks. Still another offers that she holds money to make sure she can buy lunch next week. What is the function of money that each has described? Are there any others?

3. What are two measures of money? What are the primary components of each?

4. Your friends are curious about money. At another lunchtime discussion, they ask each other two questions: Is all the money deposited in the bank in the bank's vaults? Can banks create money? Since they are stumped, you answer the questions for them.

5. Using the simple money multiplier, what will happen to the money supply if the reserve ratio is 0.2 and the Fed gives a bank $100 in reserves?

6. You and your friends are arguing about the financial sector. One friend says that real fluctuations are measured by real economic activity in the goods market and therefore the financial sector has nothing to do with the business cycle. You know better and set him straight.

7. How does the recent experience in Greece highlight the effect of expectations and risk on interest rates and on an economy?

8. Why is the money multiplier more complicated than calculating 1/r?

9. Because people don't earn interest on the money they hold in their pockets, why do they hold any money at all? (There are three reasons.)

MATCHING THE TERMS
Match the terms to their definitions

___ **1.**	asset management	**a.**	Cash that a bank keeps on hand that is sufficient to manage the normal cash inflows and outflows.
___ **2.**	bank	**b.**	The need to hold money for spending.
___ **3.**	excess reserves	**c.**	Component of the money supply that consists of M_1 plus savings and money market accounts, small-denomination time deposits, and retail money funds.
___ **4.**	Federal Reserve Bank (the Fed)	**d.**	Component of the money supply that consists of cash in the hands of the public plus checking account balances.
___ **5.**	liability management	**e.**	Holding money for unexpected expenses and impulse buying.
___ **6.**	M_1	**f.**	How a bank attracts deposits and what it pays for them.
___ **7.**	M_2	**g.**	How a bank handles its loans and other assets.
___ **8.**	money	**h.**	Measure of the amount of money ultimately created, per dollar deposited, in the banking system when people hold no currency. The mathematical expression is $1/r$.
___ **9.**	money multiplier		
___ **10.**	precautionary motive	**i.**	Holding cash to avoid holding financial assets whose prices are falling.
___ **11.**	reserve ratio	**j.**	Ratio of cash or deposits a bank holds at the central bank to deposits a bank keeps as a reserve against withdrawals of cash.
___ **12.**	reserves	**k.**	Reserves above what banks are required to hold.
___ **13.**	speculative motive	**l.**	The U.S. central bank. Its liabilities serve as cash in the United States.
___ **14.**	transactions motive	**m.**	A highly liquid financial asset that is generally accepted in exchange for other goods and is used as a reference in valuing other goods and as a store of wealth.
		n.	A financial institution whose primary function is accepting deposits from, and lending money to, individuals and firms.

PROBLEMS AND APPLICATIONS

1. For each, state whether it is a component of M_1, M_2, both, or neither:

    a. Retail money funds.

    b. Savings and money market accounts.

    c. Stocks.

    d. Twenty-dollar bills.

2. Calculate the money multiplier for each of the following reserve requirements:

    a. 15%

    b. 30%

    c. 60%

    d. 80%

    e. 100%

3. While Jon is walking to school one morning, a helicopter flying overhead drops $300. Not knowing how to return it, Jon keeps the money and deposits it in his bank. (No one in this economy holds cash.) If the bank keeps only 10 percent of its money in reserves and is fully loaned out, calculate the following:

    a. How much money can the bank now lend out?

    b. After this initial transaction, by how much has the money in the economy changed?

    c. What's the money multiplier?

    d. How much money will eventually be created by the banking system from Jon's $300?

4. For each of the following determine if it is an example of the precautionary, transaction, or speculative motive for holding money:

    a. You always carry a $10 bill in your pocket when you go on a date because your mother always said to be prepared for an emergency.

    b. You've lost your ATM card, so you have to carry more money in your pocket for daily purchases.

    c. An entrepreneur who has been "flipping" houses (buying houses, renovating them only to sell them within a short period of time), sees that housing prices are beginning to decline, so he sells his remaining holdings, keeping the proceeds in a money market account.

    d. It always seems like there is something in the grocery aisle that catches your eye. So you always keep a little extra in your pocket in case you want to buy something.

A1. Choose which of the following offerings you would prefer having: (Refer to the present value table A28-1 in the text.)

    a. $1,500 today or $2,000 in 5 years. The interest rate is 4%.

    b. $1,500 today or $2,000 in 5 years. The interest rate is 9%.

    c. $2,000 today or $10,000 in 10 years. The interest rate is 15%.

    d. $3,000 today or $10,000 in 15 years. The interest rate is 9%.

A2. A bond has a face value of $5,000 and a coupon rate of 10 percent. (A 10 percent coupon rate means that it pays annual interest of 10 percent of its face value.) It is issued in 2013 and matures in 2018. Using this information, calculate the following:

    a. What is the annual payment for that bond?

    b. If the bond is currently selling for $6,000, is its yield greater or less than 10 percent?

    c. If the bond is currently selling for $4,000, is its yield greater or less than 10 percent?

    d. What do your answers to parts *a* and *b* tell you about what the bond must sell for, relative to its face value, if the interest rate is 10%? Rises above 10%? Falls below 10%?

A3. For each, state whether a financial asset has been created. What gives each financial asset created its value?

    a. Your friend promises to pay you $5 tomorrow and expects nothing in return.

    b. You buy an apple at the grocery store.

    c. The government sells a new bond with a face value of $5,000, a coupon rate of 8%, and a maturity date of 2016.

    d. A firm issues stock.

    e. An existing stock is sold to another person on the stock market.

● MULTIPLE CHOICE

Circle the one best answer for each of the following questions:

1. Which of the following is not a function of money?
   a. Medium of exchange.
   b. Unit of account.
   c. Store of wealth.
   d. Equity instrument.

2. Which of the following is not included in the M_1 definition of money?
   a. Checking account balances.
   b. Retail money funds.
   c. Time deposits.
   d. Savings and money market accounts.

3. Which of the following components is not included in the M_2 definition of money?
   a. M_1.
   b. Savings and money market accounts.
   c. Small-denomination time deposits.
   d. Bonds.

4. In an advertisement for credit cards, the statement is made, "Think of a credit card as smart money." An economist's reaction to this would be that a credit card is:
   a. not money.
   b. dumb money.
   c. simply money.
   d. actually better than money.

5. Using a credit card creates a financial:
   a. liability for the holder and a financial asset for the issuer.
   b. asset for the holder and a financial liability for the issuer.
   c. liability for both the holder and issuer.
   d. asset for both the holder and issuer.

6. Why do people often hold money instead of bonds?
   a. Money is less liquid than bonds.
   b. Money is needed for transactions.
   c. Bonds pay interest.
   d. Of the two only money is a store of wealth.

7. Modern bankers:
   a. focus on asset management.
   b. focus on liability management.
   c. focus on both asset management and liability management.
   d. are unconcerned with asset and liability management and instead are concerned with how to make money.

8. If the reserve requirement is 20 percent, and banks keep no excess reserves, an increase in an initial inflow of $100 into the banking system will cause an increase in the money supply of:
   a. $20.
   b. $50.
   c. $100.
   d. $500.

9. If the reserve requirement is 10 percent, and banks keep no excess reserves, an increase in an initial $300 into the banking system will cause an increase in total money of:
   a. $30.
   b. $300.
   c. $3,000.
   d. $30,000.

10. If banks hold excess reserves whereas before they did not, the money multiplier:
    a. will become larger.
    b. will become smaller.
    c. will be unaffected.
    d. might increase or might decrease.

11. The money supply is best described as being:
    a. determined by the size of the money multiplier.
    b. determined by the amount of reserves.
    c. endogenously determined by the monetary system.
    d. fixed, to avoid inflation.

12. For every financial asset there is a:
    a. corresponding financial liability.
    b. corresponding financial liability if the financial asset is financed.
    c. real liability.
    d. corresponding real asset.

13. What is the function of risk premium?
    a. To make sure that the value of the bond rises with inflation.
    b. To compensate bondholders for the chance the borrower will not repay the loan.
    c. To distinguish short- from long-term bonds.
    d. To raise the return to holding government bonds.

14. If you expect interest rates to rise, you will want to be holding:
    a. more money because bond prices will likely fall.
    b. less money because bond prices will likely rise.
    c. more money because bond prices will likely rise.
    d. less money because bond prices will likely fall.

15. If interest rates fall,
    a. bond prices rise.
    b. bond prices fall.
    c. bond prices do not change.
    d. bond prices could either rise or fall.

16. If housing prices are expected to fall by 10 percent, one could say that the interest rate on housing assets is:
    a. 10 percent.
    b. -10 percent.
    c. nothing—interest rates are on bonds, not on other assets.
    d. the answer depends on what the inflation rate in the economy is.

A1. If the interest rate falls, the value of a fixed rate bond:
  a. rises.
  b. falls.
  c. remains the same.
  d. cannot be determined as to whether it rises or falls.

A2. Two bonds, one a 30-year bond and the other a 1-year bond, have the same interest rate. If the interest rate in the economy falls, the value of the:
  a. long-term bond rises by more than the value of the short-term bond rises.
  b. short-term bond rises by more than the value of the long-term bond rises.
  c. long-term bond falls by more than the value of the short-term bond falls.
  d. short-term bond falls by more than the value of the long-term bond falls.

POTENTIAL ESSAY QUESTIONS

You may also see essay questions similar to the "Problems & Applications" exercises.

1.   Why is it important for the macroeconomy that the financial sector operates efficiently?

2.   Why aren't credit cards money? What is the difference between money and credit?

ANSWERS

SHORT-ANSWER QUESTIONS

1. In one sense your friend is right; cash is money. But money is more than just cash. Money is a highly liquid financial asset that is accepted in exchange for other goods and is used as a reference in valuing other goods. It includes such things as checking account balances.

2. The first friend has described money as a medium of exchange. The second has described money as a unit of account. And the third has described money as a store of wealth. These are the three functions of money. There are no others.

3. Two measures of money are M_1 and M_2. M_1 consists of currency and checking account balances. M_2 consists of M_1 plus savings and money market accounts, small-denomination time deposits, and retail money funds.

4. No, banks do not hold all their deposits in their vaults. They keep a small percentage of it for normal withdrawal needs and lend the remainder out. Banks' maintenance of checking accounts is the essence of how banks create money. You count your deposits as money since you can write checks against them and the money that is lent out from bank deposits is counted as money. Aha! The bank has created money.

5. The equation for the simple money multiplier is $(1/r)$ where r is the reserve ratio. Plugging the values into the equation, we see that the money multiplier is 5, so the money supply increases by $500.

6. The financial sector is important to the business cycle because it facilitates trade and channels the leakage of savings out of the circular flow back into the circular flow either as consumer loans, business loans, or government loans. If the financial sector did not translate enough of the saving out of the spending stream back into the spending stream, output would decline and a recession might result. Likewise, if the financial sector increased flows into the spending stream (loans) that exceeded flows out of the spending stream (saving), an upturn might result and inflation might rise.

7. In 2011 bondholders didn't expect Greece would pay its loans and the risk premium on bonds rose tremendously. This raised interest rates and the likelihood Greece couldn't repay the loans. Eventually Greece received a bailout from the EU.

8. Banks hold excess reserves and people hold cash, both of which lower the multiplier. These variables are affected by the money supply, making it endogenous.

9. People hold money to buy goods (transactions motive); in the event of an emergency (precautionary motive); and to avoid holding other financial assets whose asset prices are falling (speculative motive).

ANSWERS

MATCHING

1-g; 2-n; 3-k; 4-l; 5-f; 6-d; 7-c; 8-m; 9-h; 10-e; 11-j; 12-a; 13-i; 14-b.

ANSWERS

PROBLEMS AND APPLICATIONS

1. a. M_2.
   b. M_2.
   c. Neither.
   d. Both.

2. a. 6.67. multiplier = (1/.15).
   b. 3.33. multiplier = (1/.30).
   c. 1.67. multiplier = (1/.6).
   d. 1.25. multiplier = (1/.8).
   e. 1.0. multiplier = (1/1).

3. a. $270.

b. $270: The increase in loans that are then deposited (.9 × 300) represents the change in money.

c. 10: $1/r = 1/.1$.

d. $3,000: money multiplier × initial deposit = 10 × 300.

4. **a.** Precautionary motive.
   b. Transactions motive.
   c. Speculative motive.
   d. Precautionary motive.

A1. Using the table to calculate the present value of $1 to be received in the future, we find that the better value is:

   a. $2,000 in 5 years when the interest rate is 4% is valued today at $1,640.

   b. $1,500 today. $2,000 in 5 years when the interest rate is 9% is worth only $1,300 today.

   c. $10,000 in 10 years. $10,000 in 10 years is valued at $2,500 when the interest rate is 15%.

   d. $3,000 today. $10,000 in 15 years when interest rate is 9% is worth only $2,700 today.

A2. a. The annual payment for that bond is $500.

   b. If the bond is currently selling for $6000, its yield is less than 10 percent.

   c. If the bond is currently selling for $4,000, its yield is greater than 10 percent.

   d. The answer to (b) and (c) tell us that the bond must sell for its face value if the interest rate is 10%, less than face value if it rises above 10%, and more than face value if it falls below 10%.

A3. a. A financial asset has been created. Your friend's promise to pay you $5 is what gives that asset its value.

   b. No, a financial asset has not been created, although a financial transaction did occur.

   c. Yes, a financial asset has been created. The government's promise to pay you $5,000 at maturity and $400 each year until then are what give that asset its value.

   d. Yes, a financial asset has been created. A claim to future profits is what gives that asset its value.

   e. No, a financial asset has not been created. The financial asset sold already existed.

======== **ANSWERS** ========

MULTIPLE CHOICE

1. **d**   Money is not a type of stock so it is not an equity instrument.

2. **a** M_1 is currency plus savings account balances.

3. **d**   Bonds are not part of M_2.

4. **a**   A credit card is not money and thus *a* would be the best answer. A credit card replaces money, making the same amount of money able to handle many more transactions.

5. **a**   One is borrowing money when one uses a credit card, thereby incurring a financial liability.

6. **b**   Money is used for most transactions because it is more liquid than bonds. Bonds pay interest (at least higher interest than money) and therefore c is not a reason why people hold money rather than bonds. Both are stores of wealth.

7. **c**   Banks are concerned with both asset management and liability management. The second part of answer d is obviously true, but it's through management of assets and liabilities that they make money, so the first part is wrong.

8. **d**   The money multiplier is $1/r = 1/.2 = 5$, which gives an increase in total money of $500.

9. **c**   The money multiplier is $1/r = 1/.1 = 10$ which gives an increase of total money of $3,000.

10. **b**   Holding excess reserves would be the equivalent to increasing the reserve requirement, which would decrease the money multiplier.

11. **c**   The money supply is endogenously determined. Because of this, instead of targeting a specific supply of money, policy makers target an interest rate. From this interest rate, they can calculate the needed money supply, from which they can determine the needed level of reserves.

12. a The very fact that it is a financial asset means that it has a financial liability, so the qualifier in b is unnecessary.

13. b Bondholders need to be compensated for the potential for loan default. This compensation is paid through a higher interest rate and is called a risk premium. While bonds might be indexed to inflation, that is not called a risk premium. While long-term bonds might pay higher interest rates compared to short-term bonds, this is not always the case.

14. a If interest rates rise, bond prices fall, which means that you prefer to be holding money rather than bonds.

15. a Bond prices move inversely with interest rates.

16. b The expected percentage change in price of an asset is its implicit interest rate.

A1. a The present value formula tells us that the value on any fixed interest rate bond varies inversely with the interest rate in the economy.

A2. a Since bond values vary inversely with interest rate changes, the answer must be a or b. Judging between a and b will be hard for you at this point unless you have studied present value in another course. However, based on the discussion in the text on pages 665-666, you can deduce that since a long-term bond is not paid back for a long time, it will be much more strongly affected by interest rate changes.

ANSWERS

POTENTIAL ESSAY QUESTIONS

The following are annotated answers. They indicate the general idea behind the answer.

1. Recall that for every real transaction there is a financial transaction that mirrors it. The financial sector's role is to ensure the smooth flow of savings out of the spending stream back into the economy. Whenever the financial sector is not operating efficiently then it is quite possible that the flow of savings out of the spending stream could be greater than the amount of money going through the financial sector and back into the economy. If this happens, we will experience a recession. The opposite would create inflationary problems.

2. Money is a financial asset of individuals and a financial liability of banks. Credit card balances cannot be money since they are assets of a bank and a liability of the nonbanking public. In a sense, credit card balances are the opposite of money. Credit is savings made available to be borrowed. Credit is not an asset for the holder of the card. However, ready availability of credit through the use of credit cards does reduce the amount of money people need or wish to hold.

MONETARY POLICY

29

CHAPTER AT A GLANCE

1. Monetary policy is a policy that influences the economy through changes in the money supply and available credit. In the AS/AD model, monetary policy works as follows:

   Contractionary monetary policy shifts the AD curve to the left:
   $M\downarrow \rightarrow i\uparrow \rightarrow I\downarrow \rightarrow Y\downarrow$

   Expansionary monetary policy shifts the AD curve to the right:
   $M\uparrow \rightarrow i\downarrow \rightarrow I\uparrow \rightarrow Y\uparrow$

2a. The Fed is a semiautonomous organization composed of 12 regional banks. It is run by the Board of Governors.

   The Fed (Federal Reserve Bank) is in charge of monetary policy (changing the money supply, credit availability, and interest rates).

   The Federal Open Market Committee (FOMC) decides monetary policy.

2b. Congress gave the Fed six explicit duties. In normal times, the most important is conducting monetary policy.

   Six functions of the Fed:
   1. *Conducting monetary policy (influencing the supply of money and credit in the economy).*
   2. *Supervising and regulating financial institutions.*
   3. *Serving as a lender of last resort to financial institutions.*
   4. *Providing banking services to the U.S. government.*
   5. *Issuing coin and currency.*
   6. *Providing financial services (such as check clearing) to commercial banks, savings and loan associations, savings banks, and credit unions.*

   In a financial crisis, the most important role is as lender of last resort.

3a. Three conventional policy tools are open market operations, the reserve requirement, and the discount rate.

   1. The primary way the Fed changes reserves is through open market operations.

      Open market operations are the Fed's buying and selling of U.S. government securities. This is the most frequently used and most important tool to change the money supply.

      Recently, banks have held significant excess reserves, limiting the effect of open market operations.

   2. Changing the reserve requirement and the discount rate also affect reserves.

      The Fed doesn't use these tools often. The reserve requirement affects (1) banks' excess reserves and (2) the money multiplier. The discount rate is the interest rate the Fed charges banks for loans.

      If the economy is in a recession, the Fed could increase the money supply (pursue an expansionary monetary policy) by doing any one or more of the following:
      - *Decrease the reserve requirement.*
      - *Decrease the discount rate.*
      - *Buy government bonds.*

3b. The Fed recently began paying interest on reserves.

The rate is 0.25%. The Fed hasn't used this rate as a policy tool yet.

4. The Federal funds rate is the interest rate banks charge one another for overnight bank reserve loans. The Fed determines whether monetary policy is loose or tight depending upon what's happening to the Fed funds rate. The Fed funds rate is an important intermediate target.

The Fed targets a range for the Fed funds rate. If the Fed funds rate goes above (below) that target range, the Fed buys (sells) bonds. These are "defensive" actions by the Fed.

5. Formally, the Taylor rule is:

Fed funds rate = 2 percent + current inflation
+ 0.5 × (actual inflation - desired inflation)
+ 0.5 × (percent deviation of aggregate output from potential)

This rule has described Fed policy since the late 1990s. The Fed deviated from this rule from 2001 to 2006 and again beginning in 2008.

The Taylor rule depends on one's estimate of potential output. Structural stagnationists suggest a higher Fed funds rate target.

6. The yield curve is a graph of the interest rate of bonds of various maturities, ordered from the shortest to longest term to maturity.

Normally, the yield curve is upward sloping. That is, bonds that mature in a shorter time (for example, 1 year) have lower interest rates than bonds that mature in a longer time (for example 30 years).
The Fed most directly affects short-term interest rates, but monetary policy affects the economy through its effect on the long-term interest rate. The assumption is that the short- and long-term rates move together.

Sometimes when the Fed raises the short-term rate and the long-term rate doesn't change, or even falls, the yield curve becomes inverted (downward sloping). When this happens, the Fed is less effective in influencing the economy than it would like.

Inflation expectations affect the long-term interest rate. The interest rate has two components: the real and nominal rate.

Real interest rate = nominal interest rate −expected inflation

SHORT-ANSWER QUESTIONS

1. You have been asked to speak to the first-year Congresspeople. Your talk is about the Fed. They want to know what monetary policy is. You tell them.

2. Another Congressperson asks how monetary policy can keep the economy from overheating. You reply from the perspective of the standard AS/AD model.

3. Suppose the economy is below potential output. Now how can monetary policy boost output? You reply again from the perspective of the standard AS/AD model.

4. To clarify your answer to Question #1 you tell them when the Fed was created and what its specific duties are.

5. Another Congressperson asks what monetary policy actions the Fed can take. You answer, mentioning three specific actions.

6. You are asked to elaborate on your answer to Question #3. Now that you have told them how the Fed can change the money supply, how does each of the ways to affect reserves work?

7. One Congressperson realizes that the Fed does not have complete control over the money supply. She states that people could demand more cash, which will reduce the money supply. How does the Fed know whether its buying and selling of bonds is having the desired effect? You answer by explaining the Fed's intermediate target.

8. Another Congressperson asks whether there are any rules that they could use to predict what the Fed will do to the Fed's intermediate target. You explain the rule that described Fed policy from the late 1990s until 2006.

9. Still another Congressperson asks, "It doesn't seem that the Fed is doing a good job. I read in the paper that the Fed has wanted to raise long-term interest rates, but is having difficulty doing so." How do you respond to this concern?

10. You take one final question and it is a difficult one: "The economy seems to be stagnating and monetary policy isn't effective in addressing slow growth. What do you think is going on?" You answer from the perspective of the structural stagnation model.

MATCHING THE TERMS
Match the terms to their definitions

____ 1. central bank

____ 2. contractionary monetary policy

____ 3. discount rate

____ 4. expansionary monetary policy

____ 5. Fed funds

____ 6. Federal Open Market Committee (FOMC)

____ 7. Federal funds rate

____ 8. inverted yield curve

____ 9. monetary base

____ 10. monetary policy

____ 11. monetary regime

____ 12. open market operations

____ 13. reserve requirement

____ 14. Taylor rule

____ 15. yield curve

a. Rate of interest the Fed charges on loans it makes to banks.

b. The Fed's day-to-day buying and selling of government securities.

c. The percentage the Federal Reserve System sets as the minimum amount of reserves a bank must have.

d. A banker's bank; it conducts monetary policy and supervises the financial system.

e. Currency in circulation, vault cash plus reserves that banks have at the Fed.

f. Monetary policy aimed at raising the money supply and raising the level of aggregate demand.

g. Monetary policy aimed at reducing the money supply and reducing the level of aggregate demand.

h. The Fed's chief policy making body.

i. The interest rate banks charge one another for Fed funds.

j. Set the Fed funds rate at 2 plus current inflation plus ½ the difference between actual and target inflation and ½ the deviation of actual output from potential.

k. A predetermined statement of the monetary policy that will be followed in various situations.

l. A curve that shows the relationship between interest rates and bonds' time to maturity.

m. A yield curve in which the short-term rate is higher than the long-term rate.

n. Loans of excess reserves banks make to one another.

o. A policy of influencing the economy through changes in the banking system's reserves that influence the money supply, credit availability, and interest rates in the economy.

PROBLEMS AND APPLICATIONS

1. Demonstrate the effect of the following on price and output using the AS/AD model:

   a. Expansionary monetary policy..

   b. Expansionary fiscal policy.

2. The Fed wants to change the reserve requirement in order to change the money supply (which is currently $3,000). For each situation below, calculate the current reserve requirement and the amount by which the Fed must change the reserve requirement to achieve the desired change in the money supply. Assume no cash holdings.

   a. Money multiplier is 3 and the Fed wants to increase the money supply by $300.

   b. Money multiplier is 2.5 and the Fed wants to increase the money supply by $300.

c. Money multiplier is 4 and the Fed wants to decrease the money supply by $500.

d. Money multiplier is 4 and the Fed wants to increase the money supply by $1,000.

3. How do your answers change for Question #2 parts *a* through *d* if instead of changing the reserve requirement, the Fed wants to use an open market operation to change the money supply? Assume the reserve requirement remains unchanged. What should the Fed do to achieve the desired change? (The multiplier and desired change in money supply for each are listed.)

a. Money multiplier is 3 and the Fed wants to increase the money supply by $300.

b. Money multiplier is 2.5 and the Fed wants to increase the money supply by $300.

c. Money multiplier is 4 and the Fed wants to decrease the money supply by $500.

d. Money multiplier is 4 and the Fed wants to increase the money supply by $1000.

4. Instead of changing the reserve requirement or using open market operations, the Fed wants to change the discount rate to achieve the desired change in the money supply. Assume that for each 1 percentage-point fall in the discount rate, banks borrow an additional $20. How do your answers to Question #2 parts *a* through *d* change? (The multiplier and desired change in money supply for each are listed below.)

a. Money multiplier is 3 and the Fed wants to increase money supply by $300.

b. Money multiplier is 2.5 and the Fed wants to increase the money supply by $300.

c. Money multiplier is 4 and the Fed wants to decrease the money supply by $500.

d. Money multiplier is 4 and the Fed wants to increase the money supply by $1,000.

5. Using the Taylor rule, what do you predict will be the Fed's target for the Fed funds rate in the following situations?

a. Inflation is at the Fed's target of 2 percent, but output is 1 percent below potential.

b. Output is at potential, but inflation is 5 percent, 2 percentage points above the Fed's target.

c. Inflation is 4 percent, 1 percentage point above the Fed's target and output is 1 percent above potential.

d. Inflation is 4 percent, 2 percentage points above the Fed's target and output is 2 percent below potential.

6. Fill in the blanks in the following table:

	Expected Inflation Rate	Nominal Interest Rate	Real Interest Rate
a.	5%	10%	___
b.	___	15%	7%
c.	−3%	___	9%
d.	4%	___	10%

7. What does the Taylor Rule suggest the Fed funds should be for the following cases:

a. Inflation is 1%, target inflation is 2% and output is 2% below potential.

b. Inflation is 4%, target inflation is 2% and output is 1% above potential.

c. Inflation is 3%, target inflation is 3% and output is 2% below potential.

8. Given the following yields on Treasury bills and bonds, draw a yield curve.

a. 3-month 1 year 5 years 10 years 30 years
    2%   3%   5%   5.75%   6.25%

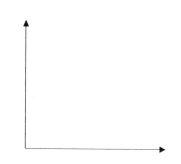

b. 3-month 1 year 5 years 10 years 30 years
    5%   4.5%   3%   2%   1%

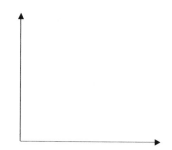

c. Which is a standard and which is an inverted yield curve?

● MULTIPLE CHOICE

Circle the one best answer for each of the following questions:

1. In the short run if the Fed undertakes expansionary monetary policy, the effect will be to shift the:
   a. AD curve out to the right.
   b. AD curve in to the left.
   c. SAS curve up.
   d. SAS curve down.

2. In the short run if the Fed undertakes contractionary monetary policy, the effect will be to shift the:
   a. AD curve out to the right.
   b. AD curve in to the left.
   c. SAS curve up.
   d. SAS curve down.

3. Which of the following is the path through which contractionary monetary policy works?
   a. Money down implies interest rate up implies investment down implies income down.
   b. Money down implies interest rate down implies investment down implies income down.
   c. Money down implies interest rate up implies investment up implies income down.
   d. Money down implies interest rate down implies investment up implies income down.

4. The central bank of the United States is:
   a. the Treasury.
   b. the Fed.
   c. the Bank of the United States.
   d. Old Lady of Threadneedle Street.

5. Monetary policy is:
   a. a variation of fiscal policy.
   b. undertaken by the Treasury.
   c. undertaken by the Fed.
   d. the regulation of monetary institutions.

6. There are seven Governors of the Federal Reserve, who are appointed for terms of:
   a. 5 years.
   b. 10 years.
   c. 14 years.
   d. 17 years.

7. Explicit functions of the Fed include all the following *except:*
   a. conducting monetary policy.
   b. conducting fiscal policy.
   c. providing banking services to the U.S. government.
   d. serving as a lender of last resort to financial institutions.

8. FOMC stands for:
   a. Federal Open Money Committee.
   b. Federal Open Market Committee.

c. Fixed Open Market Commitments.
d. Federation of Open Monies Committee.

9. The Fed can conduct monetary policy in all the following ways *except:*
   a. changing the reserve requirement.
   b. changing the discount rate.
   c. executing open market operations.
   d. running deficits.

10. The discount rate refers to the:
    a. lower price large institutions pay for government bonds.
    b. rate of interest the Fed charges for loans to banks.
    c. rate of interest the Fed charges for loans to individuals.
    d. rate of interest the Fed charges for loans to government.

11. The primary way the Fed conducts monetary policy is:
    a. open market operations.
    b. changing the discount rate.
    c. changing the reserve requirement.
    d. imposing credit controls.

12. If the Fed wants to increase the money supply, it should:
    a. buy bonds.
    b. sell bonds.
    c. pass a law that interest rates rise.
    d. pass a law that interest rates fall.

13. When the Fed sells bonds, the money supply:
    a. expands.
    b. contracts.
    c. sometimes rises and sometimes falls.
    d. Selling bonds does not have any effect on the money supply.

14. An open market purchase:
    a. raises bond prices and reduces interest rates.
    b. raises both bond prices and interest rates.
    c. reduces bond prices and raises interest rates.
    d. reduces both bond prices and interest rates.

15. The Federal funds rate is the interest rate:
    a. the government charges banks for Fed funds.
    b. the Fed charges banks for Fed funds.

c. the banks charge individual investors for Fed funds.

d. the banks charge each other for Fed funds.

16. If banks are short of reserves, the Fed funds rate will:
a. increase.
b. decrease.
c. stay the same.
d. rise or fall; it cannot be determined with the information given.

17. One of the ultimate Fed's targets is:
a. the Fed funds rate.
b. the reserve requirement.
c. stable prices.
d. the Taylor rule.

18. Assuming the Fed is following the Taylor Rule, if inflation is 3 percent, target inflation is 2 percent, and output is 1 percent above potential, what would you predict would be the Fed funds rate target?
a. 4 percent.
b. 5 percent.
c. 5.5 percent.
d. 6 percent.

19. Many economists argue that the Fed contributed to the housing bubble by:
a. passing laws that allowed financial institutions to create credit default swaps.
b. paying interest on bank reserves.
c. keeping the Fed funds rate lower than what the Taylor rule predicts.
d. buying mortgage-backed securities for foreclosed homes.

20. In general, the yield curve:
a. is flat.
b. is upward sloping.
c. is downward sloping.
d. is shaped like a mountain.

21. If short-term and long-term interest rates are currently equal and the Fed contracts the money supply, the yield curve will most likely:
a. become downward sloping.
b. become upward sloping.
c. become vertical.
d. be unaffected.

22. If inflation becomes expected, and all other things remain as they were, the yield curve would most likely:
a. become steeper.
b. become flatter
c. become flat.
d. become vertical.

POTENTIAL ESSAY QUESTIONS

You may also see essay questions similar to the "Problems & Applications" exercises.

1. According to the AS/AD model, what is considered to be appropriate monetary policy during different phases of the business cycle? What is the cause-effect chain relationship through which a change in the money supply will affect the level of economic activity? How would this cause-effect relationship be reflected graphically?

2. Why do economists keep an eye on the Fed funds rate in determining the state of monetary policy?

3. Explain why the yield curve is important for the implementation of monetary policy.

ANSWERS

SHORT-ANSWER QUESTIONS

1. Monetary policy is a policy that influences the economy through changes in the money supply and available credit. The Fed conducts U.S. monetary policy.

2. The Fed should decrease the money supply by increasing the reserve requirement, increasing the discount rate, and/or selling U.S. government bonds. This contractionary monetary policy in the AS/AD model increases interest rates, and lowers investment. This shifts the AD curve to the left and reduces income.

3. The Fed should increase the money supply by decreasing the reserve requirement, decreasing the discount rate, and/or buying U.S. government bonds. This expansionary monetary policy in the AS/AD model decreases interest rates, and raises investment. This shifts the AD curve to the right and increases income.

4. The Fed was created in 1913. Its six explicit duties are (1) conducting monetary policy, (2) regulating financial institutions, (3) serving as a lender of last resort, (4) providing banking services to the U.S. government, (5) issuing coin and currency, and (6) providing financial services to financial institutions.

5. The three tools of monetary policy at the disposal of the Fed are (1) changing the reserve requirement, (2) changing the discount rate, and (3) executing open market operations (buying and selling bonds). The Fed can also use the interest it pays on reserves, but hasn't used this tool.

6. Changing the reserve requirement changes the amount of reserves the banks must hold and thus changes the amount of loans they can make. This changes the money supply. Changing the discount rate changes the willingness of banks to borrow from the Fed to meet reserve requirements, thus changing the amount of loans they are willing to make. This changes the money supply. Open market operations change the reserves banks hold by directly increasing or decreasing cash held by banks and simultaneously decreasing or increasing their holdings of government bonds. This changes the amount of loans banks can make and changes the money supply.

7. Economists and policymakers keep a close eye on the Fed funds rate, the rate banks charge one another for loans of reserves, as an intermediate target to determine the effect of an open market operation—whether it indeed was expansionary or contractionary. An expansionary action will lower the Fed funds rate and contractionary action will raise the Fed funds rate. In effect, the Fed chooses a range for the Fed funds rate and buys and sells bonds to keep the Fed funds rate within that range. If the Fed funds rate is below (above) the target, the Fed sells (buys) bonds.

8. The Taylor rule has described recent Fed policy relatively well until 2006 and again in 2008. It states: Set the Fed funds rate at 2% plus the rate of inflation plus one-half the difference between actual and desired inflation and one-half the deviation of actual output from desired output.

9. You tell the Congressperson that conducting monetary policy is difficult. The standard discussion of monetary policy is based on the assumption that when the Fed pushes up (down) the short-term interest rate, the long-term interest rate moves up (down) as well. This is based on the relationship between short and long-term interest rates shown in the yield curve. The yield curve is generally upward sloping. But sometimes the shape of the yield curve changes. That is, when the Fed attempts to contract the money supply, the yield curve can become inverted, or downward sloping. Similarly, if the Fed tries to expand the money supply, the yield curve will generally become steeper.

10. According to the structural stagnation hypothesis, while expansionary monetary policy increases aggregate demand, because goods prices are capped, all of the increase in aggregate demand is met by foreign producers. Domestic output doesn't increase, while the trade deficit does. I might also warn the Congressperson that continued expansionary

monetary policy might lead to the return of asset price inflation.

ANSWERS

MATCHING

1-d; 2-g; 3-a; 4-f; 5-n; 6-h; 7-i; 8-m; 9-e; 10-o; 11-k; 12-b; 13-c; 14-j; 15-l.

ANSWERS

PROBLEMS AND APPLICATIONS

1. **a.** In the standard AS/AD model, expansionary monetary policy shifts the AD curve to the right (from AD_0 to AD_1). In the short run, the price level rises to P_1 and output rises to Y_1.

    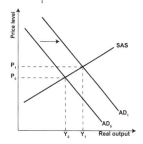

    b. Expansionary fiscal policy has the same effect as expansionary monetary policy.

2. **a.** To find the reserve requirement solve $1/r = 3$ for r. $r = 1/3$. These calculations are based on the formula $M = (1/r) \times MB$, where M is the money supply, r is the reserve ratio, and MB is the monetary base (here it equals reserves). We first find out the monetary base that supports $3,000 money supply with a money multiplier of 3. It is $1,000. We want the money supply to be $3,300. So the multiplier we want is $3,300/1,000 = 3.3$. Again solving $1/r = 3.3$ we find r must be 0.3.

    b. To find the reserve requirement solve $1/r = 2.5$ for r. $r = .4$. Reserves must be $1,200 to support money supply of $3,000. The Fed must reduce the reserve requirement to

    .3636 to increase the money supply by $300. Use the method described in (a) to find the answer.

    c. To find the reserve requirement solve $1/r = 4$ for r. $r = .25$. Reserves must be $750 to support money supply of $3,000. The Fed must increase the reserve requirement to .3 to decrease the money supply by $500. Use the method described in part a to find the answer.

    d To find the reserve requirement solve $1/r = 4$ for r. $r = .25$. Reserves must be $750 to support money supply of $3,000. The Fed must reduce the reserve requirement to .1875 to increase the money supply by $1,000. Use the method described in part a to find the answer.

3. These calculations are based on the formula $M = (1/r) \times MB$, where M is the money supply, r is the reserve ratio, and MB is the monetary base which equals reserves.

    a. The Fed should buy bonds to increase reserves in the system by $100. We find this by dividing the desired increase in the money supply by the money multiplier.

    b. The Fed should buy bonds to increase reserves in the system by $120. We find this by dividing the desired increase in the money supply by the money multiplier.

    c. The Fed should sell bonds to decrease reserves in the system by $125. We find this by dividing the desired decrease in the money supply by the money multiplier.

    d The Fed should buy bonds to increase reserves in the system by $250. We find this by dividing the desired increase in the money supply by the money multiplier.

4. These calculations are based on the formula $M = (1/r) \times MB$, where M is the money supply, r is the reserve ratio, and MB is the monetary base (here it equals reserves). Find out how much reserves must be changed and divide by 20 to find how much the discount rate must be lowered (if reserves are to be raised) or increased (if reserves are to lowered).

    a. To increase reserves in the system by $100, the discount rate should be reduced by 5 percentage points. We find how much reserves must be increased by dividing the desired increase in the money supply by the money multiplier. We find how much the discount rate must be lowered by dividing the desired increase in reserves by 20 (the amount reserves will increase with each percentage point decline in the discount rate).

b. To increase reserves in the system by $120, the discount rate should be reduced by 6 percentage points. See introduction to answer number 3 for how to calculate this.

c. To decrease reserves in the system by $125, the discount rate should be increased by 6.25 percentage points. See introduction to answer number 3 for how to calculate this.

d. To increase reserves in the system by $250, the discount rate should be reduced by 12.5 percentage points. See introduction to answer number 3 for how to calculate this.

5. a. Begin with 2 + rate of inflation, or 4. Since output is 1 percent below potential, subtract 0.5 to get to 3.5%.

b. Begin with 2 + inflation, or 7. Because inflation is 2 percentage points above target, add 1 percent to get to 8%.

c. Begin with 2 + inflation, or 6. Since inflation is 1 percentage point above its target add 0.5 and since output is 1 percent above potential, add another 0.5 to get 7%.

d. Begin with 2 + inflation, or 6. Since inflation is 2 percentage points above its target, add 1 but since output is 2 percent below potential subtract 1 to get 6%.

6.

	Expected Inflation Rate	Nominal Interest Rate	Real Interest Rate
a.	5%	10%	5%

Real rate = nominal - inflation.

b.	8%	15%	7%

Inflation = nominal - real rate.

c.	−3%	6%	9%

Nominal = inflation + real rate.

d.	4%	14%	10%

Nominal = inflation + real rate.

7. a. 3.5% [2+1+.5(1+2)+.5(−2)].
b. 8% [2+4+.5(4−2)+.5(2)].
c. 4% [2+3+.5(3−3)+.5(−2)].

8. a. The graph below shows the yield curve associated with the values given.

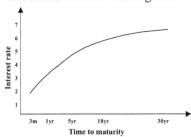

b. The graph below shows the yield curve associated with the values given.

c. Yield curve for part *a* is a standard yield curve. Yield curve for par*t b* is an inverted yield curve.

ANSWERS

MULTIPLE CHOICE

1. a Expansionary monetary policy reduces interest rates and investment increases. Hence, AD shifts out to the right by a multiple of the increase in investment.

2. b Contractionary monetary policy increases interest rates which reduces investment, a component of aggregate expenditures. The AD curve shifts in to the left by a multiple of the decline in investment.

3. a Contractionary monetary policy increases interest rates which decreases investment, thereby decreasing income by a multiple of that amount.

4. b See text.

5. c The correct answer is "policy undertaken

by the Fed." The last answer, d, involves regulation, which is also done by the Fed, but such regulation generally does not go under the name "monetary policy." Given the accuracy of answer c, answer d should be avoided.

6. c   See text.

7. b   Fiscal policy is definitely not a function of the Fed.

8. b   See Figure 29-2.

9. d   Deficits are a tool of fiscal policy.

10. b.   The Fed makes loans only to other banks, and the discount rate is the rate of interest the Fed charges for these loans.

11. a   Open market operations is mostly how the Fed changes the money supply.

12. a   The last two answers, c and d, cannot be right, because the Fed does not pass laws. When the Fed buys bonds, it lowers the interest rate but it does not lower interest rates by law. Therefore, only a is correct.

13. b   People pay the Fed for those bonds with money—Fed IOUs—so the money supply in private hands is reduced.

14. a   As the Fed buys bonds this increases their demand and their prices rise. Since bond prices and interest rates are inversely related, interest rates will fall.

15. d   See text.

16. a   Because there is a shortage of Fed funds, those who do have excess reserves can ask for a higher return to lend them to banks who need reserves.

17. b   The Fed has four ultimate targets: stable prices, sustainable growth, acceptable employment, and moderate long-term interest rates. The Fed funds rate is an operating target. The Taylor rule is not a target.

18. d   The Taylor rule states that the Fed targets the Fed funds rate with this formula: 2 + rate of inflation + one-half the difference between actual and desired inflation plus one-half the deviation of output over its target. Thus, it will set a Fed funds target of 6%, (2+3+.5+.5).

19. c   The Fed kept the Fed fund rates lower than what the Taylor rule predicted from 2001 to 2006. Economists believe this contributed to the housing bubble.

20. b   The yield curve is generally upward sloping. Interest rates for short-term bonds are generally lower than interest rates for long-term bonds because of the risk premium for long-term bonds.

21. a   If the Fed contracts the money supply, the short-term interest rate will rise. This will tend to make the yield curve inverted, or downward sloping.

22. a   If expectations of inflation rise, long-term interest rates will likely rise, so other things equal, the yield curve will become steeper.

ANSWERS

POTENTIAL ESSAY QUESTIONS

The following are annotated answers. They indicate the general idea behind the answer.

1.   Use expansionary monetary policy (Fed reduces reserve requirements, reduces the discount rate, and/or buys government securities) during a recession; use contractionary policy during an upturn in the business cycle. Use expansionary monetary policy during an expansion above trend. Expansionary monetary policy will increase the money supply, which will reduce the interest rate and increase investment spending. This shifts the AD curve out to the right by a multiple of the initial increase in investment spending and brings about a multiple increase in the income level.

2. A high Fed funds rate indicates contractionary monetary policy and a low rate indicates expansionary monetary policy. When the Fed funds rate is above its targeted range many banks have shortages of reserves and there-fore money must be tight (credit is tight); and vice versa. The Fed will buy (sell) bonds when the Fed funds rate is above (below) its target and monetary policy is too tight (loose).

3. Economists look at the yield curve because it shows the relationship between short-term and long-term interest rates. It's important to monetary policy because the Fed can only directly impact short-term interest rates. As long as the relationship between short-term and long-term interest rates remains constant, the Fed can also affect long-term interest rates, and therefore investment expenditures, and ultimately output and the price level. But if the relationship changes, the Fed has less control. One possibility is that the Fed raises short-term interest rates and long-term interest rates fall. This might happen if by raising short-term interest rates, inflation expectations fall. But if the Fed wanted long-term interest rates to rise, raising short-term rates will not be effective.

FINANCIAL CRISES, PANICS, AND UNCONVENTIONAL MONETARY POLICY

30

CHAPTER AT A GLANCE

1. Economists worry more about the collapse of the financial sector than about the collapse of other sectors because all the other sectors depend on a functioning financial sector.

   When credit is not available, the real economy can quickly come to a halt. That is why one of the roles of a central bank is to be the lender of last resort—lend to banks and other institutions when no one else will.

2. Two central ingredients of a bubble are herding and leveraging. Herding creates a run-up in prices through extrapolative expectations. Leveraging increases people's ability to herd. Combined, they can lead to price bubbles that feed upon themselves.

   Herding is the human tendency to follow the crowd. Leveraging increases people's ability to herd.

   Extrapolative expectations work this way: Rise in price →expectations of a further rise in price →rise in demand at the current price →rise in price →expectations of a further rise in price . . . and so on.

3. According to the efficient market hypothesis, bubbles can't happen since people are rational, taking into account the real value of assets today and in the future when making decisions.

   The financial bubble that burst in 2008 challenged the efficient market hypothesis. The collective irrationality that contributed to the bubble created an argument for regulation.

4. After the financial crisis in the 1930s, government set up rules for banks to prevent financial crises. The Glass-Steagall Act was one such regulatory law that set up a system of deposit insurance.

   Guarantees of deposits and expectation of bailouts create a moral hazard problem. The too-big-to-fail problem is an example of the moral hazard problem. Know what the moral hazard problem is!

   Any regulation is subject to the law of diminishing control—it will become less and less effective as time goes by as institutions find ways to get around them.

5. Economics provides general guidelines for regulation. They are based on requiring people to take responsibility for their actions.

   - Set as few bad precedents as possible.
   - Deal with moral hazard.
   - Deal with the law of diminishing control.

   Economics doesn't say whether regulations are good or bad. It points out regulation's costs and benefits.

6. Because of structural stagnation conventional expansionary monetary policy was ineffective. To get around this problem the Fed instituted unconventional policies. After the 2008 financial crisis, the Fed has wound down its policies of being the lender of last resort.

   - *Quantitative easing: Printing money to buy financial assets directly from financial institutions.*

- *Credit (or qualitative) easing: Purchasing long-term bonds to take risky assets out of the market.*
- *Operation twist: Sell short-term bonds and buy long-term bonds (not printing new money) to lower long-term interest rates.*
- *Precommitment policy: Committing to follow a particular policy for a prolonged period of time.*
- *Negative interest rates: Charging individuals to hold their money rather than paying them interest or having a nominal interest rate below the rate of inflation.*

7. In conventional monetary policy, inflation is something to be avoided. In unconventional monetary policy, inflation can be too low.

   Higher inflation allows the real interest rate to be negative, giving government more room for expansionary policy.

8. Some economists are concerned about unconventional monetary policy. Know the criticisms!

- *They prop up asset prices keeping the economy from making necessary structural adjustments.*
- *They allow the government to run high deficits, which are unsustainable.*
- *They leave the Fed open to enormous losses.*
- *Precommitments give the Fed no ability to reverse its stance should the situation change.*
- *The Fed doesn't have a viable exit plan.*

● SHORT-ANSWER QUESTIONS

1. Why are economists more concerned about the collapse of the financial sector than the collapse of other sectors?

2. How can extrapolative expectations lead to a financial bubble?

3. What roles do herding and leverage play in creating a financial bubble?

4. How does the Fed's role as lender of last resort lead to the moral hazard problem? What implications does it have for government policy?

5. How does the efficient market hypothesis differ from the structural stagnationist view of asset bubbles?

6. What is the law of diminishing marginal control? How does it undermine regulations?

7. What are three precepts that should be kept in mind when developing regulations?

8. Name four unconventional policies the Fed implemented after the financial crises.

9. Why would the Fed target an inflation rate not as an upper bound to be achieved, but as a precise target, which means that inflation can be too low?

10. What are five criticisms of the Fed's post-financial crisis policies?

MATCHING THE TERMS
Match the terms to their definitions

___ **1.** asset price bubble

___ **2.** credit easing

___ **3.** deposit insurance

___ **4.** Dodd-Frank Wall Street Reform and Consumer Protection Act

___ **5.** efficient market hypothesis

___ **6.** extrapolative expectations

___ **7.** Federal Deposit Insurance Corporation

___ **8.** Glass-Steagall Act

___ **9.** herding

___ **10.** law of diminishing control

___ **11.** lender of last resort

___ **12.** leverage

___ **13.** liquid

___ **14.** mortgage-backed securities

___ **15.** operation twist

___ **16.** precommitment policy

___ **17.** quantitative easing

___ **18.** solvent

___ **19.** too-big-to-fail problem

a. The human tendency to follow the crowd.

b. A government institution that guarantees bank deposits of up to $250,000.

c. Unsustainable rapidly rising prices of some type of financial asset.

d. Any regulation will become less effective over time as individuals will figure out ways to circumvent those regulations.

e. Buying a financial asset with borrowed money.

f. Expectations that a trend will accelerate.

g. Financial assets whose flow of income comes from a combination of mortgages.

h. A system under which the federal government promises to reimburse an individual for any losses due to bank failure.

i. Have sufficient assets that can be converted into cash and money.

j. An act of Congress passed in 1933 that established deposit insurance and implemented a number of banking regulations.

k. Lending when no one else will.

l. Having sufficient assets to cover long-run liabilities.

m. Regulations to limit risk taking and require banks to report their asset holdings.

n. All financial decisions are made by rational people and are based on all relevant and accurate information.

o. Commitment to a policy for a long period of time.

p. The belief that large financial institutions are so essential to the economy that government must prevent their failure.

q. Purchase long-term bonds to change the mix of securities by the Fed toward less liquid and more risky assets.

r. The Fed's selling short-term bonds to buy long-term bonds.

s. Policy of targeting a particular quantity of money by buying financial assets from banks and other financial institutions with newly created money.

PROBLEMS AND APPLICATIONS

1. Define each of the following unconventional monetary policy tools and explain their intended effects:

    a. Quantitative easing.

    b. Credit easing.

    c. Operation twist.

    d. Precommitment policy.

2. Define each of the following regulations and explain why they were implemented:

    a. Glass-Steagall Act.

    b. FDIC.

    c. Dodd-Frank Wall Street Reform and Consumer Protection Act.

3. Draw the effect on the yield curve associated with the following policies and explain your answer.

    a. Credit easing.

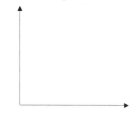

    b. Operation twist.

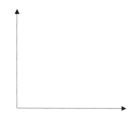

    c. Quantitative easing.

MULTIPLE CHOICE

Circle the one best answer for each of the following questions:

1. During the 2008 financial crisis, a financial bailout made better sense on economic grounds than a bailout of the automotive industry because:
    a. automobile companies are less deserving than financial companies.
    b. the automobile industry is smaller than the financial industry.
    c. the finance industry is necessary for other industries to function.
    d. the automobile industry brought the problem on itself.

2. In which two markets did a bubble form that led to a financial crisis in 2008?
    a. Housing and mortgage-backed securities.
    b. Housing and automobiles.
    c. Mortgage-backed securities and tulips.
    d. South Sea Company and tulips.

3. What role do almost all economists agree the central bank has in a financial crisis?
    a. Contractionary fiscal policy to reduce leverage.
    b. Lender of last resort.
    c. Expansionary fiscal policy to reduce herding.
    d. No role.

4. A bank that is liquid:
    a. has assets that can be readily converted into cash and money.
    b. has sufficient assets to cover its long-term liabilities.
    c. can sell short-term bonds to buy long-term bonds.
    d. is diversified in its holdings of financial assets.

5. Extrapolative expectations are expectations that:
    a. the Fed will bail out failing banks.
    b. a trend will reverse.
    c. a trend will accelerate.
    d. assets are priced at their true value.

6. A person purchases a stock worth $200, borrowing $190 and putting down $10 of her own money. The bank charges 2% a year and the stock rises by 5% in the first year. If she sells the stock, the return on her investment will be:

a. 2%

b. 5%

c. 50%

d. 62%

7. Borrowing money to increase returns is an example of:

a. herding.

b. operation twist.

c. moral hazard

d. leverage.

8. The implication of the efficient market hypothesis is that:

a. globalization was keeping prices low so that expansionary monetary policy was creating a bubble.

b. the market will continue to be efficient regardless of people's unsustainable extrapolative expectations.

c. policy makers can use monetary and fiscal policy to attain an efficient market result if banks will not.

d. monetary policy makers didn't have to pay attention to the growing bubble in the 2000s because it wasn't a bubble.

9. Moral hazard is a problem that arises when:

a. people are required to bear the negative consequences of their actions.

b. people don't have to bear the negative consequences of their actions.

c. people benefit from the negative actions of others.

d. government discourages companies from taking risks.

10. The problem created by the Federal Deposit Insurance Act is:

a. Herding.

b. Leverage.

c. Moral hazard.

d. Deregulation.

11. The recent regulation that was designed to limit risk-taking by banks by requiring them to report their holdings is called the:

a. The Glass-Steagall Act.

b. Dodd-Frank Wall Street Reform and Consumer Protection Act.

c. Troubled Asset Relief Program.

d. Federal Deposit Insurance Act.

12. All of the following are examples of the law of diminishing control that followed banking regulations put in place after the Great Depression *except*:

a. Banks created new instruments to circumvent the law.

b. Financial business migrated to unregulated institutions.

c. Depositors demanded financial institutions be responsible for their financial decisions.

d. Politicians were pressured to dismantle the regulations.

13. A policy of targeting a particular quantity of money by buying financial assets from banks and other financial institutions with newly created money is called:

a. precommitment policy.

b. operation twist.

c. credit easing.

d. quantitative easing.

14. The difference between quantitative easing and credit easing is:

a. credit easing is designed to change the mix of securities held by the Fed while quantitative easing is designed to increase the amount of money in the economy.

b. quantitative easing is designed to change the mix of securities held by the Fed while credit easing is designed to increase the amount of credit in the economy.

c. credit easing is designed to shift the yield curve up while quantitative easing is designed to twist the yield curve.

d. quantitative easing is designed to raise long-term and lower short-term interest rates while credit easing is designed to lower long-term and raise short-term interest rates.

15. A problem with a precommitment policy is that it:

a. determines the Fed's response for a period of time.

b. binds the hands of the Fed from responding to unexpected events.

c. will cause the Fed to lose credibility.

d. locks the Fed into contractionary policy.

16. Negative real interest rates:
    a. are impossible.
    b. can be desirable.
    c. reflect asset deflation.
    d. are a form of hyperinflation.

17. One of structural stagnationist's criticisms of Fed policy after the financial crisis is that it:
    a. broke up banks into commercial and non-commercial banks.
    b. required workers to take pay cuts so that they would find jobs.
    c. caused the economy to go through structural adjustments.
    d. enabled government to run large deficits through lower interest rates.

18. The problem with the Fed's exit strategy following the financial crisis is that it:
    a. likely involves loosening bank regulations.
    b. would increase the trade deficit.
    c. didn't have the support of Congress.
    d. didn't have one.

POTENTIAL ESSAY QUESTIONS

You may also see essay questions similar to the "Problems & Applications" exercises.

1. Define the law of diminishing control and explain how it relates to the history of financial regulation in the United States since the 1930s. Be sure to mention particular laws, their provisions, and the responses by financial institutions.

2. Were the four unconventional policies the Fed implemented after the financial crises effective? What problems might they create in the future?

3. What guidelines do economists suggest for creating regulatory policies? Upon what principles are these guidelines based?

ANSWERS

SHORT-ANSWER QUESTIONS

1. The collapse of the financial sector is of more concern than the collapse of other sectors because it is necessary for all other sectors of the economy to operate. Without access to credit that the financial sector provides, businesses cannot pay workers or invest in new technologies.

2. Extrapolative expectations lead to financial bubbles because they give investors the impression that prices will continue to rise. This causes traders to purchase the asset, which further raises its price. As more and more people buy the asset, its price rises dramatically.

3. Herding is when people "follow the crowd." Once some people purchase assets whose price is rising, others follow, which causes their price to rise further. Leveraging gives people the opportunity to buy assets with mostly borrowed money and provides huge returns on the initial investment. With such potential returns, more and more people leverage their purchases, which raises the price of the asset, which then allows more leveraging, further inflating the bubble.

4. The Fed's role as a lender of last resort leads to the moral hazard problem because when firms know they will be bailed out and will not suffer the negative consequences of their actions, they are more inclined to take big risks. This is problematic for government policy because regulations that are meant to stabilize the financial system can create an incentive to make risky decisions, which might actually create instability. The implication for policy is that institutions and individuals that could be bailed out must be regulated.

5. The efficient market hypothesis view is that all financial decisions are made by rational people and are based on all relevant information that accurately reflects the value of assets today and in the future. In contrast, the structural stagnationist view holds that while people can be individually rational, they could be collectively irrational, following herding behavior, which can lead to bubbles.

6. The law of diminishing marginal control holds that any regulation will become less effective over time as individuals or firms being regulated will figure out ways to circumvent those regulations through innovation, technological change, and political pressure. It undermines regulation because firms find ways around regulation, new products emerge that are not covered by the regulations, and periods of stability put pressure on politicians to lift some regulations.

7. The three precepts are that government should set as few bad precedents as possible, deal with moral hazard when it arises, and adjust regulations to reflect the law of diminishing control.

8. Four unconventional policies are quantitative easing, credit (or qualitative) operation twist, and precommitment devices.

9. A precise inflation rate target creates the possibility of negative real interest rates. This would give the Fed more room for expansionary monetary policy to spur investment and growth.

10. Five criticisms of the Fed's post-crisis policies are that they prop up asset prices to prevent structural adjustments, allow the government to run unsustainably high deficits, expose the Fed to potentially huge losses, precommitment ties the hands of the Fed should the situation change, and the lack a realistic exit plan.

ANSWERS

MATCHING

1-c; 2-q; 3-h; 4-m; 5-n; 6-f; 7-b; 8-j; 9-a; 10-d; 11-k; 12-e; 13-i; 14-g; 15-r; 16-o; 17-s; 18-l; 19-p.

ANSWERS

PROBLEMS AND APPLICATIONS

1. **a.** Quantitative easing is a policy of targeting a particular quantity of money by buying financial assets from banks and other financial institutions with newly created money. It typically takes the form of buying long-term and non-government bonds. It is meant to directly increase the money supply, by bypassing the banking sector, and support prices for financial assets by creating demand for them.

    b. Credit easing is the purchase of long-term government bonds and securities from private financial corporations for the purpose of changing the mix of securities held by the Fed toward less liquid and more risky assets. It involves purchasing different types of financial assets, such as mortgage-backed securities, and is intended to provide credit and a market for such assets to private firms.

    c. Operation twist is the sale of short-term Treasury bills in order to buy long-term Treasury bonds without creating new money. Its purpose to twist the yield curve—lowering long-term interest rates and raising short-term interest rates.

    d. A precommitment policy is a commitment to continue a given policy for a certain period of time. It is meant to create some degree of certainty for future economic conditions among investors, eliminating the risk of policy changes and encouraging investment.

2. **a.** The Glass-Steagall Act was a 1933 law that created deposit insurance and added a number of new regulations for banks, including the prohibition of commercial bank investments in securities markets. The law was enacted to bolster public faith in banks by making commercial banking safe and to limit moral hazard from deposit insurance by preventing relatively risky investments.

    b. The FDIC, or Federal Deposit Insurance Corporation, is the government's deposit insurer, guaranteeing deposits of up to $250,000 per account. It was created in the wake of the 1930s bank failures to revive public faith in banking and prevent runs on the banks.

    c. The Dodd-Frank Wall Street Reform and Consumer Protection Act is a 2010 law that seeks to limit risktaking and require banks to report holdings so that systemic risk can be assessed more easily. It includes a process for liquidating firms in an attempt to minimize the too-big-to-fail problem.

3. In normal times, long-term interest rates are higher than short-term interest rates, creating an upward-sloping yield curve such as curve A in the figure on the left below.

    a. Credit easing is designed to leave the yield curve unchanged.

    b. Operation twist is designed to lower long-term rates and raise short-term rates. This is shown by twisting the yield curve from A to B as shown in the graph on the left.

    c. Quantitative easing is designed to add credit to the economy in general and lower all interest rates. This is shown by lowering the yield curve as shown in the graph on the right.

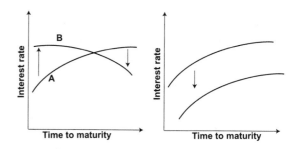

ANSWERS

MULTIPLE CHOICE

1. c   The financial industry's role in providing credit and financing to all other sectors of the economy makes it important to the health of the overall economy.

2. a   There were bubbles in neither markets for tulips nor for automobiles. The housing bubble helped create that mortgage-backed securities bubble.

3. b   The central bank has no control over fiscal policy but can act as a lender of last resort, providing funds to banks that are failing.

4. a   Liquidity means that assets can be readily turned into cash.

5. c   See the definition in the text.

6. d   The stock price rises to $210. She must pay the bank $3.80, making her a profit of $6.20 (10-3.80). The return on her investment is 62% (6.20/10 × 100).

7. d   Leverage is borrowing a significant percent of the cost of an investment that results in greater gains than if the person used only one's own assets to invest.

8. d   Under efficient markets, the current valuations are correct, so there is no possibility of bubbles developing.

9. b   See the definition in the text.

10. c   The Federal Deposit Insurance Act guarantees deposits, creating an incentive to take on risky investments because the depositor did not have to suffer the consequences of losses on those risky investments. This is known as the moral hazard problem.

11. b   The Dodd-Frank Act is a recent regulation that sought to limit risk taking. The Glass-Steagall Act was passed in the 1930s.

12. c   Depositors did not pressure institutions to be responsible in part because of guarantees by the FDIC.

13. d   See the definition in the text.

14. a   Credit easing is designed to change the quality of the assets held by the Fed instead of increasing the credit available. Quantitative easing increases the total amount of credit in the economy. Neither twists the yield curve.

15. b   By precommitting to a policy, the Fed is unable to reverse course.

16. b   Negative real interest rates means that investors will be paid to borrow. This may spur investment and growth.

17. d   The Fed's policy of keeping interest rates low kept the cost of increasing the debt low. This enabled government to run a higher deficit than it otherwise would have.

18. d   The Fed didn't have an exit policy. The Fed doesn't need congressional support to implement policy.

ANSWERS

POTENTIAL ESSAY QUESTIONS

The following are annotated answers. They indicate the general idea behind the answer.

1. The law of diminishing control is the idea that, over time, government regulations in the financial sector become less effective because financial firms create new products that the laws do not apply to, circumvent regulations with new services, and pressure politicians to relax the laws. This has created a cycle of regulation and deregulation, beginning largely with the Great Depression. After significant bank failures, the government passed the Glass-Steagall Act to insure deposits and stop banks from taking excessive risks by prohibiting commercial banks from investing in securities markets. Over time, however, those regulations became less effective as Congress removed Glass-Steagall provisions, banks evolved to offer a variety of new instruments that were not considered in the law, and tactics like the use of offshore banking provided a way around the law. The weakening of Glass-Steagall's provisions contributed to the recent financial crisis, causing the government to establish new regulations such as the Dodd-Frank Act.

2. It is unclear whether the Fed's unconventional measures were successful. While the economy averted a depression (which suggests a successful policy), the expansion was weak (the success was limited). Criticisms of the measures are that the expansionary policies propped up asset prices, risking another

bubble; they kept interest rates low, allowing the government to run deficits; they have left the Fed open to huge losses due to its holdings of bad assets; the Fed does not have flexibility to deal with new issues because of its precommitment; and the Fed doesn't have an exit policy.

3. The guidelines are to avoid setting bad precedents, deal with moral hazard, and deal with the law of diminishing control. These guidelines are intended to prevent future crises and eliminate the need for future regulation. Setting bad precedents justifies harmful behavior in the future, which could contribute to problems such as moral hazard. Legislation also must deal with moral hazard by restricting future actions for those who could benefit from government interventions. This stops people from taking advantage of regulations meant to prevent crises. Lastly, laws must deal with the law of diminishing control so that financial firms cannot avoid the regulation, create a crisis, and necessitate further legal action.

DEFICITS AND DEBT: THE AUSTERITY DEBATE

31

CHAPTER AT A GLANCE

1a. A deficit is a shortfall of revenues under payments. A surplus is an excess of revenues over payments. (Surpluses are negative deficits and vice versa.)

Surpluses and deficits are flow concepts; all deficits must be financed.

1b. Surpluses and deficits are simply summary measures of the financial health of the economy. To understand that summary you must understand the methods that were used to calculate it.

Different accounting procedures yield different figures for surpluses and deficits.

2. A structural deficit or surplus is that part of a budget deficit or surplus that would exist even if the economy were at its potential level of income. A cyclical surplus or deficit is that part that exists because the economy is operating below or above its potential income.

Cyclical deficit = Tax rate ×(Potential output −Actual output.)

Cyclical deficits or surpluses are largely due to the automatic stabilizers.

Recent deficits have exceeded projected deficits.

3. The real deficit is the nominal deficit adjusted for inflation.

Real deficit = Nominal deficit − (Inflation × Total debt.)

Inflation wipes out debt. Inflation also causes the real deficit to be less than the nominal deficit. However, inflation means a higher percentage of the deficit (and spending) will be devoted to debt service (paying interest on the debt).

4. Debt is accumulated deficits minus accumulated surpluses. It is a stock concept.

Debt is a summary measure of a country's financial situation.

The greater the GDP (income) the greater the ability to handle debt. However, government debt is different from an individual's debt. Government is ongoing; it can pay off the debt by printing money; and much of it is internal—owed to its citizens.

5a. Since in a growing economy a continual deficit is consistent with a constant debt-to-GDP ratio, and since GDP serves as a measure of the government's ability to pay off the debt, a country can run a continual deficit.

The more you earn, the more debt you can handle.

If debt continues to rise, at some point, creditors may be unwilling to buy U.S. bonds.

5b. Since World War II, the U.S. government ran almost continual deficits, which has led to a large debt.

One aspect of the debt burden is interest payments.

SHORT-ANSWER QUESTIONS

1. How much importance do most economists give to the budget deficit or surplus?

2. If the U.S. economy is below potential and the surplus is $40 billion, is the structural surplus greater or less than $40 billion?

3. If the nominal interest rate is 6%, the inflation rate is 4%, the nominal deficit is $100 billion, and the debt of the country is $2 trillion, what is the real deficit?

4. If the nominal interest rate is 5%, the inflation rate is 5%, the real deficit is $100 billion, and the debt of the country is $1 trillion, what is the nominal deficit?

5. In an expanding economy a government should run a continual deficit. True or false? Why?

6. If a politician presents you with a plan that will reduce the nominal budget deficit by $40 billion, but will not hurt anyone, how would you in your capacity as an economist likely respond?

MATCHING THE TERMS
Match the terms to their definitions

___	1. cyclical deficit	a.	A partially unfunded pension system of the U.S.
___	2. debt	b.	A shortfall per year of incoming revenue under outgoing payments.
___	3. deficit	c.	An excess of revenues over payments.
___	4. external debt	d.	Government debt owed to individuals in foreign countries.
___	5. fiscal austerity	e.	That portion of the deficit that results from economic fluctuations.
___	6. internal debt	f.	The deficit or surplus determined by looking at the difference
___	7. nominal deficit or surplus		between expenditures and receipts.
___	8. real deficit	g.	Government debt owed to its own citizens.
___	9. Social Security system	h.	The deficit that would remain when the cyclical or passive elements
___	10. structural deficit		have been netted out.
___	11. surplus	i.	The nominal deficit adjusted for inflation's effect on the debt.
		j.	Accumulated deficits minus accumulated surpluses.
		k.	Increasing taxes and decreasing spending.

PROBLEMS AND APPLICATIONS

1. Calculate the debt and deficit in each of the following:

    a. Your income has been $30,000 per year for the last five years. Your expenditures, including interest payments, have been $35,000 per year for the last five years.

    b. This year your income is $50,000; $15,000 of your $65,000 expenditures are for the purchase of the rights to an invention.

    c. Your wage income is $20,000 per year. You have a bond valued at $100,000, which pays $10,000 per year. The market value of that bond rises to $110,000. Expenses are $35,000 per year. Use the opportunity cost approach in your calculations.

2. For each of the following calculate the real deficit:

    a. Inflation is 5%. Debt is $2 trillion. Nominal deficit is $100 billion.

    b. Inflation is −3%. Debt is $500 billion. Nominal deficit is $20 billion.

    c. Inflation is 10%. Debt is $3 trillion. Nominal deficit is $100 billion.

    d. Inflation is 8%. Debt is $20 billion. Nominal deficit is $5 billion.

3. Assume a country's nominal GDP is $7 trillion, government expenditures less debt service are $1.5 trillion, and revenue is $1.3 trillion. The nominal debt is $4.9 trillion. Inflation is 2% and real interest rates are 5%. Expected inflation is fully adjusted.

    a. Calculate debt service payments.

    b. Calculate the nominal deficit.

    c. Calculate the real deficit.

    d. Suppose inflation rose to 4%. Again, expected inflation is fully adjusted. Recalculate parts *a-c*.

4. Potential income is $8 billion. The income in the economy is $7.2 billion. Revenues do not vary with income, but taxes do; they increase by 20% of the change in income. The current deficit is $400 million.

    a.   What is the economy's structural deficit?

    b.   What is the economy's cyclical deficit?

● MULTIPLE CHOICE

Circle the one best answer for each of the following questions:

1. "Because private investment is more productive than government investment, the government ought to run surpluses" reflects which framework?
    a. Long-run.
    b. Short-run.
    c. Structural stagnation.
    d. Cyclical.

2. A deficit is:
    a. the total amount of money that a country owes.
    b. the shortfall of payments under revenues in a particular time period.
    c. the shortfall of revenues under payments in a particular time period.
    d. accumulated debt.

3. If the U.S. government raised the retirement age to 72, the current budget deficit would be:
    a. reduced.
    b. increased.
    c. unaffected.
    d. eliminated.

4. The nominal deficit is $100 billion; inflation is 4 percent; total debt is $2 trillion. The real deficit is:
    a. zero.
    b. $20 billion.
    c. $80 billion.
    d. $100 billion.

5. If the nominal surplus is $200 billion, inflation is 10 percent, and total debt is $2 trillion:
    a. the real surplus is zero.
    b. the real deficit is $100 billion.
    c. the real surplus is $400 billion.
    d. the real surplus is $2.2 trillion.

6. The real deficit is $100 billion; inflation is 4 percent; total debt is $2 trillion. The nominal deficit is:
    a. zero.
    b. $120 billion.
    c. $180 billion.
    d. $200 billion.

7. If creditors are able to forecast inflation perfectly and there are no institutional constraints on interest rates:
    a. the government will not have to make interest payments.
    b. interest payments will rise by the amount that the real debt is reduced by inflation.
    c. the real deficit will equal the nominal deficit.
    d. the government will be unable to finance the debt.

8. Country A has a debt of $10 trillion. Country B has a debt of $5 trillion.
    a. Country A is in a better position than Country B.
    b. Country B is in a better position than Country A.
    c. One cannot say what relative position the countries are in.
    d. Countries A and B are in equal positions.

9. As a percentage of GDP, since World War II:
    a. debt in the United States has been rising.
    b. debt in the United States has been falling.
    c. debt in the United States has been sometimes rising and sometimes falling.
    d. the U.S. government has had no debt.

10. The portion of the budget deficit or surplus that would exist even if the economy were at its potential level of income is called the:
    a. structural deficit or surplus.
    b. cyclical deficit or surplus.
    c. primary deficit or surplus.
    d. secondary deficit or surplus.

11. If an economy is $100 billion below potential, the tax rate is 20 percent, and the deficit is $180 billion, the cyclical deficit is:
    a. $20 billion.
    b. $160 billion.
    c. $180 billion.
    d. $200 billion.

12. One of the reasons government debt is different from individual debt is:
    a. government does not pay interest on its debt.
    b. government never really needs to pay back its debt.
    c. all government debt is owed to other government agencies or to its own citizens.
    d. the ability of a government to pay off its debt is unrelated to income.

13. If there is growth and a country with a debt of $1 trillion has decided it wants to keep its ratio of debt-to-GDP constant:
    a. it should run a deficit.
    b. it should run a surplus.
    c. it should run a balanced budget.
    d. the deficit has no effect on debt.

14. The nominal debt is:
    a. unaffected by inflation.
    b. the shortfall of revenue under payments.
    c. a flow concept.
    d. a stock concept.

15. The United States:
    a. has run almost continuous surpluses since WWII.
    b. has reached a debt-to-GDP ratio of about 100%.
    c. has a national deficit over $19 billion.
    d. generally financed its deficit by printing money.

POTENTIAL ESSAY QUESTIONS

You may also see essay questions similar to the "Problems & Applications" exercises.

1. What are three reasons why government debt is different from individual debt?

2. How can a growing economy reduce the concern over deficits and the debt?

━━━ ANSWERS ━━━

SHORT-ANSWER QUESTIONS

1. How much economists are concerned about budget deficits depends on one's framework. In the long run surpluses are good because they provide savings needed for investment to increase potential output. In the short run framework, if an economy is in a recession, increased deficit spending can bring the economy back to its potential. In the structural stagnation framework, deficit spending will not bring an economy out of recession. It will only add to the economy's structural problems.

2. Since the economy is below potential, the structural surplus is larger than the nominal surplus.

3. To calculate the real deficit, you multiply inflation times the total debt (4% $\times$ $2 trillion), giving $80 billion; then subtract that from the nominal deficit of $100 billion. So in this example the real deficit equals $20 billion. The interest rate does not enter into the calculations.

4. To calculate the nominal deficit, you multiply inflation times the total debt (5% $\times$ $1 trillion), giving $50 billion, and add that to the real deficit of $100 billion. So in this example the nominal deficit equals $150 billion. The interest rate does not enter into the calculation.

5. It depends. In an expanding economy with no deficits, the ratio of debt to GDP will be falling; if the government wants to hold the debt-to-GDP ratio constant it will need to run a continual deficit. If it wants to reduce that ratio, then it need not run a continual deficit.

6. TANSTAAFL. I would check to see what accounting gimmick the politician was proposing and what the plan would do to the long-run financial health of the country.

━━━ ANSWERS ━━━

MATCHING

1-e; 2-j; 3-b; 4-d; 5-g; 6-f; 7-i; 8-a; 9-h; 10-c.

━━━ ANSWERS ━━━

PROBLEMS AND APPLICATIONS

1. a. Deficit is $5,000 per year; debt is $25,000. On page 712, deficit is defined as income less expenditures and on page 718 debt is defined as accumulated deficits minus accumulated surpluses. For each of the past 5 years, you have incurred an annual deficit of $5,000. Total debt is $5,000 times five years, or $25,000.

    b. Deficit is $15,000; debt is $15,000. If you count the purchase of the rights to the invention as a current expenditure, the deficit is $15,000. If you had no previous debt, debt is also $15,000. If, however, you count the purchase of the invention as an investment and include it in your capital budget, then your expenses are only $50,000 and your budget will be in balance.

    c. Surplus of $5,000. Using an opportunity cost approach, a person holding bonds should count the rise in the bonds' market value as revenue. Here, wage income is $20,000 per year, interest income is $10,000, and the bond's value has increased by $10,000. Total income is $40,000. Income of $40,000 less expenses of $35,000 per year yields a budget surplus of $5,000. Unless there was a previous debt, there is no debt.

2. The real deficit is the nominal deficit adjusted for inflation's effect on the debt. The definition of real deficit states: Real deficit = Nominal deficit − (Inflation $\times$ Total debt).
    a. $0: $100 billion − .05 $\times$ $2 trillion.
    b. $35 billion: $20 billion − (−.03) $\times$ $500.
    c. Surplus of $200 billion: $100 billion − .10 $\times$ $3 trillion.
    d. $3.4 billion: $5 billion − .08 $\times$ $20 billion.

3. a. $343 billion: Debt service payment = nominal interest rate $\times$ nominal debt. The nominal interest rate when expected inflation is fully adjusted for is the real interest rate plus inflation (5+2). Debt service payment = .07 $\times$ $4.9 trillion.
    b. $543 billion deficit: The nominal deficit is revenues less government expenditures (including debt service), $1.3 trillion − ($1.5 trillion + $.343 trillion).

c. $445 billion deficit: The real deficit = Nominal deficit − (Inflation × Total debt) = $.543 trillion − (.02 × $4.9 trillion).

d. Since bondholders must be compensated for the loss in the value of their bonds, they demand a nominal interest rate of 9% (5 + 4). Debt service payment is now $441 billion (.09 × $4.9 trillion). The nominal deficit is higher at $641 billion. ($1.3 trillion − ($1.5 trillion + $.441 trillion)). The real deficit has not changed. It is still $445 billion (The real deficit = Nominal deficit − (Inflation × Total debt) = $.641 trillion − (.04 × $4.9 trillion)).

4. a. If the economy were at potential, government would collect $160 million more in taxes, reducing the deficit by that amount. There would be a structural deficit of $400 − $160 = $240 million.

b. The cyclical deficit is the deficit that occurs because the economy is below potential. The passive deficit is $800 million × 20 percent, or $160 million.

ANSWERS

MULTIPLE CHOICE

1. a The long-run framework generally believes government should run surpluses because they will increase potential output. The short-run framework supports deficits when the economy is in a recession and surpluses when the economy is in an expansion. Cyclical is not a framework.

2. c A country has a budget deficit if it does not collect sufficient revenue to cover expenditures during the year.

3. c The U.S. uses a cash flow accounting method, so changes affecting the future are not seen in the current budget.

4. b Real deficit = nominal deficit − (inflation × total debt).

5. c Real surplus = nominal surplus + (inflation × total debt).

6. c Real deficit = nominal deficit − (inflation × total debt).

7. b If creditors can forecast inflation perfectly, the interest rate will rise when inflation rises and the subsequent increase in interest payments will match the decline in the real debt due to higher inflation.

8. c Debt must be judged relative to assets and to total GDP.

9. c See Figure 31-2.

10. a The cyclical deficit or surplus is the deficit or surplus that exists because the economy is below or above potential. The structural deficit or surplus is the deficit or surplus that exists even when the economy is at potential. The text doesn't define primary or secondary deficits or surpluses.

11. a The cyclical deficit is the deficit that exists because the economy is below potential. The government would collect $20 billion more in revenue if the economy were at potential, so the passive deficit is $20 billion.

12. b Because government goes on forever it doesn't ever need to pay back its debt. Only about 75 percent of government debt is owed to other government agencies or to its own citizens. The other government debt is owed to foreign individuals. Government is better able to pay off debt when income rises. Both government and individuals pay interest on debt.

13. a Real growth will reduce the ratio of existing debt-to-GDP ratio, so to hold the ratio constant a continual deficit is necessary.

14. d The debt is a stock concept while deficit is a flow concept. Debts are affected by inflation to the extent that interest payments rise.

15. b   The debt-to-GDP ratio is currently about 100%. Except from 1998 until 2001 when it ran surpluses, the United States has run nearly continual deficits. The *debt* is currently over $19 trillion. The United States pays for its deficit by selling bonds, not printing money as is done in a number of developing countries.

━━━━━━━ ANSWERS ━━━━━━━

POTENTIAL ESSAY QUESTIONS

The following are annotated answers. They indicate the general idea behind the answer.

1. First, the government's life is unlimited and therefore it never has to settle its accounts. Second, it can pay off debt by creating money (which is not recommended, however). Third, much of the government's debt is internally held and therefore, on average as a group, people are neither richer nor poorer because of the debt (even though it may redistribute income from lower-income individuals to upper-income individuals).

2. When a society experiences real growth (growth adjusted for inflation), it becomes richer, and, being richer, it can handle more debt. Moreover, since in a growing economy a continual deficit is consistent with a constant ratio of debt to GDP, and since GDP serves as a measure of the government's ability to pay off debt, a country can run a continual deficit. Deficits should be viewed relative to GDP to determine their importance.

THE FISCAL POLICY DILEMMA

32

1. Ricardian equivalence is the theoretical proposition that deficits do not affect the level of output in the economy because individuals increase their savings to account for expected future tax payments to repay the deficit.

   Basically, the Ricardian equivalence theorem says that increases in government spending are offset by equal declines in private spending. Although this argument is logical, it isn't the reason why economists before the 1930s didn't support activist fiscal policy. They didn't support it for political reasons.

2a. The precept of sound finance is that the government budget should always be balanced except in wartime.

   This precept was driven less by economic logic and more by a tradition of believing the government should not direct the economy. During the Depression economists modified this precept to support government involvement under extreme conditions.

2b. Functional finance is the theoretical proposition that government should make spending and taxing decisions based on their effect on the economy, not on the moralistic grounds that budgets should be balanced.

   In this view, fiscal policy provides government with a steering wheel with which to direct the economy.

3. Economists began to recognize assumptions of the *AS/AD* model could lead to problems with fiscal policy as they applied functional finance precepts.

a. Financing the deficit has no offsetting effects.

   In reality, it often does. A particular problem is crowding out, which is the offsetting effect on private expenditures caused by the government's sale of bonds to finance expansionary fiscal policy.

b. The government knows the situation.

   In reality the government must estimate what the situation is.

c. The government knows the economy's potential income.

   In reality the government may not know what this level is.

   Economists often use the relationship between the unemployment rate and income to estimate potential income: A percentage point fall in the target rate of unemployment is associated with a 2% increase in potential income.

d. The government has flexibility in terms of spending and taxes.

   In reality, the government cannot change them quickly.

e. The size of the government debt doesn't matter.

   In reality, the size of the debt often does matter. This is particularly true today with total debt that is 100% of GDP.

f. Fiscal policy doesn't negatively affect other government goals.

   In reality, it often does.

4. An automatic stabilizer is any government program or policy that will counteract the business cycle without any new government action.

    Automatic stabilizers include:
    *   *welfare payments*
    *   *unemployment insurance, and*
    *   *the income tax system.*

    In a recession, government expenditures automatically rise (because of increased welfare payments and unemployment claims). Taxes automatically decrease (because income has declined). The budget deficit increases because total spending increases. The opposite occurs during an upturn in the business cycle. Automatic stabilizers help smooth out the business cycle.

SHORT-ANSWER QUESTIONS

1. What is the Ricardian equivalence theorem?

2. How could Classical economists believe in both sound finance and the Ricardian equivalence theorem?

3. How does sound finance differ from functional finance?

4. How do the six problems of fiscal policy limit its usefulness?

5. Why might the size of the U.S. debt be a problem?

6. Some economists argue that crowding out totally undermines the activist view of fiscal policy. Explain their argument.

7. A country has just discontinued its unemployment insurance program and is experiencing a recession. How will this recession differ from earlier recessions?

8. In the short-run model, you want to lower interest rates and increase income. Would you propose expansionary monetary or fiscal policy? What concerns would you voice about this policy?

9. Suppose you are the featured speaker at a primer for the first-year Congresspeople. You have been asked to speak about fiscal policy. A Congressperson asks what fiscal policy tools Congress has to affect the economy, and what effect they have on the level of output. You tell her.

MATCHING THE TERMS
Match the terms to their definitions

____ **1.** automatic stabilizer

____ **2.** crowding out

____ **3.** functional finance

____ **4.** procyclical fiscal policy

____ **5.** Ricardian equivalence theorem

____ **6.** sound finance

a. A theoretical proposition that governments should make spending and taxation decisions on the basis of their effect on the economy, not on the basis of some moralistic principle that budgets should be balanced.

b. A view of public finance and fiscal policy that the government budget should always be balanced except in wartime.

c. The theoretical proposition that deficits do not affect the level of output in the economy because individuals increase their savings to account for expected future tax payments to repay the deficit.

d. Any government program or policy that will counteract the business cycle without any new government action.

e. The offsetting effect on private expenditures caused by the government's sale of bonds to finance expansionary fiscal policy.

f. Changes in government spending and taxes that increase the cyclical fluctuations in the economy instead of reducing them.

PROBLEMS AND APPLICATIONS

1. Demonstrate your answers to the following questions both in words and with graphs:

    a. How does a government deficit affect the long-term interest rate in the loanable funds market (the market for saving and investment)?

    b. How does the change in interest rates in part *a* impact the effectiveness of fiscal policy in the *AS/AD* model?

2. What fiscal policy did the United States adopt in 2008?

    a. Demonstrate your answer using the AS/AD model.

    b. Did most economists think this was the correct policy choice? Why or why not?

3. How did the government respond to the Great Depression?

a. What effect did it have on the economy?

b. Which economists supported this action?

● MULTIPLE CHOICE

Circle the one best answer for each of the following questions:

1. Sound finance holds that:
   a. government spending is directed toward sound investments.
   b. the government budget should always be balanced except in wartime.
   c. the government budget should be judged by its effect on the economy.
   d. government should always borrow money in a sound fashion when it runs a deficit.

2. The Ricardian equivalence theorem holds that:
   a. government spending is equivalent to private spending.
   b. financing a deficit by bonds will have the same effect as financing it through taxes.
   c. imposing taxes is equivalent to confiscation of property by government.
   d. all spending in the economy is equivalent.

3. Economists who held that theoretically the Ricardian equivalence theorem was true:
   a. would not support sound finance.
   b. would not support functional finance.
   c. could support sound finance and/or functional finance.
   d. could support either sound finance or functional finance but not both.

4. Functional finance holds that:
   a. budgets should always deal with functional issues.
   b. government should make monetary policy decisions on the basis of their effect on the economy.
   c. government should make fiscal policy decisions on the basis of their effect on the economy.
   d. government's budgets should be balanced.

5. Crowding out is caused by:
   a. government running a deficit and selling bonds to finance that deficit.
   b. government printing money.
   c. government running a surplus and selling bonds and the people who buy those bonds selling their older bonds to the government.
   d. the tendency for new workers to replace more expensive older workers.

6. Using the relationship between a change in the target rate of unemployment and potential income, if the target rate of unemployment rises by 2 percent, potential income is expected to:
   a. fall 2%.
   b. rise 2%.
   c. fall 4%.
   d. rise 4%.

7. Fiscal policy in the United States in 2008:
   a. reflected sound finance.
   b. reflected functional finance.
   c. was driven by a concern about the debt.
   d. was a neutral policy.

8. Automatic stabilizers:
   a. are government programs to employ workers during recessions.
   b. create government budget surpluses during economic recessions.
   c. are designed to reduce the price level directly.
   d. counteract both recessions and expansions through changes in spending without government action.

9. A state constitutional provision to maintain a balanced budget is an example of:
   a. an automatic stabilizer.
   b. monetary policy.
   c. procyclical policy.
   d. countercyclical policy.

10. If the government borrows money, the interest rate will likely:
    a. fall.
    b. rise.
    c. remain unchanged.
    d. rise and then fall.

POTENTIAL ESSAY QUESTIONS

You may also see essay questions similar to the "Problems & Applications" exercises.

1. How do the automatic stabilizers add stability to the business cycle? Are there any time lag (delay) problems associated with the use of the automatic stabilizers?

2. What is the crowding-out effect? What impact does this have on the effectiveness of fiscal policy in stimulating the economy during a recession? How large is the crowding-out effect, according to economists who support sound finance and those who support functional finance?

3. Say you are a policy adviser to the government of a country that is growing at 6%, has inflation of 1%, and unemployment of 2%. You are hired by the government to advise them on how they can improve the economy. What advice would you give?

■■■■ ANSWERS ■■■■

SHORT-ANSWER QUESTIONS

1. It is a theoretical proposition that deficits do not affect the level of output in the economy because individuals increase their savings to account for expected future tax payments to repay the deficit.

2. They supported sound finance on the basis of politics; they supported the Ricardian equivalence theorem as a logical proposition that had only limited relevance to the real world.

3. Sound finance holds that the budget should be balanced at all times; functional finance holds that spending and taxing decisions should be made on the basis of their effect on the economy.

4. The six problems with fiscal policy limit its usefulness in the following ways: (1) Financing the deficit might have offsetting effects, reducing the net effect. (2) The government doesn't always know the current state of the economy and where it is headed, meaning they must be forecast; if you don't know the state of the economy you don't know what fiscal policy to use. (3) The government doesn't know what potential income is, meaning it must be estimated; if you estimated it wrong, you get the wrong fiscal policy. (4) The government cannot implement policy easily; if you can't implement it you can't use it. (5) The size of the debt might matter and since deficits create debt, you might not want to use it. (6) finally, fiscal policy often negatively affects other government goals; if it does you might not use the policy even though it would change the economy in the direction you want. The bottom line is: In extreme cases, the appropriate fiscal policy is clear, but in most cases, the situation is not extreme.

5. If those who buy government debt begin to worry that the U.S. government cannot repay the bonds, interest rates may rise, increasing total spending and making the debt an even greater problem.

6. If crowding out is so strong that the reduced investment totally offsets the expansionary effect of fiscal spending, the net effect of fiscal policy can be zero.

7. Unemployment insurance is an automatic stabilizer, a government program that counteracts the business cycle without any new government action. If income falls, automatic stabilizers will increase aggregate expenditures to counteract that decline. Likewise with increases in income: when income increases, automatic stabilizers decrease the size of the deficit. Eliminating unemployment insurance will eliminate this stabilization aspect of the policy and will contribute to making the recession more severe than it otherwise would have been. However, it would also make people more likely to accept lower wages and search harder for a job, thereby reducing the amount of unemployment. As usual, the answer depends.

8. I would propose expansionary monetary policy. Expansionary fiscal policy would raise interest rates. I would emphasize that while the effect on income may be expansionary in the short run, in the long run, the expansionary monetary policy may simply lead to inflation.

9. The tools of fiscal policy are changing taxes and changing government spending. Increasing taxes and lowering spending contract the economy; decreasing taxes and increasing spending expand the economy.

■■■■ ANSWERS ■■■■

MATCHING

1-d; 2-e; 3-a; 4-f; 5-c; 6-b.

■■■■ ANSWERS ■■■■

PROBLEMS AND APPLICATIONS

1. **a.** A government deficit increases the demand for loanable funds. The following graph

shows this as a shift in the demand curve from D_0 to D_1. An increase in the demand for loanable funds increases the long-term interest rate, in the graph, from i_0 to i_1.

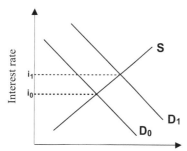

Quantity of loanable funds

b. An increase in the deficit (caused by increased government spending or a reduction in taxes) shifts the AD curve to the right. This is illustrated in the graph below as a shift in the AD curve to the right from AD_0 to AD_1. The increase in the interest rate increases the cost of borrowing for investment, which reduces investment expenditures, causing the AD curve to shift to the left by a multiple of the decrease in investment expenditures. This offsets the impact of fiscal policy on the economy somewhat and is shown in the graph as a shift in the AD curve from AD_1 to AD_2

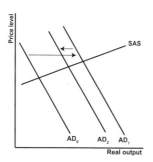

2. The U.S. adopted expansionary fiscal policy.
  a. Expansionary fiscal policy will shift the AD curve to the right (AD_0 to AD_1), increasing income and the price level. The expansionary fiscal policy will likely result in some crowding out of private investment, meaning it will shift back to the left slightly (AD_1 to AD_2). (732-733)
  b. Most economists agreed that expansionary fiscal policy was necessary to help get the U.S. out of the severe recession. In general,

if the economy is headed towards a depression, most economists support functional finance in the form of expansionary fiscal policy. Still, economists were concerned about the U.S. debt and potentially negative effects on the economy.

3. The government responded with government spending without increasing taxes, that is, ran a deficit.
  a. Government spending, particularly during World War II pulled the economy out of its depression.
  b. Both Classical and Keynesian economists supported this action. While Classical economists believed that in general policymakers should follow the principle of sound finance, given the depression that the economy was stuck in, they were willing to entertain the notion that it was possible that if the government spent more than it collected in taxes—ran a deficit— the economy would be jump-started.

━━━━━━ **ANSWERS** ━━━━━━

MULTIPLE CHOICE

1.   b   Sound finance holds the moral stance that government should stay out of the economy, that is, the government budget should always be balanced.

2.   b   According to the Ricardian equivalence theorem people will save the money needed to repay bonds that will come due in the future, so that financing by bonds will have the same effect as financing through taxes.

3.   c   The Ricardian equivalence theorem states that it doesn't matter if spending is financed by taxes or by bonds. The effect will be the same — none. Sound finance doesn't depend on the Ricardian equivalence theorem, it is a moral position. Functional finance just says that government should make the decision whether to run a deficit based on how it will affect the economy. Someone who holds the Ricardian equivalence theorem to be true would recommend a sound finance policy of no deficit.

4. c   Functional finance rejects the moralistic position of sound finance and says government should make decisions based on how fiscal policy will affect the economy.

5. a   Crowding out is the offsetting of a change in government expenditures by a change in private expenditures in the opposite direction. Answer c, if you could follow it, is nonsensical.

6. c   The relationship is that a 1% change in unemployment is related to a 2% change in income in the opposite direction. Therefore income is expected to fall by 4% (2×2).

7. b   Economic policy in 2008 was significantly expansionary in an attempt to avert a depression. This fits the functional finance view of using policy to direct the economy.

8. d   Automatic stabilizers are welfare payments, unemployment insurance, and taxes that raise income during recessions and lower income during expansions.

9. c   State balanced budget provisions mean that states cut spending and increase taxes during recessions and raise spending and reduce taxes during expansions. These actions exacerbate the business cycle and are therefore procyclical.

10. b   When the government borrows money, the demand for bonds rises, leading to a rise in the interest rate.

■ ANSWERS ■

POTENTIAL ESSAY QUESTIONS

The following are annotated answers. They indicate the general idea behind the answer.

1.   When the economy is in a recession and total spending is too low, then government spending automatically rises while tax collections automatically fall (the government automatically incurs a deficit). This helps to stimulate total spending and cushion the downturn in the economy. The opposite is true when the economy is expanding. Note that these changes take place when the income level falls and expands. Therefore, there are no time lag problems accompanying the automatic stabilizers.

2.   The crowding-out effect states that deficit spending financed by borrowing will increase interest rates and therefore crowd out private spending. Any "crowding out" associated with deficit spending renders fiscal policy less effective in stimulating total spending and therefore the economy during a recession. Both sides see some crowding out. Total crowding out will render fiscal policy impotent in stimulating total spending. The effect of deficit spending may even be negative on the economy if private spending is more productive than government spending.

3.   I would start by pointing out that by most western economy standards the economy is going quite well, and that perhaps they should be satisfied with what they have. If they insist on policy actions, I would try to find out more information about the economy. For example, I would be worried that with high growth and low unemployment, inflation may soon become a problem. Thus I would be very hesitant to use any demand-based policy. With growth of 6%, I would assume that supply incentives are working, but I would ask them to carefully see if a technology or pro-savings policy may make sense. Opinions may differ among economists.

JOBS AND UNEMPLOYMENT

33

1. Some microeconomic categories of unemployment are: demographics, duration of unemployment, and reason for unemployment.

   Microeconomic policies are needed to address structural unemployment.

2. Okun's rule of thumb: A 1 percentage point change in the unemployment will be associated with a 2 percent deviation in output from its trend in the opposite direction.

   Productivity and the number of people choosing to work fluctuates, which will affect unemployment and potential output independently, making this rule of thumb highly imperfect.

3. Cyclical unemployment is temporary unemployment that rises during recessions and falls with expansions. Structural unemployment does not change with recessions or expansions.

   When an economy is in a structural stagnation, much of unemployment is structural and can be lowered only through structural policies, such as those that lower reservation wages and those that make the tradable sector more competitive.

4. The target rate of unemployment has risen in recent years.

   Three reasons are (1) a younger workforce, (2) changing social and institutional structures, (3) changing government programs, and (4) globalization.

   Be able to explain each!

5. Whether one sees someone as unemployed involves a normative judgment.

   The individual responsibility framework says that jobs are the responsibility of individuals. The social responsibility framework says that government owes individuals a job commensurate with one's education and experience at a respectable wage.

6. A guaranteed jobs program could provide a "job" for everyone who wants one.

   Any realistic jobs program could not provide the type of "job" that most people want.

   The proposal offered in the text is unlikely to be implemented because it benefits only the least well off. Politics usually supports policies that also help the middle class, making the policies much more expensive.

SHORT-ANSWER QUESTIONS

1. What happened to the duration of unemployment during the recent recession?

2. State two categories of unemployment for which microeconomic policies are appropriate. Why are such categories important to follow?

3. How is the target rate of unemployment related to potential output?

4. What is the difference between cyclical and structural unemployment? Which can be lowered with expansionary policies?

5. What are four reasons the target rate of unemployment has risen in recent years?

6. What are the two frameworks for judging unemployment? Which framework is right?

7. Why don't jobs in the author's job proposal provide useful output for the economy?

MATCHING THE TERMS
Match the terms to their definitions

___	1. cyclical unemployment	a.	A 1 percentage point change in the unemployment rate will be associated with a 2 percent deviation in output from its trend in the opposite direction.
___	2. Okun's rule of thumb	b.	Long-term unemployment that occurs because of changes in the structure of the economy.
___	3. reservation wage	c.	Temporary unemployment that can be expected to end as the economy recovers.
___	4. structural unemployment	d.	The wage a person requires before accepting a job.

PROBLEMS AND APPLICATIONS

1. For each of the following changes in the unemployment rate, state what will likely happen to output relative to its trend in the United States:

   a. falls from 10 to 8 percent.

   b. rises from 4 percent to 5 percent.

   c. rises from 5 percent to 9 percent.

2. Calculate the expected change in output given the following:

   a. Total output is $10 trillion, the unemployment rate rises from 5 to 6 percent, and trend growth is 2 percent.

   b. Total output is $10 trillion, the unemployment falls from 8 to 7 percent and trend growth is 3 percent.

3. For each, state whether the unemployment is structural or cyclical.

   a. As the United States becomes a more high-tech producer, labor-intensive factories relocate to low-wage countries. Factory workers lose their jobs and the unemployment rate rises.

   b. As it becomes more acceptable for mothers to work, more women enter the labor market looking for work. The unemployment rate rises.

   c. Foreign economies slow and demand fewer U.S. exports. Unemployment rate rises.

4. State whether the following opinions reflect the individual or social responsibility frameworks:

   a. Anyone can begin a business.

   b. Government should implement a jobs program during recessions.

   c. People expect a higher wage than they can reasonably get.

MULTIPLE CHOICE

Circle the one best answer for each of the following questions:

1. During and after the 2008/09 recession:
   a. the duration of unemployment fell.
   b. the duration of unemployment rose.
   c. the duration of unemployment stayed constant.
   d. the government ceased targeting the unemployment rate.

2. What will likely lower cyclical unemployment?
   a. Workers move to the nontradable sector.
   b. The Fed sells bonds.
   c. The economy expands.
   d. Okun's law changes.

3. What will likely lower structural unemployment?
   a. People lower their reservation wages.
   b. The labor force participation rate rises.
   c. The Fed sells bonds.
   d. The economy expands.

4. If the unemployment rate rises by 0.5 percent by how much is output expected to change relative to potential output?
   a. Fall by 1 percentage point.
   b. Rise by 1 percentage points.
   c. Fall by 2 percentage points.
   d. Rise by 2 percentage points.

5. If output is $15 trillion, the unemployment rate falls by 3 percentage points, and trend growth is 2 percent, what is expected to happen to output?
   a. Rise to $15.6 trillion.
   b. Rise to $16.2 trillion.
   c. Fall to $14.7 trillion.
   d. Fall to $13.8 trillion.

6. Globalization accompanied by large trade deficits most likely raises:
   a. utilized unemployment.
   b. cyclical unemployment.
   c. structural unemployment.
   d. None of the above.

7. A decline in the number of immigrants into the United States would most likely reduce:
   a. reserved unemployment.
   b. utilized unemployment.
   c. cyclical unemployment.
   d. structural unemployment.

8. According to the individual responsibility framework, which of the following would be most likely counted as unemployed?
   a. A person graduates from a job-training program but cannot find a job.
   b. A person has a lower reservation wage than the equilibrium wage, and cannot find a job.
   c. A person has a higher reservation wage than the equilibrium wage and cannot find a job.
   d. A person who has looked for a job for 24 months and can't find one.

9. A jobs program that offers higher wages to those with higher education:
   a. is better than a jobs program that offers equal wages to all.
   b. is worse than a jobs program that offers equal wages to all.
   c. raises the costs of the program.
   d. lowers the cost of the program.

POTENTIAL ESSAY QUESTIONS

You may also see essay questions similar to the "Problems & Applications" exercises.

1. What are the main characteristics of the job program proposed in the chapter? What is the purpose of each of these characteristics?

2. Which framework for looking at unemployment is right—the individual responsibility framework or social responsibility framework?

ANSWERS

SHORT-ANSWER QUESTIONS

1. As can be seen in Figure 33-2 the duration of unemployment rose dramatically in the most recent recession. While in previous recessions about 2 million people were unemployed for more than 27 weeks, during the 2008/09 recession 7 million people were unemployed for more than 27 weeks.

2. Two categories are unemployment by sex and age. Other possible answers are unemployment by race, duration of unemployment and reason for unemployment. They are important to follow because macro policies are designed to address economic problems as a whole while specific micro policies targeted to the needs of specific populations are needed to address various categories of unemployment.

3. The relationship between the target rate of unemployment and potential output is stated by Okun's rule of thumb—a 1 percentage point rise in the unemployment rate is associated with a 2 percent fall in output from its trend (potential) and vice versa.

4. Cyclical unemployment is temporary unemployment that can be expected to end as the economy recovers. Structural unemployment is long-term unemployment that occurs because of changes in the structure of the economy. Cyclical unemployment can be lowered with expansionary policies; structural unemployment must be addressed by structural adjustments in an economy.

5. Four reasons the target rate of unemployment has risen are: a younger workforce, changing social institutions such as women entering the labor force, the establishment of economic safety nets, and globalization.

6. Two frameworks for looking at unemployment are the individual responsibility framework and the social responsibility framework. In the individual responsibility framework, individuals are responsible for finding work. According to this view, a person who isn't working is choosing not to work. There is always a job available. And if there isn't, a person can create his/her own job. In the social responsibility framework, society owes people jobs commensurate with their training and job experience at a respectable wage. Which is right is a matter of debate and depends a person's values.

7. The author's jobs proposal doesn't provide jobs useful to society so that those jobs do not compete with jobs of existing institutions whose role is to provide useful output to society. The goal is not to replace market jobs, simply to supplement them.

ANSWERS

MATCHING

1-c; 2-a; 3-d; 4-b.

ANSWERS

PROBLEMS AND APPLICATIONS

1. a. Output rises by 4 percent relative to its trend.
    b. Output falls by 2 percent relative to its trend.
    c. Output falls by 8 percent relative to its trend.

2. a. Output falls by 2 percent relative to its trend. Output remains unchanged at $10 trillion.
    b. Output rises by 2 percent relative to its trend, or 5 percent to $10.50 trillion.

3. a. Structural unemployment falls. Cyclical unemployment remains unchanged.
    b. To the extent that lowering taxes raise output, cyclical unemployment falls. To

the extent that lower taxes increase potential output, structural unemployment falls.

c. Cyclical unemployment falls if expansionary policy raises output.

4. a. Individual responsibility.
    b. Social responsibility.
    c. It definitely fits the individual responsibility view. It may fit the social responsibility view if the reservation wage is higher than what one believes is a wage society owes the worker.

ANSWERS

MULTIPLE CHOICE

1. b   The duration of unemployment generally rises during a recession, but rose especially high in the 2008/09 recession.

2. c   Cyclical unemployment rises with contractions and falls with expansions. Workers who are unemployed while the move from sector to sector reflects structural unemployment and the Fed selling bonds tends to contract the economy.

3. a   Structural unemployment is caused by structural problems in the economy, including reservation wages that are too high. Higher labor force participation would raise structural unemployment

4. a   Okun's rule of thumb is that a 1 percent rise in the unemployment rate is associated with a 2 percent fall in output relative to potential. Multiply the change in unemployment by 2 to find the answer.

5. b   Again, use Okun's rule of thumb. Output is expected to rise by 6 percent relative to potential. Because trend growth is 2 percent, output is expected to rise by 8 percent to $16.20 trillion (15 x 1.08).

6. c   Globalization with large trade deficits lowers output. Because the cause is not cyclical, but rather related to the competitiveness of the economy, it leads to structural unemployment. The text does not mention utilized unemployment.

7. d   To the extent that immigrants compete for jobs that American-born citizens would take, fewer immigrants would open jobs for Americans and lower structural unemployment. The unemployment is not caused by a change in output and therefore is not cyclical.

8. b   The fact that the person has a lower reservation wage than the equilibrium suggests that the person truly cannot find a job. The person who has a higher reservation than the market could likely find work if he/she settled for a lower wage. A person whose reservation wage is below the going wage might still be above the equilibrium wage. We don't know enough about the retrained worker.

9. c   It will cost more both because it pays more wages and more people will participate. Whether it is better or worse is a matter of opinion.

ANSWERS

POTENTIAL ESSAY QUESTIONS

The following are annotated answers. They indicate the general idea behind the answer.

1. The main characteristics of the job proposal are (1) set maximum wage for all workers, (2) have jobs with no useful output except to the individual, (3) monitor workers and (4) get eligibility requirements (no students). The maximum wage means that people will not be taking the job because it pays well. Only those who really want a job would be willing to work for this pay. The job has no useful output

because the jobs are meant to supplement, not replace, the marketplace. If the output were useful private companies would be hiring the employees to produce those goods. The monitoring component assures that people who apply are eligible, people show up to work do the job they were assigned, and are paid. Monitoring will keep the program costs lower than they would be otherwise. The eligibility requires also keep the costs low—students are excluded because many are not looking for permanent work.

2. Which framework is right is debatable. An argument for the individual responsibility framework is this: People are inherently creative and able to create jobs if they *really* want them, even if it is cleaning the house for your neighbor at a wage of $10 an hour. The people who choose not to create such jobs because they don't utilize their education or pay too little are choosing not to work. Those who argue for this framework point to the difficult and low-paying jobs that Americans are not willing to do. In fact the government has programs to bring in immigrants to do this work. Otherwise it won't get done.

    An argument for the social responsibility framework is that one's job is inherently related to one's identity and value. Taking a job that does not reflect one's skills and education undermines one's identity as a valuable contributor to society. Such jobs represent underutilization of a person's potential. Another reason to support the social responsibility framework is that there are people who are perceived as not being able to contribute to the economy. An example is people who are either physically or intellectually disabled. They deserve to work as well and government has a role in providing them jobs.

INFLATION, DEFLATION, AND MACRO POLICY

CHAPTER AT A GLANCE

1. Asset price inflation is an important measure of inflation.

   Asset price inflation matters because it cannot last. When it turns into asset price deflation, the economy can face significant problems as it did in 2008.

   Economists focus on goods inflation because they haven't developed a good measure for asset price inflation.

2. Inflation has costs and benefits. They may not be the ones you'd expect.

   Inflation does not make society as a whole better off or worse off. It makes those who do not raise their prices worse off and those who raise their prices better off.

   Inflation imposes informational costs, institutional costs, and distributional costs.

   In an asset inflation, cautious borrowers are helped. Less cautious borrowers are hurt.

   Benefits of inflation are that it facilitates relative price changes, allows more expansionary monetary policy, and may encourage investment.

3. Three ways expectations of inflation are formed are:
   1. Rational expectations→ expectations that the economists' model predicts.

   2. Adaptive expectations→ expectations based in some way on the past.

   3. Extrapolative expectations→ expectations that a trend will accelerate.

   Expectations can change the way an economy operates. Expectations play a key role in policy.

   Policy makers use the following equation to determine whether inflation may be coming:

   Inflation = Nominal wage increase − productivity growth.

4. The quantity theory of money basically states that inflation is directly related to the rise in the money supply. It is based upon the equation of exchange: $MV = PQ$.

   Three assumptions made in the quantity theory of money:

   1. *Velocity (V) is constant.*
   2. *Real output (Q) is independent of the money supply (M).*
   3. *Causation goes from money (M) to prices (P). That is, an increase (decrease) in M causes an increase (decrease) in P.*
   Note: The price level rises because the money supply rises.

   Some institutionally focused economists believe the source of inflation is the price-setting process of firms. Inflation causes the money supply to increase.

   Economists now focus less on the quantity theory of money because the connection between the money supply and inflation has broken down and velocity is not constant.

   In the 1990s, the close relationship between money and inflation broke down.

5a. The long-run Phillips curve is vertical as shown in the graph below; it takes into account the feedback of inflation on expectations of inflation.

Along the long-run Phillips curve, expected inflation equals actual inflation.

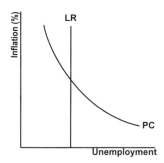

5b. The short-run Phillips curve is downward sloping. Expectations of inflation are constant along a single short-run Phillips curve.

The short-run Phillips curve reflects the empirically observed trade-off between inflation and unemployment. It is shown as PC in the graph above. Expectations of inflation are constant along the short-run (PC) Phillips curve. Increases (decreases) in inflationary expectations shift the short-run Phillips curve to the right (left).

In the Phillips curve model, expansionary policy can lower unemployment in the short run at a cost of higher inflation. Eventually inflation expectations rise and the economy returns to its target rate of unemployment at a higher inflation rate.

6. Because globalization puts a ceiling on the domestic price level, it leads to a flat short-run Phillips curve as shown as PC_2 in the graph below.

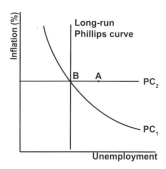

Expansionary policy during a period of globalization will reduce the unemployment rate without leading to inflation. An example is moving from point A to B in the figure above. The inflation expectations do not rise and the short-run Phillips curve does not shift. It's sustainable as long as foreign countries are willing to finance the trade deficit.

SHORT-ANSWER QUESTIONS

1. What is asset price inflation and how is it related to a financial bubble?

2. Why can asset price inflation be detrimental to an economy?

3. Your study partner states that inflation only hurts society. It has no benefits. How do you respond?

4. What are three ways people form expectations of future inflation?

5. Write the equation of exchange. What assumptions make the equation of exchange into the quantity theory of money?

6. Who is more likely to favor a monetary rule: economists who support the quantity theory or institutionally focused economists? Why?

7. Which of the two curves in the graph below is a short-run Phillips curve, and why?

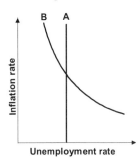

8. How does globalization change the Phillips curve trade-off?

9. Why does government generally fight deflation?

MATCHING THE TERMS
Match the terms to their definitions

___ **1.** adaptive expectations	**a.** Expectations based in some way on the past.
___ **2.** asset price inflation	**b.** MV=PQ.
___ **3.** equation of exchange	**c.** A curve showing the trade-off between inflation and unemployment when expectations of inflation are constant.
___ **4.** extrapolative expectations	
___ **5.** hyperinflation	**d.** A curve showing the trade-off (or complete lack thereof) between inflation and unemployment when expectations of inflation equal actual inflation.
___ **6.** long-run Phillips curve	
___ **7.** quantity theory of money	**e.** The price level varies in response to changes in the quantity of money.
___ **8.** rational expectations	**f.** Combination of high and accelerating inflation and high unemployment.
___ **9.** short-run Phillips curve	**g.** Expectations that a trend will accelerate.
___ **10.** stagflation	**h.** The number of times per year, on average, a dollar goes around to generate a dollar's worth of income.
___ **11.** velocity of money	**i.** Expectations that the economists' model predicts.
___ **12.** zero interest rate lower bound	**j.** The prices of assets rise more than their "real" value.
	k. When inflation hits triple digits — 100 percent or more per year.
	l. A limit on how much interest rates can fall.

PROBLEMS AND APPLICATIONS

1. Inflation has both costs and benefits.
  a. What are three benefits?

  b. What are three costs?

2. Fill in the blanks below:

Inflation	Nominal wage increase	Productivity growth
6%	3%	____
____	2%	2%
2%	3%	____

3. a. What are the three assumptions that translate the equation of exchange into the quantity theory of money?

  b. State the equation of exchange and show how the three assumptions lead to the conclusion that inflation is always and everywhere a monetary phenomenon.

4. With the equation of exchange, answer the following questions:

  a. Nominal GDP is $2,000 and the money supply is 200. What is the velocity of money?

b. The velocity of money is 5.60 and the money supply is $1,100 billion. What is nominal output?

c. Assuming velocity is constant and the money supply increases by 6%, by how much does nominal output rise?

5. Suppose the economy is operating at potential output. Inflation is 3% and expected inflation is 3%. Unemployment is 5.5%.

   a. Draw a long-run Phillips curve and a short-run Phillips curve consistent with these conditions.

   b. The government implements an expansionary monetary policy. As a result, unemployment falls to 4.5% and inflation rises to 6%. Expectations do not adjust. Show where the economy is on the graph you drew for 5(a). What happens to the short-run Phillips curve? Inflation? Unemployment?

   c. The economy returns to its potential, and expectations equal the inflation rate at potential. What happens to the short-run Phillips curve?

6. Suppose the economy is operating at potential output. Inflation is 6%, which equals inflation expectations. Unemployment is 5%. Explain the effect of the following on inflation and unemployment using the curves you have drawn.

   a. The government implements a contractionary monetary policy. As a result, unemployment rises to 6.5% and inflation falls to 5%. Expectations do not adjust.

   b. Expectations now fully adjust.

7. For each of the following points that represents the economy on the Phillips curve, make a prediction for unemployment and inflation.

   a.

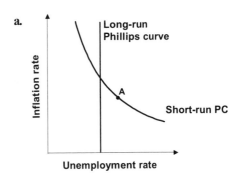

   b.

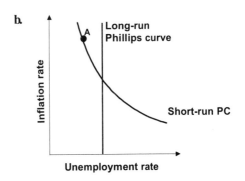

c.

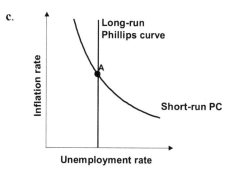

d.

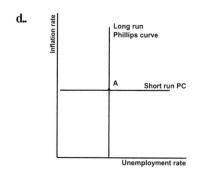

● MULTIPLE CHOICE

Circle the one best answer for each of the following questions:

1. Asset inflation is when:
    a. asset prices rise regardless of their real value.
    b. the money supply rises and leads to inflation.
    c. asset prices rise more than their real value.
    d. expansionary fiscal policy leads to inflation.

2. Asset deflation generally:
    a. is more harmful than the preceding inflation was helpful.
    b. is less harmful than the preceding inflation was helpful.
    c. is neither good nor bad, it merely redistributes income.
    d. cannot occur because people will know that it will follow asset inflation.

3. A cost of inflation is that it:
    a. makes everyone poorer.
    b. makes the poor poorer and the rich richer.
    c. reduces the informational content of prices.
    d. it raises real interest rates.

4. A benefit of inflation is that it:
    a. gets around the zero interest rate lower bound.
    b. can raise nominal interest rates while keeping real interest rates constant.
    c. benefits lenders in fixed contracts.
    d. more accurately reveals relative price changes.

5. If there is asset inflation and no goods inflation:
    a. wealth will not be redistributed because there is no goods inflation.
    b. wealth will not be redistributed because there is asset inflation for everyone.
    c. wealth will be redistributed even though there is no goods inflation.
    d. There is no relationship between inflation and wealth distribution.

6. In an unexpected inflation, lenders will generally:
    a. gain relative to borrowers.
    b. lose relative to borrowers.
    c. neither gain nor lose relative to borrowers.
    d. The effect will be totally random.

7. According to the text if individuals base their expectations on the past we say that their expectations are:
    a. rational.
    b. historical.
    c. adaptive.
    d. extrapolative.

8. If productivity growth is 2 percent and inflation is 5 percent, on average nominal wage increases will be:
    a. 2 percent.
    b. 3 percent.
    c. 5 percent.
    d. 7 percent.

9. One assumption that changes the equation of exchange into the quantity theory of money is:
    a. Velocity remains constant.
    b. Real output varies with the money supply.
    c. Expectations change with inflation.
    d. Price times quantity equals nominal output.

10. According to the quantity theory:
    a. unemployment is everywhere and always a monetary phenomenon.
    b. inflation is everywhere and always a monetary phenomenon.
    c. the equation of exchange does not hold true.
    d. real output is everywhere and always a monetary phenomenon.

11. A reason why the quantity theory of money is problematic is that:
    a. money supply increases generally affect only goods prices.
    b. the Fed generally runs expansionary monetary policy.
    c. the velocity of money has fluctuated over time.
    d. real output rises during expansions and falls during contractions.

12. Institutionally focused economists argue:
    a. the equation of exchange is incorrect.
    b. the equation of exchange should be read from right to left.
    c. the equation of exchange should be read from left to right.
    d. both the quantity theory and the equation of exchange are incorrect.

13. The Phillips curve represents a relationship between:
    a. inflation and unemployment.
    b. inflation and real income.
    c. money supply and interest rates.
    d. money supply and unemployment.

14. The short-run Phillips curve shifts around because of changes in:
    a. the money supply.
    b. expectations of employment.
    c. expectations of inflation.
    d. expectations of real income.

15. The slope of the long-run Phillips curve is thought by many economists to be:
    a. horizontal.
    b. vertical.
    c. downward sloping.
    d. backward bending.

16. If the economy is at point A in the Phillips curve graph following, what prediction would you make for unemployment in the long run?

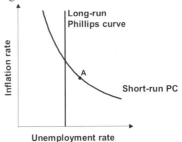

    a. It will increase.
    b. It will decrease.
    c. It will remain constant.
    d. It will explode.

17. If the economy is at point A in the Phillips curve graph below and the government runs expansionary monetary policy, what prediction would you make for inflation?

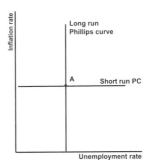

    a. It will increase.
    b. It will decrease.
    c. It will remain constant.
    d. It will explode.

18. Globalization will tend to:
    a. flatten the short-run Phillips curve.
    b. flatten the long-run Phillips curve.
    c. shift the short-run Phillips curve.
    d. shift the long-run Phillips curve.

19. If the economy is at Point A in the Phillips curve graph below, what prediction would you make for unemployment in the long run?

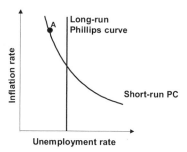

a. It will increase.
b. It will decrease.
c. It will remain constant.
d. It will immediately fall to zero.

20. Stagflation is:
a. a combination of low and decelerating inflation and low unemployment.
b. a combination of low and decelerating inflation and high unemployment.
c. a combination of high and accelerating inflation and low unemployment.
d. a combination of high and accelerating inflation and high unemployment.

POTENTIAL ESSAY QUESTIONS

You may also see essay questions similar to the "Problems & Applications" exercises.

1. What problems can be created for an economy by expansionary monetary policy that leads to asset price inflation?

2. How does globalization affect the Phillips curve analysis? What is the implication for expansionary monetary and fiscal policies?

ANSWERS

SHORT-ANSWER QUESTIONS

1. Asset price inflation is when the prices of assets rise more than the "real" value. If expansionary monetary policy does not lead to goods price inflation, it may raise asset prices. If these prices are unsustainable, it will lead to a bubble.

2. Asset price inflation that is unsustainable will eventually lead to asset deflation. Asset deflation means that people's perceived wealth has declined. To the extent that they borrowed against that wealth to increase consumption, once asset prices fall, they may be unable to repay those loans. Likewise, firms that are doing well during an asset price inflation may have purchased things such as office buildings. Once asset deflation sets in, they might owe more on the building than it is worth. If asset deflation reduces its sales (consumers cut back demand), the firm may even go out of business.

3. While inflation has costs (informational, institutional and distributional), it can also benefit society. The benefits are: facilitating relative price changes, allowing more expansionary monetary policy, and distributional consequences among borrowers and lenders that encourages investment and spurs growth.

4. People formulate expectations in a variety of ways. Three types of expectations are adaptive expectations (expectations based in some way on the past), rational expectations (the expectations that the economists' model predicts), and extrapolative expectations (expectations that a trend will accelerate).

5. The equation of exchange is $MV = PQ$. Three assumptions turn this equation into the quantity theory of money: (1) real output is determined independently, (2) velocity is constant, and (3) the direction of causation goes from left to right.

6. Economists who support the quantity theory of money are more likely to favor a monetary rule, because they see the economy gravitating toward a natural (or target) rate of unemployment regardless of monetary policy. Thus expansionary monetary policy can lead only to inflation. A monetary rule will limit the government's attempt to expand the economy with monetary policy and hence will achieve the target rate of unemployment and low inflation. Institutional economists are less likely to see the economy gravitating toward the target rate of unemployment, so they would favor some discretionary policy to improve the operation of the macroeconomy.

7. Curve B is the short-run Phillips curve. The short-run Phillips curve represents a trade-off between inflation and unemployment. It is an empirically determined phenomenon, and based on that empirical evidence, economists generally believe that whenever unemployment decreases, inflation increases, and vice versa. They explain that this empirical occurrence is due to slowly adjusting expectations and institutions. In the long run, expectations and institutions can change and hence the reason for the trade-off is eliminated, making the vertical line represent the long-run Phillips curve—it represents the lack of a trade-off between inflation and unemployment in the long run.

8. Globalization holds down domestic prices at the world price level, making the short-run Phillips curve horizontal. If the government runs expansionary monetary policies, unemployment will fall while inflation does not change.

9. Governments try to prevent deflation because deflation in goods and services is generally associated with asset price deflation. Asset price deflation creates the illusion of the loss of wealth, which will likely cause a decline in aggregate demand and a recession.

ANSWERS

MATCHING

1-a; 2-j; 3-b; 4-g; 5-k; 6-d; 7-e; 8-i; 9-c; 10-f; 11-h; 12-l.

ANSWERS

PROBLEMS AND APPLICATIONS

1. **a.** Three benefits of inflation are (1) facilitating relative price changes; (2) allowing more expansionary monetary policy; and (3) giving the illusion of increased wages.

    b. Three costs of inflation are it (1) makes it difficult to tell what is a relative price change; (2) may cause people to lose faith in government and hurt growth; and (3) harms thoses who cannot raise their prices.

2. | Inflation | Nominal wage increase | Productivity growth |
    | --- | --- | --- |
    | 6% | 3% | -3% |
    | 0% | 2% | 2% |
    | 2% | 3% | 1% |

3. **a.** 1. Velocity is constant, 2. Real output is independent of the money supply, 3. Causation goes from money supply to prices.

    b. $MV = PQ$ is the equation of exchange. Since V is constant and Q exogenous, the only remaining variables that change within the system are M and P. Since the causation runs from M to P, to keep the equation balanced, a rise in M must lead to a rise in P (and only P since Q is exogenous).

4. **a.** $V = 10$: $MV = PQ$; $200V = \$2,000$; $V = 10$.
    b. $\$6,160$ billion: $MV = PQ$; $(5.6)(1,100) = \$6,160$ billion.
    c. By 6%.

5. **a.** The long-run Phillips curve is vertical at the rate of unemployment consistent with potential output, here at 5.5%. The short-run Phillips curve is the downward-sloping curve shown in the graph below as PC_0. In this case, we drew a short-run Phillips curve where expected inflation equals the 3% actual inflation. It intersects the long-run Phillips curve at 5.5% unemployment and 3% inflation. The economy is at point A.

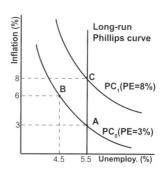

b. The economy moves along the short-run Phillips curve up and to the left to point B. The short-run Phillips curve does not shift since inflation expectations have not changed. At point B, inflation is 6% and the unemployment rate is 4.5%.

c. As expectations of inflation increase the short-run Phillips curve begins to shift up. As long as the economy is below the target rate of unemployment, inflation continues to rise. When inflation pressures subside, including those caused by adjustment of inflation expectations, the PC curve intersects the LR curve at the target rate of unemployment, in this case 8%. How much inflation is unknown, except it must be equal to or above the rate it was as a result of the initial increase in aggregate spending.

6. **a.** The economy moves along the short-run Phillips curve down and to the right to point B in the graph on the next page. The short-run Phillips curve does not shift since inflation expectations have not changed. At point B, inflation is 5% and the unemployment rate is 6.5%.

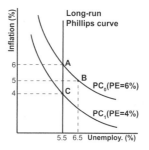

b. The decrease in spending lowers the unemployment rate and inflation falls.

Price level expectations reduce the price level further, shifting the PC curve to the left. Once price pressures stop, unemployment returns to 5.5% at a lower rate of inflation, in this case 4%. The specific decline in inflation is unknown, but must be less than or equal to the rate of inflation caused by the initial drop in aggregate spending.

7. **a.** Inflation is below expected inflation and unemployment is higher than the natural rate of unemployment. As expectations adjust, the short-run Phillips curve shifts to the left and unemployment falls.

b. Inflation is above expected inflation and unemployment is lower than the natural rate of unemployment. As expectations adjust, the short-run Phillips curve shifts to the right and unemployment rises.

c. Inflation equals expected inflation and unemployment equals the target rate of unemployment. Inflation and unemployment will not change.

d. Because globalization is keeping the price level down, there is no reason for inflation expectations to shift, so the short-run Phillips curve remains where it is as does unemployment and inflation.

ANSWERS

MULTIPLE CHOICE

1. c　See the definition of asset price inflation in text.

2. a　Asset deflation is more harmful than an asset inflation because people cannot reverse purchases.

3. c　Inflation makes those who can't raise their prices poorer and helps those who can. Therefore it doesn't make everyone poorer. While it may raise nominal interest rates, it does not raise real interest rates.

4. a　An inflation can lead to lower real interest rates and, if inflation exceeeds nominal

interest rates, zero real interest rates. This allows for more expansionary monetary policy.

5. c　Both goods and asset inflation redistribute wealth. Asset price inflation increases wealth for those who make risky investments (thoses whose value rise quickly) while not benefiting the cautious investor who misses out on the rise asset prices on risky investments.

6. b　With an unexpected inflation borrowers gain and lenders lose because the money borrowers are paying back will buy less because of the inflation.

7. c　Rational expectations are based on models; extrapolative expectations are based on expectations that a trend will continue. Historical expectations are not mentioned in the text.

8. d　Inflation is the difference between nominal wage increases and productivity growth.

9. a　There are three reasons that change the equation of exchange into the quantity theory. They are: (1) velocity is constant, (2) real output is determined independently and (3) causation goes from left to right. The only option listed in the question is (1).

10. b　The quantity theory directly relates money and inflation.

11. c　One assumption of the quantity theory is that velocity is constant. If it is not, which it has not been, the theory breaks down. What happens to real output does not change the quantity theory of money.

12. b　The equation of exchange is a tautology; it cannot be incorrect. Institutionally focused economists see price changes causing money and velocity changes so MV=PQ should be read from right to left.

13. a　The Phillips curve is drawn with inflation on the vertical axis and unemployment on the horizontal axis.

14. c   The short-run Phillips curve holds expectations of inflation constant. Therefore, it shifts because changes in expectations of inflation cause everybody to build those expectations into their nominal price requests.

15. b   As discussed in the text, the long-run Phillips curve is vertical. Actually, there is some debate about whether it is downward sloping, but the text focuses on the vertical nature of the curve, so b is the answer that should be given. Remember, you are choosing the best answer relative to what is presented in the text.

16. b   Since point A is to the right of the long-run Phillips curve, actual unemployment exceeds the natural rate of unemployment. Therefore we would expect unemployment to decrease. See pages 785-786.

17. c   Because globalization is keeping the price level down, the policy will have no effect on goods inflation.

18. a   Since globalization keeps the price level constant, there is no trade-off between unemployment and inflation. Inflation remains constant. Therefore the short-run Phillips curve is flat. In the long run unemployment is still fixed.

19. a   Since point A is to the left of the long-run Phillips curve, actual unemployment is below the natural rate of unemployment. Therefore, we would expect unemployment to increase.

20. d   Stagflation is defined as a combination of high and accelerating inflation and high unemployment.

━━━━━━   ANSWERS   ━━━━━━

POTENTIAL ESSAY QUESTIONS

The following are annotated answers. They indicate the general idea behind the answer.

1.   Expansionary monetary policy that leads to asset price inflation can allocate resources into unsustainable risky investments and speculation. Over the long run, asset prices can rise only as much as the real economy grows. If they grow faster, eventually some adjustment will have to occur, and when that does there will be an asset deflation.

When an asset inflation turns into a deflation, the adjustment can be difficult. Consumers who leveraged their spending may not be able to pay back what they borrowed. Firms that over-expanded find they do not have sufficient sales and may not be able to sell the assets they purchased during the asset price inflation. Both can lead to a severe economic contraction.

2.   Because globalization sets a ceiling on domestic price inflation of tradable goods, it will lead to a flat Phillips curve where the government can expand the economy—lower unemployment—without causing goods inflation. As long as other countries are willing to finance the resulting trade deficit, this allows the economy to expand consumption beyond potential. If government tries to hold domestic potential output up, the result will be either an unsustainable asset inflation or increased unemployment in the nontradable sector, creating an imbalance between the tradable and nontradable sectors. Those with jobs in the nontradable sector do reasonably well, and those without jobs in the nontradable sector do poorly. The implication for expansionary policy is that in a globalized economy where trade deficits can be large, policy makers should be on the lookout for negative side effects of expansionary policy, and not use the lack of goods inflation as the only indicator that the economy has not exceeded its sustainable potential output.

Pretest
Chapters 28-34

Take this test in test conditions, giving yourself a limited amount of time to complete the questions. Ideally, check with your professor to see how much time he or she allows for an average multiple choice question and multiply this by 34. This is the time limit you should set for yourself for this pretest. If you do not know how much time your teacher would allow, we suggest 1 minute per question, or about 34 minutes.

1. Which of the following is not included in the M_1 definition of money?
    a. Checking accounts balances.
    b. Retail money funds.
    c. Time deposits.
    d. Savings and money market accounts.

2. Which of the following components is not included in the M_2 definition of money?
    a. M_1.
    b. Savings and money market accounts.
    c. Small-denomination time deposits.
    d. Bonds.

3. If the reserve requirement is 20 percent, and banks keep no excess reserves, an increase in an initial inflow of $100 into the banking system will cause an increase in the money supply of:
    a. $20.
    b. $50.
    c. $100.
    d. $500.

4. If banks hold excess reserves whereas before they did not, the money multiplier:
    a. will become larger.
    b. will become smaller.
    c. will be unaffected.
    d. might increase or might decrease.

5. What is the function of risk premium?
    a. To make sure that the value of the bond rises with inflation.
    b. To compensate bondholders for the chance the borrower will not repay the loan.
    c. To distinguish short- from long-term bonds.
    d. To raise the return to holding government bonds.

6. Which of the following is the path through which contractionary monetary policy works?
    a. Money down implies interest rate up implies investment down implies income down.
    b. Money down implies interest rate down implies investment down implies income down.
    c. Money down implies interest rate up implies investment up implies income down.
    d. Money down implies interest rate down implies investment up implies income down.

7. Monetary policy is:
    a. a variation of fiscal policy.
    b. undertaken by the Treasury.
    c. undertaken by the Fed.
    d. the regulation of monetary institutions.

8. When the Fed sells bonds, the money supply:
    a. expands.
    b. contracts.
    c. sometimes rises and sometimes falls.
    d. Selling bonds does not have any effect on the money supply.

9. Many economists argue that the Fed contributed to the housing bubble by:
    a. passing laws that allowed financial institutions to create credit default swaps.
    b. paying interest on bank reserves.
    c. keeping the Fed funds rate lower than what the Taylor rule predicts.
    d. buying mortgage-backed securities for foreclosed homes.

10. If short-term and long-term interest rates are currently equal and the Fed contracts the money supply, the yield curve will most likely:

a. become downward sloping.
b. become upward sloping.
c. become vertical.
d. be unaffected.

11. What role do almost all economists agree the central bank has in a financial crisis?
    a. Contractionary fiscal policy to reduce leverage.
    b. Lender of last resort.
    c. Expansionary fiscal policy to reduce herding.
    d. No role.

12. A person purchases a stock worth $200, borrowing $190 and putting down $10 of her own money. The bank charges 2% a year and the stock rises by 5% in the first year. If she sells the stock, the return on her investment will be:
    a. 2%
    b. 5%
    c. 50%
    d. 62%

13. Moral hazard is a problem that arises when:
    a. people are required to bear the negative consequences of their actions.
    b. people don't have to bear the negative consequences of their actions.
    c. people benefit from the negative actions of others.
    d. government discourages companies from taking risks.

14. All of the following are examples of the law of diminishing control that followed banking regulations put in place after the Great Depression *except*:
    a. Banks created new instruments to circumvent the law.
    b. Financial business migrated to unregulated institutions.
    c. Depositors demanded financial institutions be responsible for their financial decisions.
    d. Politicians were pressured to dismantle the regulations.

15. The difference between quantitative easing and credit easing is:
    a. credit easing is designed to change the mix of securities held by the Fed while quantitative easing is designed to increase the amount of money in the economy.
    b. quantitative easing is designed to change the mix of securities held by the Fed while credit easing is designed to increase the amount of credit in the economy.
    c. credit easing is designed to shift the yield curve up while quantitative easing is designed to twist the yield curve.
    d. quantitative easing is designed to raise long-term and lower short-term interest rates while credit easing is designed to lower long-term and raise short-term interest rates.

16. Negative real interest rates:
    a. are impossible.
    b. can be desirable.
    c. reflect asset deflation.
    d. are a form of hyperinflation.

17. A deficit is:
    a. the total amount of money that a country owes.
    b. the shortfall of payments under revenues in a particular time period.
    c. the shortfall of revenues under payments in a particular time period.
    d. accumulated debt.

18. The nominal deficit is $100 billion; inflation is 4 percent; total debt is $2 trillion. The real deficit is:
    a. zero.
    b. $20 billion.
    c. $80 billion.
    d. $100 billion.

19. The real deficit is $100 billion; inflation is 4 percent; total debt is $2 trillion. The nominal deficit is:
    a. zero.
    b. $120 billion.
    c. $180 billion.
    d. $200 billion.

20. The portion of the budget deficit or surplus that would exist even if the economy were at its potential level of income is called the:
    a. structural deficit or surplus.
    b. cyclical deficit or surplus.
    c. primary deficit or surplus.
    d. secondary deficit or surplus.

21. Sound finance holds that:
    a. government spending is directed toward sound investments.
    b. the government budget should always be balanced except in wartime.
    c. the government budget should be judged by its effect on the economy.
    d. government should always borrow money in a sound fashion when it runs a deficit.

22. The Ricardian equivalence theorem holds that:
    a. government spending is equivalent to private spending.
    b. financing a deficit by bonds will have the same effect as financing it through taxes.
    c. imposing taxes is equivalent to confiscation of property by government.
    d. all spending in the economy is equivalent.

23. Crowding out is caused by:
    a. government running a deficit and selling bonds to finance that deficit.
    b. government printing money.
    c. government running a surplus and selling bonds and the people who buy those bonds selling their older bonds to the government.
    d. the tendency for new workers to replace more expensive older workers.

24. Using the relationship between a change in the target rate of unemployment and potential income, if the target rate of unemployment rises by 2 percent, potential income is expected to:
    a. fall 2%.
    b. rise 2%.
    c. fall 4%.
    d. rise 4%.

25. Automatic stabilizers:
    a. are government programs to employ workers during recessions.
    b. create government budget surpluses during economic recessions.
    c. are designed to reduce the price level directly.
    d. counteract both recessions and expansions through changes in spending without government action.

26. What will likely lower structural unemployment?
    a. People lower their reservation wages.
    b. The labor force participation rate rises.
    c. The Fed sells bonds.
    d. The economy expands.

27. If output is $15 trillion, the unemployment rate falls by 3 percentage points, and trend growth is 2 percent, what is expected to happen to output?
    a. Rise to $15.6 trillion.
    b. Rise to $16.2 trillion.
    c. Fall to $14.7 trillion.
    d. Fall to $13.8 trillion.

28. Globalization accompanied by large trade deficits most likely raises:
    a. utilized unemployment.
    b. cyclical unemployment.
    c. structural unemployment.
    d. None of the above.

29. A jobs program that offers higher wages to those with higher education:
    a. is better than a jobs program that offers equal wages to all.
    b. is worse than a jobs program that offers equal wages to all.
    c. raises the costs of the program.
    d. lowers the cost of the program.

30. Asset inflation is when:
    a. asset prices rise regardless of their real value.
    b. the money supply rises and leads to inflation.
    c. asset prices rise more than their real value.
    d. expansionary fiscal policy leads to inflation.

31. If there is asset inflation and no goods inflation:
    a. wealth will not be redistributed because there is no goods inflation.
    b. wealth will not be redistributed because there is asset inflation for everyone.
    c. wealth will be redistributed even though there is no goods inflation.
    d. There is no relationship between inflation and wealth distribution.

32. The short-run Phillips curve shifts around
because of changes in:
a. the money supply.
b. expectations of employment.
c. expectations of inflation.
d. expectations of real income.

33. Globalization will tend to:
a. flatten the short-run Phillips curve.
b. flatten the long-run Phillips curve.
c. shift the short-run Phillips curve.
d. shift the long-run Phillips curve.

34. If the economy is at Point A in the Phillips
curve graph below, what prediction would
you make for unemployment in the long run?

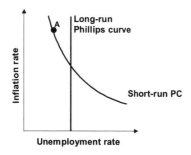

a. It will increase.
b. It will decrease.
c. It will remain constant.
d. It will immediately fall to zero.

ANSWERS

1.	a	(28:2)		**18.**	b	(31:4)
2.	d	(28:3)		**19.**	c	(31:6)
3.	d	(28:8)		**20.**	a	(31:10)
4.	b	(28:10)		**21.**	b	(32:1)
5.	b	(28:13)		**22.**	b	(32:2)
6.	a	(29:3)		**23.**	a	(32:5)
7.	c	(29:5)		**24.**	c	(32:6)
8.	b	(29:13)		**25.**	d	(32:8)
9.	c	(29:19)		**26.**	a	(33:3)
10.	a	(29:21)		**27.**	b	(33:5)
11.	b	(30:3)		**28.**	c	(33:6)
12.	d	(30:6)		**29.**	c	(33:9)
13.	b	(30:9)		**30.**	c	(34:1)
14.	c	(30:12)		**31.**	c	(34:5)
15.	a	(30:14)		**32.**	c	(34:14)
16.	b	(30:16)		**33.**	a	(34:18)
17.	c	(31:2)		**34.**	a	(34:19)

*Key: The figures in parentheses refer to multiple
choice question and chapter numbers. For example
(1:2) is multiple choice question 2 from chapter 1.*

COMPARATIVE ADVANTAGE, EXCHANGE RATES, AND GLOBALIZATION

9

CHAPTER AT A GLANCE

1. The principle of comparative advantage states that as long as the relative opportunity costs of producing goods differ among countries, there are potential gains from trade.

   When countries specialize in the production of those goods for which each has a <u>comparative advantage</u> and then trade, all economies involved benefit.

   A country has a comparative advantage in producing good "x" if its opportunity cost of producing good "x" is lower.

2. Three determinants of the gains of trade are:

   - The more competition, the less the trader gets.
   - Smaller countries get a larger proportion of the gain than larger countries.
   - Countries producing goods with economies of scale get a larger gain from trade.

   Also: countries which specialize and trade along the lines of comparative advantage are able to consume more than if they did not undertake trade (they are able to escape the confines of their own production possibility curves).

3. Four reasons for differences between economists' and laypeople's views of trade are: (1) gains from trade are often stealth gains, (2) opportunity cost is relative, (3) nations trade more than just manufactured goods, and (4) trade affects distribution of income.

   The gains from trade in the form of low consumer prices tend to be widespread and not easily recognizable, while the costs in jobs lost tend to be concentrated and readily identifiable. This affects the distribution of income. But, the gains outweigh the costs over

   time. Convincing the public of this remains a challenge, especially for policymakers.

4. Transferable comparative advantages will tend to erode over time; inherent comparative advantages will not.

   The law of one price and the convergence hypothesis will work to erode any transferable comparative advantages over time. The degree to which, and how quickly, the United States loses some of its comparative advantages depends on how transferable they are.

   Rising wages in China relative to the United States and a decline in the exchange rate value of the dollar are two ways the United States will gain comparative advantages.

5. The foreign exchange (forex) market is the market for foreign currencies. It can be analyzed using the supply and demand model to determine the price of one country's currency in terms of another country's currency; the rate at which one country's currency can be traded for that of another is the exchange rate. The graph below shows the market for euros. The equilibrium price is $1.30 per euro and 100 euros.

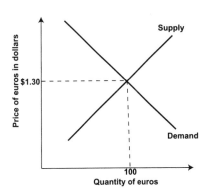

A *currency depreciation* is *a change in the exchange rate so that one currency buys fewer units of a foreign currency*. A *currency appreciation* is *a change in the exchange rate so that one currency buys more units of a foreign currency*.

When comparing two currencies with the supply and demand model, the supply of one currency equals the demand for the other currency. To demand one currency, you must supply another. For example, if a European citizen wants to purchase a US product, she must supply euros in order to demand dollars to buy the product.

6. The exchange rate plays a major role in the demand for a country's domestic goods. If a country's currency depreciates, its goods become more competitive in the global market; on the other hand, if a country's currency appreciates, its goods become less competitive in the global market.

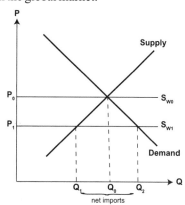

In the graph above, the nation's trade is balanced when the world supply is S_{w0} and the domestic price is P_0. If the country's currency appreciates, the world price level shifts down, in this case to S_{w1}. The nation will develop a trade deficit shown by Q_2-Q_1.

With free trade, if producers want to sell their goods, they must match the world price, and if consumers have the ability to buy all the goods they want at the world price, they will not pay more than that price.

7. The resource curse occurs when a country discovers a large amount of natural resources, which raises foreign demand for the resource and thus causes the country's currency to appreciate.

While there is increased foreign demand for the discovered resources, the appreciation of the country's currency causes other goods lose their comparative advantage.

○ SHORT-ANSWER QUESTIONS

1. What is the principle of comparative advantage?

2. What are three determinants of the gains of trade?

3. What are four reasons laypeople's and economists' views of trade differ?

4. How does trade today affect the distribution of income within the United States?

5. What are four sources of comparative advantages for the United States?

6. How do transferable comparative advantages differ from inherent advantages?

7. Why is the United States losing some of its comparative advantages?

8. What does it mean for the dollar to appreciate relative to the yuan?

9. How will an appreciation of the dollar affect the U.S. trade deficit? Explain your answer.

10. What is the resource curse? What impact does it have on exchange rates and the trade deficit?

MATCHING THE TERMS
Match the terms to their definitions

___ 1.	Balance of trade	a.	The difference between the value of exports and imports
___ 2.	Comparative advantage	b.	When a nation's exports exceed its imports
___ 3.	Currency appreciation	c.	As long as the relative opportunity costs of producing goods differ among countries, there are potential gains from trade, even if one country has an absolute advantage in everything
___ 4.	Currency depreciation		
___ 5.	Exchange rate		
___ 6.	Inherent comparative advantage	d.	A change in the exchange rate so that one currency buys fewer units of a foreign currency
___ 7.	Resource curse	e.	When a nation's imports exceed its exports
___ 8.	Trade deficit	f.	The rate at which one country's currency can be traded for another country's currency
___ 9.	Trade surplus		
___ 10.	Transferable comparative advantage	g.	Comparative advantage based on factors that are relatively unchangeable
		h.	Comparative advantage based on factors that can be changed relatively easily
		i.	The paradox that countries with an abundance of resources tend to have lower economic growth and more unemployment than countries with fewer resources
		j.	A change in the exchange rate so that one currency buys greater units of a foreign currency

PROBLEMS AND APPLICATIONS

1. **a.** State whether there is a basis for trade in the following:

   Case 1: In Country A the opportunity cost of producing one widget is two wadgets. In Country B the opportunity cost of producing two widgets is four wadgets.

   Case 2: In Country C the opportunity cost of producing one widget is two wadgets. In Country D the opportunity cost of producing two widgets is one wadget.

   Case 3: In Country E the opportunity cost of producing one widget is two wadgets. In Country F the opportunity cost of producing one widget is four wadgets.

   b. On what general principle did you base your reasoning?

   c. Assume that in Case 3 there are constant economies of scale. Country E is currently producing 10 widgets and 4 wadgets. Country F is currently producing 20 widgets and 20 wadgets. Can you make an offer involving trade that will make both countries better off?

d. How would your answer differ if each country experiences economies of scale?

2. Suppose Country A and Country B are potential trading partners. Each country produces two goods: fish and wine. If Country A devotes all of its resources to producing fish, it can produce 1,000 fish, and if it devotes all of its resources to producing wine, it can produce 2,000 bottles of wine. If Country B devotes all of its resources to producing fish, it can produce 3,000 fish, and if it devotes all of its resources to producing wine it can produce 3,000 bottles of wine. For simplicity, assume the production possibility curves of these countries are straight lines.

a. Draw the production possibility curve for Country A on the axes below. In Country A, what is the opportunity cost of one bottle of wine in terms of fish?

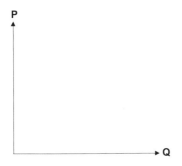

b. Draw the production possibility curve for Country B on the axes for part *a*. In Country B, what is the opportunity cost of one bottle of wine in terms of fish?

c. Does Country A have a comparative advantage in producing either wine or fish? Does Country B have a comparative advantage in producing either wine or fish?

d. Suppose Country A specialized in that good for which it has a comparative advantage and Country B specialized in that good for which it has a comparative advantage. Each country would then trade the good it produced for the good the other country produced. What would be a fair exchange of goods?

3. Suppose two countries A and B have the following production possibility tables:

% Resources devoted to Machines	Country A Production Machines	Food	Country B Production Machines	Food
A	100	200	0	40	0
B	80	160	8	32	40
C	60	120	16	28	80
D	40	80	24	24	120
E	20	40	32	16	160
F	0	0	40	0	200

a. Draw the production possibility curves for Country A and Country B on the axes below.

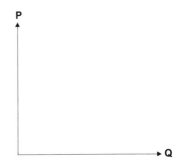

b. Which country has the comparative advantage in the production of food?

c. Suppose each country specializes in the production of one good. Explain how Country A can end up with 50 food units and 150 machines and Country B can end up with 150 food units and 50 machines. Both points are outside the production possibility curve for each country without trade.

4. Using a supply and demand curve for domestic goods with a world price level show a country with a trade balance:

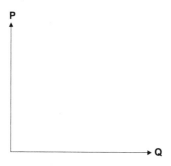

a. Show the effect of a currency appreciation on the trade balance.

b. Show the effect of a currency depreciation on the trade balance.

MULTIPLE CHOICE

Circle the one best answer for each of the following questions:

1. Refer to the graph below. Given these production possibility curves, you would suggest that:

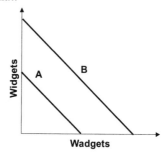

a. Country A should specialize in widgets and Country B in wadgets.
b. no trade should take place.
c. Country A should specialize in wadgets and Country B in widgets.
d. Both countries should produce an equal amount of each.

2. Refer to the graph below. The graph demonstrates Saudi Arabia's and the United States' production possibility curves for widgets and wadgets. Given these production possibility curves, you would suggest that:

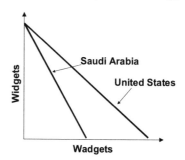

a. Saudi Arabia specialize in widgets and the United States in wadgets.
b. no trade should take place.
c. Saudi Arabia specialize in wadgets and the United States in widgets.
d. both countries should produce an equal amount of each.

3. If a nation has a comparative advantage in the production of good X then:
a. it can produce good X at the lowest opportunity cost.
b. it will import good X.

c. it can produce more of good X than any other nation.

d. the opportunity cost of producing an additional unit of good X is greater than for any other nation.

4. A widget has an opportunity cost of 4 wadgets in Saudi Arabia and 2 wadgets in the United States. Given these opportunity costs, you would suggest that:
a. Saudi Arabia specialize in widgets and the United States in wadgets.
b. no trade should take place.
c. Saudi Arabia specialize in wadgets and the United States in widgets.
d. both countries should produce an equal amount of each.

5. Country A's cost of widgets is $4.00 and cost of wadgets is $8.00. Country B's cost of widgets is 8 euros and cost of wadgets is 16 euros. Which of the following would you suggest?
a. Country A should specialize in widgets and Country B in wadgets.
b. Trade of widgets for wadgets would not benefit the countries.
c. Country A should specialize in wadgets and Country B in widgets.
d. Both countries should produce an equal amount of each.

6. In considering the distribution of the gains from trade:
a. smaller countries usually get a larger proportion of the gains from trade.
b. larger countries usually get a larger proportion of the gains from trade.
c. the gains are generally split equally between small and large countries.
d. no statement can be made about the general nature of the split.

7. Which of the following statements correctly summarizes a difference between the layperson's and the economist's views of the net benefits of trade?
a. Economists often argue that the gains from trade in the form of low consumer prices tend to be widespread and not easily recognizable while the costs in jobs lost tend to be concentrated and readily identifiable.

b. Economists often argue that most U.S. jobs are at risk of outsourcing while laypeople intuitively recognize that inherent in comparative advantage is that each country has a comparative advantage in the production of some good.
c. Economists focus on trade in manufactured goods while laypeople also focus on trade involving the services of people who manage the trade.
d. Economists most often argue that the costs of trade outweigh the benefits while laypeople often argue that the benefits of trade outweigh the costs.

8. In the United States, globalization has caused workers in the education, healthcare, and government sectors to face:
a. lower wages.
b. higher prices on consumer goods.
c. little or no downward pressure on their wages.
d. longer hours to compete with the higher production levels abroad.

9. Transferable comparative advantages are:
a. based on factors that are relatively unchangeable.
b. based on factors that can change relatively easily.
c. becoming more like inherent comparative advantages with technological innovations.
d. rarely eroded over time.

10. Which of the following is eroding the U.S. comparative advantage?
a. The spread of technology.
b. The law of one price.
c. A depreciating dollar.
d. Intellectual property rights.

11. The foreign exchange rate is the rate at which:
a. taxes are imposed on foreign imports.
b. foreign good are traded between domestic consumers.
c. one country's currency can be traded for another country's currency.
d. immigrants are exchanged between countries.

12. If civil war broke out in China, and people lost faith in the yuan:

 a. the demand for yuan would decrease and the supply of yuan would increase.

 b. the demand for yuan would increase and the supply of yuan would increase.

 c. the demand for yuan would decrease and the supply of yuan would decrease.

 d. the demand for yuan would increase and the supply of yuan would decrease.

13. In the graph below, the value of the dollar is:

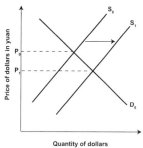

Quantity of dollars

 a. appreciating because the dollar buys more yuan.

 b. depreciating because the dollar buys more yuan.

 c. appreciating because the dollar buys fewer yuan.

 d. depreciating because the dollar buys fewer yuan.

14. In the following graph, the country has a trade:

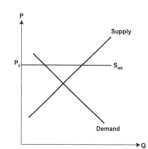

 a. deficit.
 b. surplus.
 c. balance.
 d. appreciation.

15. Which of the following would raise the world price level facing the United States?

 a. The dollar appreciates.
 b. The dollar depreciates.
 c. The trade deficit rises.
 d. The trade deficit falls.

16. The resource curse is when:

 a. a nation only has an inherent comparative advantage for one resource.

 b. a nation only has a transferrable comparative advantage for one resource.

 c. the discovery of a resource in a nation causes its currency to appreciate and thus causes the nation to lose comparative advantages in other sectors.

 d. a nation has neither an inherent nor a transferrable comparative advantage for any resource.

● POTENTIAL ESSAY QUESTIONS

You may also see essay questions similar to the "Problems & Applications" exercises.

1. What are two complications in exchange rate determination? What is the effect of each on the value of a country's currency?

2. If you were a trader would you look for potential trades between countries where production costs fall as output rises, or where production costs rise as output rises? Why?

ANSWERS

SHORT-ANSWER QUESTIONS

1. The principle of comparative advantage is that as long as the relative opportunity costs of production differ among countries, there are potential gains from trade, even if one country has an absolute advantage in everything.

2. Three determinants of the gains of trade are (1) the more competition, the less the trader gets and the more will go to the countries who are trading; (2) smaller countries get a larger proportion of the gain than larger countries; and (3) countries producing goods with economies of scale get a larger gain from trade.

3. Four reasons for differences between economists' and laypeople's views of trade are: (1) gains from trade are often stealth gains, (2) opportunity cost is relative therefore comparative advantage is determined by more than wages, (3) nations trade more than just manufactured goods, and (4) trade affects the distribution of income.

4. Currently trade has made the distribution of income in the United States more unequal. Production in the tradable sector such as manufacturing has become less competitive. Some workers in this sector have received lower wages and lost their jobs, which lowers their overall income. At the same time, people with intellectual property and workers in high tech and financial sectors have seen their incomes rise because the market for high-tech products has expanded beyond the United States and globalization has increased the demand in the financial and trade-facilitation sectors.

5. The United States has comparative advantages due to: (1) skills of the U.S. labor force, (2) U.S. governmental institutions, (3) U.S. physical and technological infrastructure, (4) English as the international language of business, (5) wealth from past production, (6) U.S. natural resources, (7) cachet, (8) inertia, (9) U.S. intellectual property rights, and (10) a relatively open immigration policy. (The question asks for four of these.)

6. Transferable comparative advantages are comparative advantages based on factors that can change relatively easily. Inherent comparative advantages are comparative advantages that are based on factors that are relatively unchangeable.

7. The United States is losing some of its comparative advantage because economic forces are pushing to spread capital and technology to other countries.

8. The appreciation of the dollar relative to the yuan means that one dollar buys more yuans.

9. The appreciation of the dollar will increase the U.S. trade deficit. The appreciation causes the relative price of U.S. goods to increase, causing U.S. goods to become less competitive in the global market. As a result, the quantity of goods exported by the United States decreases and the quantity of foreign goods imported by the United States increases, both of which cause the trade deficit to increase.

10. The resource curse is the paradox that countries with an abundance of resources tend to have lower economic growth and more unemployment than countries with fewer resources. This occurs because the large quantity of resources or discovery of resources in the country raises foreign demand for that resource and causes the country's currency to appreciate. The appreciation of the country's currency causes other goods to lose their comparative advantage and become less competitive in the global market, thus, one industrial sector gains a comparative advantage while others lose their comparative advantage. As a result, the trade deficit rises.

ANSWERS

MATCHING

1-a; 2-c; 3-j; 4-d; 5-f; 6-g; 7-i; 8-e; 9-b; 10-h.

ANSWERS

PROBLEMS AND APPLICATIONS

1. **a.** There is a basis for trade in Cases 2 and 3 because opportunity costs differ.

   b. The general principle is that there are gains from trade to be made when each country has a comparative advantage in a different good. That is, the opportunity costs differ.

   c. I would have country E specialize in widgets and country F specialize in wadgets. Since country E is currently producing 10 widgets and 4 wadgets, I would have it produce 12 widgets and no wadgets, promising that I will give it 5 wadgets for the extra two widgets it produced. I would have Country F produce 28 wadgets and 18 widgets, promising that I will give it 2 widgets in return for 7 of its wadgets. After I made this trade both countries are one wadget better off. I am two wadgets better off. (These two wadgets are the return to me for organizing the trade.)

   d. If there were economies of scale, there would be an even stronger argument for trade.

2. **a.** The production possibility curve for Country A is the curve labeled A in the graph below. In Country A the opportunity cost of one bottle of wine is 1/2 fish. Each fish forgone frees up resources sufficient to make two bottles of wine.

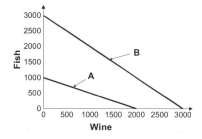

   b. The production possibility curve for Country B is the curve labeled B in the graph above. In Country B the opportunity cost of one bottle of wine is one fish. Each fish forgone frees up resources sufficient to make one bottle of wine.

   c. Country A has a comparative advantage in wine because it has to give up only 1/2 a fish for each bottle of wine while Country B has to give up 1 fish for each bottle of wine. Country B must necessarily have a comparative advantage in fish.

   d. A fair exchange for B would be giving up one fish for one bottle of wine or better because that is its opportunity cost of producing one fish. A fair exchange for A would be giving up two bottles of wine for 1 fish or better since its opportunity cost of producing two bottles of wine is one fish. Any exchange that reflects a ratio between these two values would be fair.

3. **a.** The production possibility curves for Country A and Country B are drawn below.

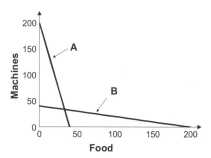

   b. Country B has the comparative advantage in the production of food since it has to give up only 1/5 of a machine to produce one unit of food while Country A has to give up 5 machines to produce one unit of food.

   c. Country A would be willing to supply 5 machines for 1 unit of food. Country B would be willing to supply 5 units of food for one machine. Let's suppose they trade 1 for 1. Country A would produce 200 machines, selling 50 to Country B for 50 units of food. Country B would produce 200 food units, and sell 50 to Country A for 50 machines. This way they each reach their higher desired level of consumption.

4. The world price level intersects the demand and supply curves at their equilibrium as shown in the graph below. There is no trade deficit.
    a. The world price level falls below the domestic price level, which causes a trade deficit shown by $Q_1 - Q_2$.
    b. The world price level rises above the domestic price level, which causes a trade surplus shown by $Q_2 - Q_1$.

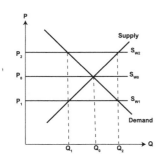

ANSWERS

MULTIPLE CHOICE

1. b   Since the curves have the same slope, no country has a comparative advantage in either good and there is no basis for trade. See Figure 9-1.

2. a   The opportunity cost for Saudi Arabia of wadgets in terms of widgets is higher than the opportunity cost for the United States. So Saudi Arabia should specialize in widgets and the United States in wadgets. See Figure 9-1.

3. a   A comparative advantage in the production of X means the nation can produce that good with a lower opportunity cost. Because the nation is relatively more efficient at producing X, it will specialize in its production and export that good. Answer c may be true, but it is also possible to have a comparative advantage in X without being able to produce more of X than any other nation.

4. c   The opportunity cost for the United States of wadgets in terms of widgets is higher than the opportunity cost for Saudi Arabia. So the United States should specialize in widgets and Saudi Arabia in wadgets.

5. b   The opportunity cost of widgets and wadgets is equal in both countries so neither country has a comparative advantage in either good and there is no basis for trade.

6. a   Smaller countries usually find that their production possibilities are changed more, and hence they benefit more.

7. a   It is because the costs of trade are more visible than the benefits that many laypeople oppose free trade. Switching "economists" and "laypeople" would make options b through d correct.

8. c   Workers in education, healthcare, and government sectors felt little or no downward pressure on their wages from globalization because these sectors produce goods and services that cannot be easily traded on the global market.

9. b   Transferable comparative advantages are based on factors that can change relatively easily and will tend to erode over time. Technological innovations are turning inherent comparative advantages into transferable comparative advantages.

10. a   As technology spreads, foreign countries can compete on a broader range of goods. As long as wages in foreign countries are lower than in the United States, this will erode U.S. comparative advantage. The law of one price describes why low wage countries will eventually lose comparative advantage. An depreciating dollar increases U.S. comparative advantage.

11. c   The foreign exchange rate is the rate at which one country's currency can be traded for another country's currency.

12. a If civil war broke out in China and caused people to lose faith in the yuan, the yuan would depreciate. Thus, the demand for yuan would decrease and the supply for yuan would increase.

13. d Since the supply of dollars is shifting out to the right, it takes fewer yuan to buy one dollar. That means the dollar is depreciating.

14. b The graph shows a country with a trade surplus, for the world price is greater than the domestic price; therefore the nation will export more and import less.

15. b When the dollar depreciates, an American gets fewer foreign currency units for every dollar exchanged, making foreign goods cost more.

16. c The resource curse occurs when the discovery of a resource in a nation causes it's currency to appreciate and thus causes the nation to lose comparative advantages in other sectors.

ANSWERS

POTENTIAL ESSAY QUESTIONS

The following are annotated answers. They indicate the general idea behind the answer.

1. If the supply and demand for currencies applied only to tradable goods, trade between two countries would generally be in balance, and both countries would have roughly equal sectors of comparative advantages in producing goods. However, that doesn't always happen because of two main complications. (1) The demand for a country's currency reflects a demand for its assets as well as its produced goods. Therefore, when the demand for a country's assets is high, the value of its currency will also be high. With a higher exchange rate, the world price of tradable goods will be low, and the domestic country will have a comparative advantage in relatively fewer sectors than other countries. (2)Another complication to determining the exchange rate is known as the resource curse, which is when a resource is discovered that increases the demand for a nation's currency and thus causes its value to appreciate. When this happens, the natural resource sector of the country gains a comparative advantage while other sectors either do not gain a comparative advantage or lose a comparative advantage due to the higher value of the currency.

2. If I were a trader, I would look for potential trades between countries where production costs fall as output rises. If a nation's production costs fall as output rises, it exhibits economies of scale, therefore, an increase in production can lower the average cost of producing a good. With lower production costs, the nation produces more and reaps more benefits from trade in the form of higher profits. As a trader, the more the trading countries make, the more I make, so I would look for nations that exhibit economies of scale and generate greater profits.

INTERNATIONAL TRADE POLICY

10

CHAPTER AT A GLANCE

1. The primary trading partners of the United States are Canada, Mexico, the European Union, and the Pacific Rim countries.

   A trade balance is the difference between a country's exports and imports. When imports exceed exports, a country has a trade deficit. When exports exceed imports a country has a trade surplus. Because the United States has had large trade deficits since the 1970s, it is a net debtor nation.

   The nature of trade is continually changing. The United States is importing more and more high-tech goods and services from India, China and other East Asian countries.

   Outsourcing is a type of trade. Outsourcing is a larger phenomenon today compared to 30 years ago because countries where jobs are outsourced today—China and India—are much larger.

2. Three policies used to restrict trade are:

   - tariffs: taxes on internationally traded goods;
   - quotas: quantity limits placed on imports; and
   - regulatory trade restrictions: government-imposed procedural rules that limit imports.

   Countries can also restrict trade through: voluntary restraint agreements, embargoes, and nationalistic appeals.

3. A tariff operates in the same way as a tax. The difference between a tariff and a quota is who gets the revenue. Government collects the revenue with the tariff. Firms receive the revenue with a quota.

   As seen in the following graph, a tariff, T, raises equilibrium price from P_0 to P_1 and equilibrium quantity declines from Q_0 to Q_1. Government collects the shaded region in tariffs. A quota of Q_1 has the same effect, except the shaded area goes to firms.

   When the domestic country is small and world price lower than domestic prices, tariffs lower a trade deficit. See Figure 10-5 for how.

   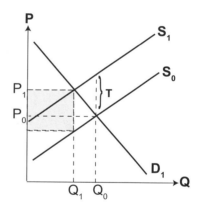

4. Arguments for restricting trade include:

   - Unequal internal distribution of the gains from trade;
   - Haggling by companies over the gains from trade;
   - Haggling by countries over trade restrictions;
   - Specialized production; learning by doing; and economies of scale;
   - Macroeconomic aspects of trade;
   - National security;
   - International politics;
   - Increased revenue brought in by tariffs.

   Understand these motives for trade barriers and be able to explain why they may not be sound.

5. Economists generally oppose trade restrictions because:

- from a global perspective, free trade increases total output;
- international trade provides competition for domestic companies;
- restrictions based on national security are often abused or evaded; and
- trade restrictions are addictive.

Economists generally argue that the benefits of free trade outweigh the costs—especially over time.

Trade restrictions limit the supply of an imported good, increasing its price and decreasing quantity. Governments prefer tariffs over quotas because they generate tax revenues, while companies prefer quotas.

6. Free trade associations help trade by reducing barriers to trade among member nations. Free trade associations could hinder trade by building up barriers to trade with nations outside the association.

A free trade association is a group of countries that allow free trade among its members and puts up common barriers against all other countries' goods.

The WTO and GATT are important international economic organizations designed to reduce trade barriers among <u>all</u> countries.

SHORT-ANSWER QUESTIONS

1. Who are the primary trading partners of the United States?

2. How has U.S. trade with the rest of the world changed in recent years?

3. What is the difference between a debtor and a creditor nation? Is the United States a creditor or debtor nation?

4. As a foreign firm, would you prefer a tariff or a quota in the country to which you export? Why?

5. In a talk to first-year members of Congress you are asked what they can do to restrict trade. You oblige.

6. You reveal to these first-year members of Congress that you believe in free trade. Hands fly up from people just waiting to tell you why they want to restrict trade. What are some of their reasons?

7. After listening to their remarks, you gather your thoughts and offer them reasons why you generally oppose trade restrictions. What do you say?

8. The first-year members of Congress ask you how joining a free trade association could help and hinder international trade. What do you say?

MATCHING THE TERMS
Match the terms to their definitions

___ **1.** economies of scale

___ **2.** embargo

___ **3.** free trade association

___ **4.** General Agreement on Tariffs and Trade (GATT)

___ **5.** infant industry argument

___ **6.** learning by doing

___ **7.** most-favored nation

___ **8.** quota

___ **9.** regulatory trade restriction

___ **10.** strategic bargaining

___ **11.** strategic trade policy

___ **12.** tariff

___ **13.** trade adjustment assistance program

___ **14.** World Trade Organization (WTO)

a. A tax governments place on internationally traded goods—generally imports.

b. All-out restriction on the import or export of a good.

c. Costs per unit output go down as output increases.

d. A country that will pay as low a tariff on its exports as will any other country.

e. Demanding a larger share of the gains of trade than you might get normally.

f. Government-imposed procedural rule that limits imports.

g. Group of countries that allow free trade among its members and put up common barriers against all other countries' goods.

h. Periodic international conference held in the past to reduce trade barriers.

i. Program designed to compensate losers for reductions in trade restrictions.

j. Quantity limit placed on imports.

k. An organization whose functions are generally the same as were those of GATT—to promote free and fair trade among countries.

l. With initial protection, an industry will be able to become competitive.

m. You become better at a task the more you perform it.

n. Threatening to implement tariffs to bring about a reduction in tariffs or some other concessions from the other country.

PROBLEMS AND APPLICATIONS

1. State whether the trade restriction is a quota, tariff, or regulatory trade restriction.

a. The EU (European Union) requires beef to be free of growth-inducing hormones in order to be traded in EU markets.

b. Hong Kong has maintained rice import controls on quantity since 1955 in order to keep local rice importers in business and to secure a steady wartime food supply.

c. To encourage domestic production of automobile parts, Japan limits the importation of automobile parts according to a rigid schedule of numbers.

d. The United States charges French wineries 10% of the value of each case of French wine imported into the United States.

2. Suppose the U.S. is considering trade restrictions against EU-produced hams. Given the demand and supply curves drawn below, show a tariff and a quota that would result in the same exports of ham to the United States.

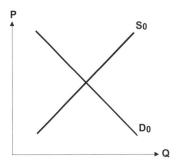

a. Would a tariff or a quota result in higher government revenue?

b. Which would the EU prefer?

c. Which would American ham producers prefer?

d. Which would American consumers prefer?

3. Refer to the graph below. The world price for a pound of coconuts is $3.00. The government of Fiji imposes a 50 cent tariff on the coconut imports to raise revenue and protect domestic producers as shown in the graph below. Assume the country is so small it takes the world price as given.

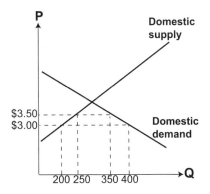

a. What are imports when the world price is $3.00?

b. What are imports if government imposes a 50-cent tariff?

c. Shade in the government revenue as a result of the tariff. What is the value of this revenue?

d. What quota would have the same effect on price and quantity as the tariff? Label the quota on the graph.

4. Coconut producers in Fiji politically lobby to get the tariff changed to a quota.

a. Why would the firms lobby for a quota instead of a tariff?

b. Why might the Fijian government resist changing the tariff to a quota?

c. What difference does the quota make for Fijian consumers compared to the tariff?

d. A member of Congress argues to eliminate restrictions altogether. What are some of the reasons she gives?

● MULTIPLE CHOICE

Circle the one best answer for each of the following questions:

1. The prime trading partners of the United States by dollar volume are:
    a. India, China, and Indonesia.
    b. Canada, Mexico, the European Union, and the Pacific Rim countries.
    c. Saudi Arabia, Israel, and Iran.
    d. South American and West African nations.

2. If a nation is a debtor nation it:
    a. is currently running a trade deficit.
    b. is currently running a trade surplus.
    c. has run trade deficits in the past.
    d. has run trade surpluses in the past.

3. Compared to the past, the United States is now:
    a. importing more high-tech goods and services from India and China and other East Asian countries.
    b. importing more goods and services that are lower down the technological ladder.
    c. outsourcing less to newly emerging industrialized countries like China and India.
    d. facing less competition from newly emerging industrialized countries like China and India.

4. If a country has a trade deficit, it is:
    a. consuming more than it is producing.
    b. lending to foreigners.
    c. buying financial assets.
    d. buying real assets.

5. A most-favored nation is a country that:
    a. pays no tariffs on exports.
    b. has a policy of no regulatory trade restrictions.
    c. prefers regulatory trade restrictions to tariffs and quotas.
    d. pays as low a tariff on its exports as will any other country.

6. Trade restrictions tend to:
    a. increase competition.
    b. increase prices to consumers.
    c. benefit consumers.
    d. have economic benefits that outweigh the economic costs.

7. A tariff is a:
    a. tax government places on imports.
    b. quantity limit placed on imports.
    c. total restriction on imports.
    d. government-imposed procedural rule that limits imports.

8. An embargo is:
    a. a tax government places on imports.
    b. a quantity limit placed on imports.
    c. a total restriction on imports.
    d. a government-imposed procedural rule that limits imports.

9. The value T on the graph below represents?

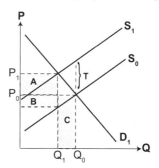

    a. an embargo.
    b. a tariff.
    c. a quota.
    d. a regulatory trade restriction.

10. In the graph for Question #9, which area represents the revenue collected by government?
    a. A.
    b. B.
    c. B and C.
    d. A and B.

11. For governments:
    a. tariffs are preferred over quotas because tariffs can help them collect revenues.
    b. quotas are preferred over tariffs because quotas can help them collect revenues.
    c. neither quotas nor tariffs can help collect revenues.
    d. both because quotas and tariffs are sources of revenues.

12. Trade adjustment assistance programs are designed to:
    a. compensate losers for trade restrictions.
    b. assist importers to conform to regulatory trade restrictions.
    c. educate firms how to trade on the global level.
    d. subsidize research on the most effective strategic trade policies.

13. Reasons for restricting trade include all of the following *except:*
    a. the existence of learning by doing and economies of scale.
    b. national security reasons.
    c. the increased revenue brought in from tariffs.
    d. the fact that trade decreases competitive pressures at home.

14. Economists generally oppose trade restrictions for all of the following reasons *except:*
    a. from a global perspective, free trade increases total output.
    b. the infant industry argument.
    c. trade restrictions lead to retaliation.
    d. international politics.

15. Free trade associations tend to:
    a. reduce restrictions on trade and thereby always expand free trade.
    b. lower trade barriers for all countries.
    c. replace multinational negotiations, and thereby always hurt free trade.
    d. expand, but also reduce, free trade.

POTENTIAL ESSAY QUESTIONS

You may also see essay questions similar to the "Problems & Applications" exercises.

1. What is the difference between a tariff and a quota? Why do governments prefer tariffs while foreign producers prefer quotas? What is the result of tariffs and quotas on the price and equilibrium quantity of the imported good?

2. What are six ways in which a country may restrict trade? Why do most economists support free trade and oppose trade restrictions?

━━━ ANSWERS ━━━

SHORT-ANSWER QUESTIONS

1. The primary trading partners of the United States are Canada, Mexico, the European Union, and Pacific Rim countries.

2. The kinds of goods and services the U.S. imports have shifted from primarily basic manufacturing goods and raw commodities to high-tech manufacturing goods and services from developing countries such as India, China, and other East Asian countries. In addition, more and more production of more sophisticated goods and services is being outsourced to these countries because their economies are much larger.

3. A debtor nation is a nation that accumulated more trade deficits than trade surpluses. The United States is currently a debtor nation. A creditor nation is a nation that is running a trade surplus; its accumulated trade surpluses exceed accumulated trade deficits.

4. I would prefer a quota to a tariff because, while in both cases the quantity I sell is lower, with a quota I collect the revenue and with a tariff, government collects the revenue.

5. Three policies countries use to restrict trade are (1) tariffs, (2) quotas, and (3) regulatory trade restrictions. There are others.

6. Answers might include: (1) although foreign competition might make society better off, some people may lose their jobs because of foreign competition (unequal internal distribution of the gains from trade); (2) some foreign companies are taking tough bargaining positions, and restricting trade is our only weapon (haggling by companies over trade restrictions); (3) some foreign countries are threatening us with trade restrictions (haggling by countries over the gains from trade); (4) trade restrictions will protect new U.S. industries until they learn to be competitive (learning by doing and economies of scale); (5) imports hurt U.S. domestic income in the short run, and the economy needs to grow in the short run (trade can reduce domestic output in the short run); (6) some restrictions are needed to protect our national security; (7) we do not want to trade with countries who violate our human rights standards or whose ideology conflicts with our democratic ideals (international politics may dominate trade considerations); and (8) tariffs bring in revenue for the U.S. government.

7. I would say that I generally oppose trade restrictions because (1) from a global perspective, free trade increases total output, (2) international trade provides competition for domestic companies, (3) restrictions based on national security are often abused, and (4) trade restrictions are addictive.

8. Free trade associations promote trade among members by reducing barriers to trade among the member nations. However, free trade associations could hinder trade by building up barriers to trade with nations outside the association.

━━━ ANSWERS ━━━

MATCHING

1-c; 2-b; 3-g; 4-h; 5-l; 6-m; 7-d; 8-j; 9-f; 10-e; 11-n; 12-a; 13-i; 14-k.

━━━ ANSWERS ━━━

PROBLEMS AND APPLICATIONS

1. **a.** Regulatory trade restriction because this is a regulation that has the final effect of reducing imports without a tax or numerical limitation.
   b. Quota. It is a numerical restriction on the amount of rice entering the country.
   c. Quota because it is a numerical restriction on imports.
   d. Tariff because it is a tax on imports.

2. A tariff would shift the supply curve up by the amount of the tariff. A quota with the same result would be at Q_1. Equilibrium quantity

would fall from Q_0 to Q_1. Equilibrium price would rise from P_0 to P_1. This is shown on the graph below. See Figure 10-4.

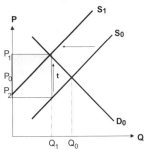

a. The government receives no revenue from the quota, but receives the shaded region as revenue from the tariff as shown on the graph above. See Figure 10-4.

b. The EU would prefer the quota since it will receive a higher price, P_1, for the same quantity of goods, Q_1 as it would with a tariff. With a tariff it would receive P_2, for Q_1. See Figure 10-4.

c. American ham producers prefer the quota because any increase in domestic demand would be met by domestic supply.

d. American consumers do not prefer either since the resulting price and quantity is the same with both. If, however, the tariff revenue were to lead to lower taxes or higher government services, they might prefer the tariff over the quota. They also might prefer the tariff to the quota because any increase in domestic demand will be partially met with imports, keeping domestic producers more efficient than under a quota system.

3. a. At a world price of $3.00 the domestic quantity demanded is 400 pounds of coconuts and imports are 200. Thus, imports are 200.

b. The tariff leads to a decline in domestic quantity demanded to 350 pounds of coconuts and an increase in domestic quantity supplied to 250 pounds of coconuts. Net imports are now 100.

c. The government of Fiji earned $50 as a result of the tariff. ($0.50x100)

d. The quota would be a limit of 100 pounds of coconut. See the accompanying graph.

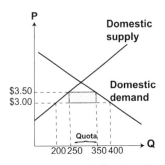

4. Considering the graph for Question #3 above;
a. Fijian coconut producers prefer a quota to a tariff because in the case of a quota, they receive the benefits from trade in the form of additional corporate revenue as domestic demand must then be met with domestic supply.

b. The government may resist changing the tariff to a quota because they would lose tariff revenue.

c. Fijian consumers have no preference. Both result in higher prices.

d. She might say that free trade increases total output and provides competition to domestic companies. She might also add that trade restrictions are addictive and soon they might be placing tariffs on all types of goods, not just coconuts.

ANSWERS

MULTIPLE CHOICE

1. b   Though the United States has recently expanded trade with China and India, the prime trade partners of the United States are Canada, Mexico, the European Union, and the Pacific Rim countries. See Figure 10-1.

2. c   A debtor nation may currently be running a surplus or a deficit. Debt is accumulated deficits. A debtor nation could be running a surplus if it ran deficits in the past.

3. a   The U.S. is importing more and more high-tech goods and services that are higher up the technological ladder from India and China and other East Asian countries. The U.S. is outsourcing more to these newly

emerging industrialized countries and is therefore facing more competition from these nations.

4. a   If a country has a trade deficit, it is importing (consuming) more than it is exporting (producing).

5. d   Most-favored nations might pay tariffs, but they receive the lowest tariffs compared to all other countries.

6. b   Trade restrictions reduce competition and therefore increase prices to consumers. Thus, consumers are hurt. The benefits of trade restrictions go to the domestic producers that do not have to compete as aggressively. The economic costs of trade restrictions (in the form of higher prices consumers must pay) far outweigh their benefits (which go to the protected domestic industries in the form of higher profits and more secure jobs).

7. a   A tariff is a tax placed on imported goods.

8. c   An embargo is an all-out restriction on the trade of goods with another country.

9. b   A tariff is a tax on goods, in this graph represented by T. Quotas are quantity restrictions. Regulatory trade restrictions cannot be illustrated with this graph.

10. d   The revenue to government is represented by the tariff times the quantity imported, Areas A+B. Area A does not reflect the entire amount of the tariff revenue. The tariff is T. Area C does not make sense.

11. a   Governments prefer tariffs because they generate revenues, quotas do not.

12. a   Trade adjustment assistance programs compensate people who have lost their jobs as a result of an increase in trade restrictions. Governments try to use trade adjustment assistance programs to facilitate free trade, but in practice, it is difficult to determine who is actually hurt by free trade.

13. d   Trade increases competitive pressures at home and increases competitiveness.

14. b   The infant industry argument is an argument in favor of trade restrictions. Economists' response to the infant industry argument is that history shows that few infant industries have ever grown up.

15. d   While free trade associations may work toward lowering trade barriers among member nations, they may result in higher trade barriers for nonmember countries.

ANSWERS

POTENTIAL ESSAY QUESTIONS

The following are annotated answers. They indicate the general idea behind the answer.

1.   A tariff is a tax on an imported item. A quota is a quantity limitation. Tariffs are preferred by governments because they raise revenues and are disliked by foreign producers because they require tax payments to the imposing government. However, notice that both tariffs and quotas raise prices and decrease the quantity of imported goods bought and sold.

2.   Countries use a variety of policies to restrict trade. These include:
- Tariffs.
- Quotas.
- Voluntary restraint agreements.
- Embargoes.
- Regulatory trade restrictions.
- Nationalistic appeals.

Economists generally oppose trade restrictions because: (1) from a global perspective, free trade increases total output—it raises standards of living; (2) international trade provides competition for domestic companies; (3) restrictions based on national security are often abused or evaded; and (4) trade restrictions often become addictive for domestic firms that benefit. Free trade forces domestic firms to be efficient—to provide higher quality goods at cheaper prices. Economists argue that trade restrictions may create some short-run benefits, but the costs (or harm done, which includes higher prices domestic consumers must pay) outweigh the benefits over time.

INTERNATIONAL FINANCIAL POLICY

35

CHAPTER AT A GLANCE

1a. The balance of payments is a country's record of all transactions between its residents and the residents of all foreign countries.

It is broken down into the current account and the financial and capital account.

The financial and capital account measures the flows of payments between countries for assets such as stocks, bonds, and real estate. The current (or trade) account measures the flows of payments for goods and services.

1b. The balance of trade is the difference between the value of goods and services a nation exports and the value of goods and services it imports.

The balance of merchandise trade is often discussed in the popular press as a summary of how the U.S. is doing in international markets. However, it only includes goods exported and imported—not services. Trade in services is just as important as trade in merchandise, so economists pay more attention to the balance of trade, which is combined balance on goods and services.

1c. By definition the financial and capital account balance and current account balance offset one another. When economists say that a country is running a balance of payments deficit, they are excluding the government's financial transactions.

The balance of payments is related to foreign exchange rate markets. When foreigners are buying our goods, services, or assets, that represents a demand for the dollar (an inflow) in international exchange rate markets. If we

buy foreign goods, services, or assets, that represents a supply of dollars (an outflow).

1d. A deficit in the balance of payments means that the private quantity supplied of a currency exceeds the private quantity demanded. A surplus in the balance of payments means the opposite.

Whenever the exchange rate is above equilibrium (below equilibrium), the country will experience a balance of payments deficit (surplus).

2. The fundamental forces affecting exchange rates are income, interest rates, the price level and trade policies. Other short-run forces can cause currencies to fluctuate wildly. see "A Reminder" box in the text.

A country can support its currency by buying or selling its currency. It can maintain a higher-than-equilibrium price as long as it has enough official reserves to do so.

A country can stabilize its currency by buying or selling it to maintain the desired value. Stabilization requires government to correctly estimate its currency's long-run value.

3a. Monetary policy affects exchange rates through the interest rate path, the income path, and the price-level path, as shown in the diagram in the text.

Expansionary monetary policy (increasing the money supply) lowers exchange rates. It decreases the relative price of a country's currency. Contractionary monetary policy has the opposite effect.

3b. Fiscal policy affects exchange rates through the interest rate path, the income path, and the price-level path, as shown in the diagram in the text.

The net effect of fiscal policy on exchange rates is ambiguous.

✔ *Be able to explain why!*

4a. Purchasing power parity is a method of calculating exchange rates so that various currencies will each buy an equal basket of goods and services.

The PPP (Purchasing Power Parity) is one method of estimating long-run exchange rates.

4b. A real exchange rate is an exchange rate adjusted for differential inflation in countries.

%Δ real exchange rate = %Δ nominal exchange rate + (domestic inflation − foreign inflation).

5a. Three exchange rate régimes are:
- *Fixed exchange rate*: The government chooses an exchange rate and offers to buy and sell currencies at that rate.
- *Flexible exchange rate*: Determination of exchange rates is left totally up to the market.
- *Partially flexible exchange rate*: The government sometimes affects the exchange rate and sometimes leaves it to the market.

Which is best is debatable.

5b. Fixed exchange rates provide international monetary stability and force governments to make adjustments to meet their international problems. (This is *also* a disadvantage.) If they become unfixed, they create monetary instability. (806-807)

✔ *Know these advantages and disadvantages!*

5c. Flexible exchange rate régimes provide for orderly incremental adjustment of exchange rates rather than sudden large jumps, and allow governments to be flexible in conducting domestic monetary and fiscal policy. (This is *also* a disadvantage.) They are, however, susceptible to private speculation.

✔ *Know these advantages and disadvantages!*

5d. Partially flexible exchange rate régimes combine the advantages and disadvantages of fixed and flexible exchange rates.

Most countries have opted for this policy. However, if the market exchange rate is below the rate the government desires, and the government does not have sufficient official reserves (to buy and increase the demand for its currency), then it must undertake policies that will either increase the private demand for its currency or decrease the private supply. Doing so either involves using traditional macro policy—fiscal and monetary policy—to influence the economy, or using trade policy to affect the level of exports and imports.

6. Four economic advantages of a common currency:
- eliminates cost of exchanging currencies,
- facilitates price comparisons,
- creates a larger single market, and
- increases the demand for currency as a store of wealth.

The disadvantages of a common currency:
- loss of national identity,
- increased economic ties among member countries, and
- loss of independent monetary policy for member countries.

✔ *Know the advantages and disadvantages of a common currency.*

The most important disadvantage is loss of independent monetary policy. A country loses the ability to increase the money supply by itself in order to fight a recession.

See also, Appendix: "History of Exchange Rate Systems."

SHORT-ANSWER QUESTIONS

1. Distinguish between the balance of payments and the balance of trade.

2. How can a country simultaneously have a balance of payments deficit and a balance of trade surplus?

3. How does each part of the balance of payments relate to the supply and demand for currencies?

4. If a country runs expansionary monetary policy, what will likely happen to the exchange rate?

5. If a country runs expansionary fiscal policy, what will likely happen to the exchange rate?

6. If the demand and supply for a country's currency depend upon demand for imports and exports, and demand for foreign and domestic assets, how can a country fix its exchange rate?

7. How do market exchange rates differ from exchange rates using the purchasing power parity concept?

8. How do inflation rate differentials affect the real exchange rate?

9. Differentiate among fixed, flexible, and partially flexible exchange rates.

11. You are advising Great Britain about whether it should join the European Monetary Union. What arguments can you give in support of joining? What arguments can you give against joining?

10. Which are preferable, fixed or flexible exchange rates?

MATCHING THE TERMS
Match the terms to their definitions

___ **1.** balance of merchandise trade

___ **2.** balance of payments

___ **3.** balance of trade

___ **4.** currency stabilization

___ **5.** currency support

___ **6.** current account

___ **7.** financial and capital account

___ **8.** fixed exchange rate

___ **9.** flexible exchange rate

___ **10.** partially flexible exchange rate

___ **11.** purchasing power parity

___ **12.** real exchange rate

a. A method of calculating exchange rates that attempts to value currencies at a rate such that each will buy an equal basket of goods.

b. A country's record of all transactions between its residents and the residents of all foreign countries.

c. A regime in which government sometimes affects the exchange rate and sometimes leaves it to the market.

d. A regime in which a government chooses an exchange rate and offers to buy and sell currencies at that rate.

e. A regime in which the determination of the value of a currency is left up to the market.

f. The buying of a currency by a government to maintain its value above its long-run equilibrium.

g. The difference between the value of goods and services a nation exports and the value of goods and services it imports.

h. The part of the balance of payments account that lists all long-term flows of payments.

i. The part of the balance of payments account that lists all short-term flows of payments.

j. The difference between the value of the goods exported and the value of the goods imported.

k. Buying and selling of a currency by the government to offset temporary fluctuations.

l. Exchange rate adjusted for inflation differentials.

PROBLEMS AND APPLICATIONS

1. State for each whether the transaction shows up on the balance of payments current account, the balance of payments financial and capital account, or neither.

   a. An American buys 100 shares of stock of Mercedes Benz, a German company.

   b. A Japanese businessperson buys Ameritec, an American bank.

   c. An American auto manufacturer buys $20 million in auto parts from a Japanese company.

   d. An American buys 100 shares of IBM stock. (IBM is an American company.)

   e. General Motors exports 10,000 cars to Germany.

   f. Toyota Motor Corporation, a Japanese firm, makes a $1 million profit from its plant in Kentucky, USA.

2. For each of the following, show graphically what would happen to the market for British pounds. Assume there are only two countries, the United States and Britain.

   a. Income in Britain rises.

   b. Income in the United States rises.

   c. The prices of goods in the United States increase.

   d. Interest rates rise in Britain.

   e. The value of the pound is expected to fall.

3. Explain the effects of the following macro policies on income, interest rates, inflation and ultimately on the value of the domestic currency.

   a. Expansionary monetary policy.

   b. Contractionary fiscal policy.

   c. Expansionary monetary and fiscal policy.

4. State what will happen to the real exchange rate of the dollar in the following instances:

   a. U.S. inflation is 2 percent, Japan's inflation is 5 percent, and the U.S. dollar rises 3 percent.

   b. U.S. inflation is 4 percent, Japan's inflation is 1 percent, and the U.S. dollar rises 2 percent.

   c. U.S. deflation is 1 percent, Japan's inflation is 1 percent, and the U.S. dollar falls 4 percent.

   d. U.S. inflation is 5 percent, Japan's inflation is 2 percent, and the U.S. dollar falls 1 percent.

● MULTIPLE CHOICE

Circle the one best answer for each of the following questions:

1. If a country has perfectly flexible exchange rates and is running a current account deficit, it is running:
   a. a financial and capital account surplus.
   b. a financial and capital account deficit.
   c. a government financial account surplus.
   d. a government financial account deficit.

2. In the balance of payments accounts, net investment income shows up in:
   a. the current account.
   b. the financial and capital account.
   c. the government financial account.
   d. Net investment income is not an entry in the balance of payments.

3. If the government financial account is significantly in surplus, the country is most likely:
   a. trying to hold its exchange rate higher than it otherwise would be.
   b. trying to hold its exchange rate lower than it otherwise would be.
   c. trying to have no effect on its exchange rate.
   d. sometimes trying to increase and sometimes trying to decrease its exchange rate.

4. In recent years, the United States has:
   a. generally run a balance of trade surplus.
   b. generally run a balance of trade deficit.
   c. sometimes run a balance of trade surplus and sometimes run a balance of trade deficit.
   d. generally run a balance of trade equality.

5. In recent years, the United States has:
   a. generally run a financial and capital account surplus.
   b. generally run a financial and capital account deficit.
   c. sometimes run a financial and capital account surplus and sometimes run a financial and capital account deficit.
   d. generally run a financial and capital account equality.

6. Assuming flexible exchange rates, if the European demand for U.S. imports increases, one would expect the price of euros in terms of dollars to:

   a. rise.
   b. fall.
   c. remain unchanged.
   d. sometimes rise and sometimes fall.

7. Assuming flexible exchange rates, if the U.S. demand for European imports increases, one would expect the price of euros in terms of dollars to:
   a. rise.
   b. fall.
   c. remain unchanged.
   d. sometimes rise and sometimes fall.

   Use the following graph of the foreign exchange market to answer Questions 8-10:

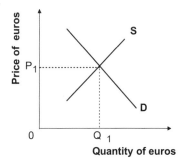

8. If U.S. income increases:
   a. the supply curve will shift out to the right.
   b. the supply curve will shift in to the left.
   c. the demand curve will shift out to the right.
   d. the demand curve will shift in to the left.

9. If European interest rates increase relative to world interest rates:
   a. only the supply curve will shift out to the right.
   b. only the demand curve will shift in to the left.
   c. the supply curve will shift in to the left and the demand curve will shift out to the right.
   d. the supply curve will shift out to the right and the demand curve will shift in to the left.

10. If European inflation increases relative to world inflation:
   a. only the supply curve will shift out to the right.
   b. only the demand curve will shift in to the left.
   c. the supply curve will shift in to the left and the demand curve will shift out to the right.
   d. the supply curve will shift out to the right and the demand curve will shift in to the left.

11. If a country with flexible exchange rates runs expansionary monetary policy, in the short run one would expect the value of its exchange rate to:
a. rise.
b. fall.
c. be unaffected.
d. sometimes rise and sometimes fall.

12. Expansionary monetary policy has a tendency to:
a. push interest rates up and exchange rates down.
b. push interest rates down and exchange rates down.
c. push income down and exchange rates down.
d. push imports down and exchange rates down.

13. Contractionary fiscal policy has a tendency to:
a. push interest rates up and exchange rates down.
b. push interest rates down and exchange rates down.
c. push income up and have an ambiguous effect on the exchange rate.
d. push imports down and have an ambiguous effect on exchange rates.

14. Refer to the graph below. If the U.S. government wants to fix its convertible currency at exchange rate P_1, it will have to:

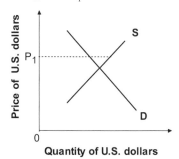

a. demand dollars, paying for them with official reserves.
b. supply dollars in exchange for official reserves.
c. disallow currency conversion except at the official rate P_1.
d. supply both official reserves and dollars because excess supply of dollars is so large.

15. If a country wants to reduce fluctuations in its currency while keeping its long-run value constant, it should establish a currency:
a. support program, buying its currency with foreign reserves if it wants to lower the value of its currency.
b. support program, selling its currency with foreign reserves if it wants to lower the value of its currency.
c. stabilization program, buying its currency when its value is too high and selling when its value is low.
d. stabilization program, buying its currency when its value is too low and selling when its value is too high.

16. Say the Bangladeshi taka is valued at 42 taka to $1. Also say that you can buy the same basket of goods for 10 taka that you can buy for $1. In terms of dollars the purchasing power parity of the taka is:
a. overvalued.
b. undervalued.
c. not distorted.
d. nonconvertible.

17. Suppose inflation in the United States is 3 percent and inflation in Europe is 4 percent. If the U.S. dollar exchange rate falls by 5 percent relative to the euro, the real exchange rate of the dollar relative to the euro has:
a. risen 2 percent.
b. risen 6 percent.
c. fallen 2 percent.
d. fallen 6 percent.

18. If a country has fixed exchange rates:
a. the government need not worry about the exchange rate.
b. governments are committed to buying and selling currencies at a fixed rate.
c. the exchange rate is set by law.
d. the exchange rate has a fixed component and a flexible component.

19. If a country has a flexible exchange rate, the exchange rate:
a. is determined by flexible government policy.
b. is determined by market forces.
c. fluctuates continually, changing by at least 1 percent per year.
d. fluctuates continually, changing by at least 10 percent per year.

20. Compared to a fixed exchange rate system, a flexible exchange rate system:
    a. allows countries more flexibility in their monetary policies.
    b. allows countries less flexibility in their monetary policies.
    c. has no effect on monetary policies.
    d. allows countries more flexibility in their industrial policies.

21. A reason why a country might choose to join a currency union is:
    a. so that its central bank can monetize the country's debt.
    b. to broaden the marketplace by reducing costs of trade.
    c. to reduce the demand for the common currency as a reserve currency.
    d. to increase its sense of nationalism.

A1. The gold standard is a type of:
    a. fixed exchange rate.
    b. partially flexible exchange rate.
    c. flexible exchange rate.
    d. nonconvertible exchange rate.

A2. The gold specie flow mechanism works primarily by flows of:
    a. money from one country to another.
    b. services from one country to another.
    c. merchandise from one country to another.
    d. exchange rates from one country to another.

A3. Under the gold standard, if a country has a balance of payments deficit:
    a. gold would flow out of the country.
    b. gold would flow into the country.
    c. the country's exchange rate would rise.
    d. the country's exchange rate would fall.

A4. SDRs refers to:
    a. Specie Draft Rights.
    b. Specie Drawing Rights.
    c. Special Drawing Rights.
    d. Special Draft Rights.

POTENTIAL ESSAY QUESTIONS

You may also see essay questions similar to the "Problems & Applications" exercises.

1. How are a government's exchange rate policy and the government financial and capital account in the balance of payments related? Is it easier for a government to push the value of its currency up or down? Why?

2. Explain how fixed, flexible (or floating), and partially flexible exchange rates are determined. What are the advantages and the disadvantages of each? Why do most nations have a partially flexible exchange rate policy?

ANSWERS

SHORT-ANSWER QUESTIONS

1. The balance of payments is a country's record of all transactions between its residents and the residents of all foreign nations. It is divided into the current account and the financial and capital account. The balance of trade is one part of the balance of payments—specifically that part dealing with the exchange of goods and services.

2. As discussed in Question #1, the balance of trade is one part of the balance of payments. Thus, if other parts of the international payments —for example, the financial and capital account—are in deficit, the balance of trade could still be in surplus. Here, we are excluding government financial transactions, which will be positive if the private balance of trade is negative.

3. The balance of payments records the flow of a currency in and out of a country (1) in order to buy and sell goods and services in the current account, and (2) in order to buy and sell assets along with payments resulting from previous purchases of assets in the financial and capital account. To buy foreign goods and assets one must supply domestic currency and demand foreign currency. Therefore, the balance of payments records the demand and supply of a country's currency during a given period of time.

4. Expansionary monetary policy tends to push income and prices up and interest rates down. All these phenomena tend to push the exchange rate down.

5. Expansionary fiscal policy tends to push income, prices, and interest rates up. Higher income and higher prices increase imports and put downward pressure on exchange rates. Higher interest rates push exchange rates in the opposite direction, so the net effect of expansionary fiscal policy on exchange rates is unclear.

6. The current account and financial and capital account reflect private demand and supply of a country's currency. If a country wants to fix

the value of its currency to maintain its value at the fixed value, the government must buy and sell its currency using official reserves. Buying (selling) one's own currency shows up as a subcomponent of net U.S. acquisitions of foreign financial assets.

7. Market exchange rates are determined by the demand and supply of a country's currency. Since not all goods, services, and assets produced in a country can be traded internationally, the value of an exchange rate may not reflect the relative prices in each country. The purchasing power parity concept adjusts the value of a country's currency by determining the rate at which equivalent baskets of goods can be purchased in each country.

8. If inflation is higher in a foreign country compared to the domestic country, and the nominal exchange rate doesn't change, the real exchange rate for the domestic country will fall. This is because the domestic currency will not be able to purchase as many foreign goods as before the foreign inflation.

9. A fixed exchange rate is an exchange rate that the government chooses and then holds, by standing ready to buy and sell at that rate. Flexible exchange rates are exchange rates that are determined by the market without any government intervention. Partially flexible exchange rates are exchange rates that are determined by the market but are sometimes also affected by government intervention.

10. It depends. Each has its advantages and disadvantages. Flexible exchange rates give a country more control over domestic policy, and generally an orderly adjustment in exchange rates, but can also cause large fluctuations in the value of the country's currency, hurting trade. With fixed exchange rates, such fluctuations can be avoided.

11. The disadvantages of joining the European Monetary Union are that Great Britain would have to give up the pound as its currency, a source of national pride, it would have to give up independent monetary policy, and it would have increased economic ties with member countries. The advantages are that if the euro

becomes an important reserve currency, Britain will enjoy lower interest rates, and its producers and consumers will have greater access to a larger market. The cost of exchanging currencies is eliminated and price comparisons will be easier.

ANSWERS

MATCHING

1-j; 2-b; 3-g; 4-k; 5-f; 6-i; 7-h; 8-d; 9-e; 10-c; 11-a; 12-l.

ANSWERS

PROBLEMS AND APPLICATIONS

1. **a.** Financial and capital account. This is a long-term outflow.
    b. Financial and capital account. This is a long-term inflow.
    c. Current account. These are merchandise imports, a short-term flow.
    d. Neither. It is a domestic transaction.
    e. Current account. These are merchandise exports, a short-term flow.
    f. Current account. This is net investment income.

2. **a.** Demand for imports by the British rises; hence demand for dollars (supply of pounds) rises. This is shown in the graph below.

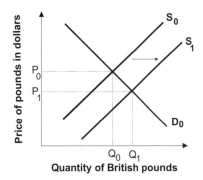

b. Demand for imports by Americans rises; hence demand for pounds rises. This is shown in the graph below.

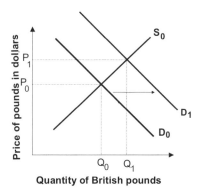

c. Demand for imports by the British falls; hence demand for dollars (supply of pounds) falls. This is shown in the graph below.

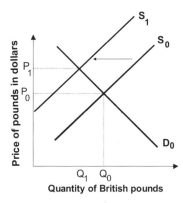

d. Demand for British assets will rise; hence the demand for the pound rises. This is shown in the graph below.

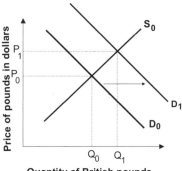

e. The demand for the pound falls. This is shown in the graph below.

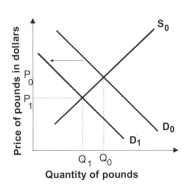

3. a. Expansionary monetary policy will increase income, lower interest rates and raise inflation. All three will lead to a lower exchange rate.

b. Contractionary fiscal policy will lower interest rates, income and inflation. Lower interest rates will put downward pressure on the exchange rate while lower income and prices will pressure the exchange rate up. The net effect is ambiguous.

c. Expansionary monetary policy will put downward pressure on the exchange rate as described in the answer to part *a*. Expansionary fiscal policy raises inflation, income and interest rates. Since not all three impact exchange rates in the same direction, the overall impact on the exchange rate is ambiguous. Since monetary policy has a certain impact, it will dominate and the exchange rate will likely fall.

4. a. Remains the same $[3 + (2 - 5)]$.
b. Rises 5 percent $[2 + (4 - 1)]$.
c. Falls 6 percent $[-4 + (-1 - 1)]$.
d. Rises 2 percent $[-1 + (5 - 2)]$.

ANSWERS

MULTIPLE CHOICE

1. a With perfectly flexible exchange rates the balance of payments must sum to zero; thus the financial and capital account must be in surplus if the current account is in deficit. The government financial account could not be negative because if there are perfectly flexible exchange rates, there are no net government transactions.

2. a Although net investment income might seem to many people as if it goes in the financial and capital account, it is a return for a service and is considered part of the current account.

3. a A surplus in the government financial account means the balance of payments would otherwise be in deficit. The country is buying up its own currency. This means it is trying to hold up its exchange rate.

4. b See text.

5. a Running a financial and capital account surplus is the other side of the balance sheet from the trade deficit.

6. b To purchase greater amounts of U.S. products, the European Union must increase the supply of euros, pushing down the value of the euro relative to the dollar. See "A Reminder" box in the text.

7. a To purchase greater amounts of European products, U.S. citizens must increase the supply of their currency, pushing down its value relative to the euro. That means that the value of the euro rises relative to the dollar. See "A Reminder" box in the text.

8. c If U.S. income increases, the U.S. demand for European imports will increase, shifting the demand for euros out to the right. See "A Reminder" box in the text.

9. c An increase in European interest rates will increase the demand for European assets. As a result, the demand for euros will shift out to the right. In addition, Europeans will substitute domestic assets for foreign assets, shifting the supply of euros to the left. See "A Reminder" box in the text.

10. d An increase in European inflation will reduce the demand for European goods.

Foreigners will demand fewer euros with which to buy European goods and Europeans will supply more euros as they exchange euros for other currencies to buy cheaper goods abroad. See "A Reminder" box in the text.

11. b   Expansionary monetary policy decreases interest rates and thereby tends to decrease the exchange rate in the short run.

12. b   See the diagram in the text.

13. c   See the diagram in the text.

14. a   At P_1, there is an excess supply of dollars. To keep the value of the dollar from falling, the U.S. will have to buy up that excess using official reserves of foreign currencies. Disallowing conversion except at an official rate would make the dollar a nonconvertible currency.

15. d   Since the country only wants to reduce fluctuations, not its long-run value, it will implement a currency stabilization program. It buys its currency (shifting the demand curve to the right) to raise its value when it is too low and selling its currency (shifting the supply curve to the right) to lower its value when it is too high.

16. b   Since the purchasing power parity exchange rate is lower than the actual exchange rate, the taka is undervalued.

17. d   The real exchange rate has fallen 6 percent: $[-5+(3-4)]$.

18. b   To keep the exchange rate at the stated amount, governments must be willing to buy and sell currencies so that the quantity supplied and quantity demanded are always equal at the fixed rate.

19. b   There are no predetermined levels of change with a flexible exchange rate.

20. a   Under a fixed exchange rate system, unless the country has sufficient official reserves, countries must use their monetary policies

to meet international commitments. Thus flexible exchange rate policies allow them more flexibility in their monetary policies. Flexible exchange rates *may* allow them more flexibility in their industrial policies, but flexible exchange rates *definitely* allow them more flexibility in their monetary policy, so a is the preferred answer.

21. b   A common currency reduces barriers to trade among member nations, thereby broadening the potential marketplace for domestic producers.

A1. a.   See the text.

A2. a.   When there is an imbalance of trade in the gold system, gold—which is money—flows from the deficit country to the surplus country, pushing the price level down in the deficit country and up in the surplus country. This process brings about a trade balance equilibrium, eventually.

A3. a   See the text about the flow of gold. The last two answers could be eliminated since the gold standard involves fixed exchange rates.

A4. c   SDRs refers to Special Drawing Rights.

━━━━━━ ANSWERS ━━━━━━

POTENTIAL ESSAY QUESTIONS

The following are annotated answers. They indicate the general idea behind the answer.

1. If a country is experiencing a balance of payments deficit (the private quantity supplied of its currency exceeds the private quantity demanded at the current exchange rate), then its currency will fall in value over time. A country's government could prevent its currency from falling (depreciating) by buying its own currency in exchange rate markets. The opposite is also true. Because a country can

create and then sell its own currency, it is easier for a country to push the value of its currency down than up.

2. Notice the "margin list" on page 774 and list of advantages and disadvantages of each on pages 774-775. Most nations have opted for a partially flexible exchange rate policy in order to try to get the advantages of both a fixed and a flexible exchange rate.

MACRO POLICY IN A GLOBAL SETTING

36

1a. There is significant debate about what U.S. international goals should be because exchange rates have conflicting effects and, depending on the state of the economy, there are arguments for high and low exchange rates.

A high exchange rate (strong value of the dollar) helps hold down the prices of imports and therefore inflation. However, it creates a trade deficit that has a depressing effect on aggregate demand for U.S. output and therefore the income level.

1b. Running a trade deficit is good in the short run but presents problems in the long run; thus there is debate about whether we should worry about a trade deficit or not.

Trade deficit→ imports > exports.

Short-run benefit: We are able to consume more than we would otherwise be able to.

Long-run cost: We have to sell off U.S. assets because we are consuming more than we are producing. All the future interest and profits on those assets will thus go to foreigners, not U.S. citizens.

A country with fixed exchange rates must give up any attempt to target domestic interest rates to achieve domestic goals.

2. Monetary policy affects the trade balance primarily through the income path as shown in the diagram in the text..

Expansionary monetary policy makes a trade deficit larger.

Contractionary monetary policy makes a trade deficit smaller.

✔ *Be able to explain why!*

3. Fiscal policy affects the trade deficit primarily though the income path as shown in the diagram in the text

Expansionary fiscal policy increases a trade deficit.

Contractionary fiscal policy decreases a trade deficit.

✔ *Be able to explain why!*

4. Governments try to coordinate their monetary and fiscal policies with other governments because their economies are interdependent.

Each country will likely do what's best for the world economy as long as it is also best for itself.

5. While internationalizing a country's debt may help in the short run, in the long run it presents potential problems, since foreign ownership of a country's debts means the country must pay interest to those foreign countries and that debt may come due.

The United States has been internationalizing its debt since the early 1980s, which means that it must, at some point in the future, export more than it imports (consume less than it produces) to pay for this.

6. Macro policy must be conducted within the setting of a country's overall competitiveness.

In recent years the U.S. comparative advantage has been in assets, and less so for produced goods. When foreigners cease wanting to purchase dollars or U.S. assets, the U.S. dollar will depreciate.

SHORT-ANSWER QUESTIONS

1. What should U.S. international goals be?

2. Why can a country achieve an interest rate target or an exchange rate target, but generally cannot achieve both at the same time?

3. Which dominates policy for a country: domestic or international goals? Why?

4. If a country runs contractionary monetary policy, what will likely happen to the trade balance?

5. If a country runs contractionary fiscal policy, what will likely happen to the trade balance?

6. Given the difficulty of doing so, why do countries try to coordinate their monetary and fiscal policies with other countries?

7. The United States in recent years has run a large current account deficit and has become the world's largest debtor nation. What are some of the potential problems that this presents?

8. If foreigners began to demand fewer U.S. assets, why might U.S. policy makers be forced to consider contractionary monetary and fiscal policy?

9. What would happen to U.S. comparative advantage in production of goods if the U.S. dollar fell?

PROBLEMS AND APPLICATIONS

1. You observe that over the past decade, a country's competitiveness has improved, reducing its trade deficit.

   a. What monetary or fiscal policies might have led to such results? Why?

b. You also observe that interest rates have steadily fallen along with a fall in the exchange rate. What monetary or fiscal policies might have led to such results?

2. You have been hired as an adviser to Fantasyland, a country with perfectly flexible exchange rates. State what monetary and fiscal policies you might suggest in each of the following situations. Explain your answers.

   a. You want to increase domestic income and to reduce the exchange rate.

   b. You want to reduce interest rates, reduce inflation, and reduce the trade deficit.

   c. You want lower unemployment, lower interest rates, a lower exchange rate, and a lower trade deficit.

MULTIPLE CHOICE

Circle the one best answer for each of the following questions:

1. Countries prefer:
   a. a high exchange rate.
   b. a low exchange rate.
   c. sometimes a low and sometimes a high exchange rate.
   d. a fixed exchange rate.

2. Countries prefer:
   a. a trade deficit.
   b. a trade surplus.
   c. sometimes a trade deficit and sometimes a trade surplus.
   d. a trade equilibrium.

3. If a country wants to maintain a fixed exchange rate above equilibrium, but does not have the necessary official reserves, it can:
   a. increase demand for its currency by running contractionary monetary policy.
   b. reduce supply of its currency by running expansionary monetary policy.
   c. increase demand for its currency by running contractionary fiscal policy.
   d. increase supply of its currency by running expansionary fiscal policy.

4. If the trade deficit has gone up, it is most likely that the government ran:
   a. an expansionary monetary policy.
   b. a contractionary monetary policy.
   c. a contractionary fiscal policy.
   d. an expansionary monetary policy and a contractionary fiscal policy.

5. Expansionary monetary policy tends to push income:
   a. down and the trade deficit down.
   b. down and the trade deficit up.
   c. up and the trade deficit down.
   d. up and the trade deficit up.

6. Contractionary fiscal policy tends to push:
   a. income down and imports up.
   b. income down and the trade deficit up.
   c. income down and the trade deficit down.
   d. prices down and imports up.

7. Assume the United States would like to raise its exchange rate and lower its trade deficit. It would pressure Japan to run:
   a. contractionary monetary policy.
   b. contractionary fiscal policy.
   c. expansionary monetary policy.
   d. expansionary fiscal policy.

8. According to the textbook, generally when international goals and domestic goals conflict:
   a. the international goals win out.
   b. the domestic goals win out.
   c. sometimes it's a toss-up which will win out.
   d. international monetary goals win out but international fiscal goals lose out.

9. When a country runs a large trade deficit, the amount of crowding out that occurs because of fiscal policy is:
   a. increased.
   b. decreased.
   c. unaffected.
   d. sometimes increased and sometimes decreased.

10. A country has the greatest domestic policy flexibility with:
   a. fixed exchange rates.
   b. flexible exchange rates.
   c. a trade deficit.
   d. a trade surplus.

11. A sudden fall in the price of the dollar in terms of other countries' currencies will most likely make policy makers face the possibility of implementing:
   a. capital inflow controls.
   b. import subsidies.
   c. contractionary macro policy.
   d. expansionary macro policy.

POTENTIAL ESSAY QUESTIONS

You may also see essay questions similar to the "Problems & Applications" exercises.

1. If there was initially a trade balance, what kind of trade imbalance would be created by an increase in the exchange rate value of the dollar (a stronger dollar)? Why?

2. What are the benefits and costs to the United States of having a strong dollar–a high exchange rate value of the dollar?

3. Why do domestic economic goals usually dominate international economic goals?

ANSWERS

SHORT-ANSWER QUESTIONS

1. By "international goals" economists usually mean the exchange rate and the trade balance that policy makers should shoot for. There is significant debate in the United States about what our international goals should be; there are arguments for both high and low exchange rates, and for both trade deficits and trade surpluses. The argument for a high exchange rate is that it lowers the cost of imports; the argument against it is that it raises the price of exports, making U.S. goods less competitive. The argument in favor of a trade deficit is that it allows a country to consume more than it produces; the argument against it is that a trade deficit will have to be paid off at some point.

2. Because monetary policy affects the value of the currency, a country cannot target both interest rates and exchange rates simultaneously. Suppose the currency value is at its desired level, but interest rates are too high. Expansionary monetary policy would lower the interest rate, but a lower interest rate reduces foreign demand for the country's interest-bearing assets. The demand for the currency will shift in to the left and its exchange rate will fall. Likewise, citizens of the country will invest elsewhere and the supply of the currency will shift out to the right. The value of the currency will be lower than its target.

3. Generally, domestic goals dominate for two reasons: (1) international goals are often ambiguous, as discussed in answer to Question #1 above, and (2) international goals affect a country's population indirectly and in politics, indirect effects take a back seat.

4. Contractionary monetary policy tends to push income down. Lower income means lower imports, lowering the trade deficit.

5. Contractionary fiscal policy pushes income down. This tends to decrease imports and decrease a trade deficit.

6. The policies of one country affect the economy of another. So it is only natural that the two countries try to coordinate their policies. It is also only natural that since voters are concerned with their own countries, coordination is difficult to achieve unless coordination is in the interest of both countries.

7. While internationalizing a country's debt may help in the short run, in the long run it presents potential problems, since foreign ownership of a country's debts means the debtor country must pay interest to the foreign countries, and also, that debt may come due.

8. If foreigners begin to demand fewer U.S. assets, the financial and capital account surplus would fall and there would be downward pressure on the price of the U.S dollar. A dramatic decline in the price of the dollar would cause inflation to rise. If that happened policy makers would likely consider contractionary monetary and fiscal policy to stem the decline in the dollar and the acceleration of inflation.

9. If the U.S. dollar fell, U.S. goods would be less expensive to foreigners, improving the U.S. comparative advantage in a number of produced goods.

ANSWERS

PROBLEMS AND APPLICATIONS

1. a. An increase in competitiveness and a decrease in the trade deficit are probably due to contractionary fiscal policy. Contractionary fiscal policy reduces inflation, improves competitiveness, and decreases income, which reduces imports. Improved competitiveness and decreased income both work to reduce the trade deficit. Contractionary monetary policy would also reduce the trade deficit, but its effect on competitiveness is ambiguous.

   b. If interest rates have also fallen, it is likely that fiscal policy has been very contractionary because contractionary monetary policy would have led to higher interest rates and a higher exchange rate value of the dollar.

2. a. Expansionary monetary policy will reduce the exchange rate through its effect on interest rates and will increase domestic income. Expansionary fiscal policy will increase domestic income. The increase in income will increase imports, which will tend to decrease the exchange rate, but higher interest rates will tend to lead to a higher exchange rate. The effect of expansionary fiscal policy on exchange rates is therefore ambiguous.

b. Contractionary fiscal policy will tend to reduce inflation and interest rates. The reduction in inflation will improve competitiveness and a reduction in income will reduce imports. Both work to reduce the trade deficit.

c. Expansionary monetary policy will reduce unemployment and reduce interest rates. Lower interest rates will tend to make exchange rates fall. Expansionary monetary policy, however, will make the trade deficit higher. Expansionary fiscal policy will also reduce unemployment. Interest rates, however, will rise and so will the trade deficit. This mix of goals is difficult to attain.

ANSWERS

MULTIPLE CHOICE

1. c   The answer is "sometimes a low and sometimes a high exchange rate" because there are rationales for both.

2. c   The domestic economy's needs change over time and as they do, so does the country's preferred trade situation. Both a deficit and a surplus have their advantages and disadvantages.

3. a   Contractionary monetary policy will increase the demand for one's currency and increase its value. Contractionary fiscal policy will reduce the supply of the currency and increase its value. Contractionary monetary and fiscal policy are two ways to fix the exchange rate without intervening in the exchange market.

4. a   Both expansionary monetary policy and expansionary fiscal policy increase the trade deficit. Thus, only a fits.

5. d   See the discussion and diagram in the text.

6. c   See diagram in the text.

7. c   The effect of fiscal policy on the exchange rate is ambiguous, so the only sure option is c. See "A Reminder" box in the text.

8. b   As discussed in the text usually, because of political considerations, domestic goals win out.

9. b   Since the trade deficit means capital is flowing into the country, the capital usually ends up as buying some government debt, which reduces crowding out.

10. b   When exchange rates are left to the market (flexible), the government does not have to change its domestic policy to meet its international goal for its exchange rate. Therefore, it is freer to follow domestic policy when exchange rates are flexible.

11. c   If the price of the dollar falls significantly in the forex market, policy makers will likely be under pressure to slow the fall and prevent inflation, which means that they will have to face the possibility of implementing contractionary policy to keep the dollar from falling too much. The other options are not ones associated with a falling price of the dollar.

—— ANSWERS ——

POTENTIAL ESSAY QUESTIONS

The following are annotated answers. They indicate the general idea behind the answer.

1. A stronger dollar means that a single dollar will now buy more units of a foreign currency. This makes foreign products cheaper to Americans. The United States would import more. At the same time, a stronger dollar means it will now take more units of a foreign currency to buy a single dollar. This will cause U.S. goods to become more expensive to foreigners. The United States would export less. The combined effects of more U.S. imports and fewer U.S. exports mean a trade deficit will be created or will get larger in the United States.

2. A strong dollar holds down the price of imports and therefore inflation. However, the cost is a trade deficit that would have a depressing effect on total spending and therefore on the nation's income level (there would be an especially depressing effect on the nation's exporting industries).

3. First, there is more agreement on domestic goals. Second, domestic goals affect people within one's country more directly and they are the ones who vote for elected officials who determine policy. Finally, pursuing domestic goals is politically more appealing.

STRUCTURAL STAGNATION AND GLOBALIZATION

CHAPTER AT A GLANCE

1. Structural stagnation is a hypothesis about the macro economy that sees the U.S.'s slow recovery as being caused by globalization accompanied by large trade deficits.

   For an economy to return to its potential output after a recession, it must grow at a higher rate than the economy declined because it must make up lost output as well as the rise in potential output that keeps the economy on its trend. See Figure 37-2.

   The secular stagnation theory was a theory in which advanced countries such as the United States would eventually stop growing because investment opportunities would be eliminated.

   Structural stagnation is different; it focuses instead on globalization accompanied by large trade deficits as the cause of slowdown.

2. With the structural stagnation hypothesis trend growth is 2 to 2.5%, which is lower than the standard growth rate of 3%.

   To return to its long-term trend, growth must be greater than the decline in output during the recession. The economy has not done so.

3. The structural stagnation model can be represented in a globalized AS/AD model that adds a flat world supply curve (WAS) at the world price level (P_w) below the domestic equilibrium price level (P_D) as shown in the graph in the next column. This reduces a country's potential output (from LAS_0 to LAS_1) while increasing its domestic consumption (from Y_0 to Y_2). Domestic production falls from Y_0 to Y_1. The difference between consumption and domestic production ($Y_2 - Y_1$) is the trade deficit.

   Remember, the WAS curve must be below the domestic price level for there to be a trade deficit.

   Potential output falls because domestic consumption limits what firms can sell, and therefore firms cut production. It's not a cyclical phenomenon.

   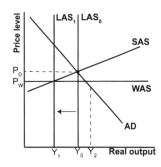

4. Three adjustments that would reduce the trade deficit are:
   ● Reduce the value of the dollar.
   ● Reduce relative wages and costs.
   ● Reduce aggregate demand.

   All three alternatives have costs. To lower production costs, workers will have to accept lower wages. Lowering the exchange rate will lead to domestic inflation, and contractionary policy will lower overall consumption.

   Expansionary policy that keeps aggregate demand high keeps these adjustments from occurring. While expansionary policies will not lead to goods inflation, they could lead to another financial bubble.

5. Expansionary fiscal and monetary policies have slowed the adjustments necessary to bring the economy to international equilibrium, and have

contributed to asset price inflation and a financial bubble.

The globalized AS/AD model relates to tradable goods. The nontradable sector is not directly affected by the world price level.

6. Eliminating structural stagnation will require workers in the tradable sector to either learn new globally competitive skills or accept lower wages. The adjustments will likely be slow and unpleasant. Eventually workers in the non-tradable sector will have to accept lower wages as well.

    Globalization makes income distribution less equal. International traders gain tremendously and workers in uncompetitive trade sectors lose the most. Those working in the nontradable sector have been hurt somewhat.

    Remember, globalization has its benefits—the ability to consume more goods at low prices and increased specialization that stimulates productivity.

7. Government has limited tools to address structural stagnation without creating more problems.

    Policies that will deal with structural stagnation include : policies that
    - *address the housing overhang.*
    - *lower the exchange rate.*
    - *slow U.S. wage growth.*
    - *raise trade restrictions (undesirable policy).*
    - *increase productivity.*

    See also Appendix "A: Creating a Targeted Safety Net to Help the Least Well Off."

SHORT-ANSWER QUESTIONS

1. How is a structural stagnation different from a standard recession?

2. What is the difference between the structural stagnation view of trend growth and the conventional view?

3. In the structural stagnation hypothesis, once structural changes related to globalization are complete, what is expected to happen to economic growth in the United States? What will have happened to the U.S. share of global output?

4. Demonstrate the globalized AS/AD model with a trade deficit. What is true about the world aggregate supply curve relative to the domestic price level?

5. Demonstrate the effect of contractionary policy in the globalized AS/AD model.

6. According to the structural stagnation hypothesis, why didn't policy makers realize that the economy had exceeded potential output?

7. What is the value-added chain and how does it relate to globalization?

8. Name three policies the government can implement to deal with the long-run structural problems facing the United States. Demonstrate the effects of these policies in the globalized AS/AD model.

MATCHING THE TERMS
Match the terms to their definitions

___ 1. commodities

___ 2. globalization

___ 3. globalized AS/AD model

___ 4. reservation wage

___ 5. secular stagnation theory

___ 6. stagflation

___ 7. structural stagnation hypothesis

___ 8. value-added chain

___ 9. world supply curve

a. An hypothesis of the macro economy that sees the recent problems of the U.S. economy to be directly related to the structural problems caused by globalization.

b. A theory in which advanced countries such as the United States would eventually stop growing because investment opportunities would be eliminated.

c. The increasing economic connections among economies around the world that increase competition among countries.

d. The standard AS/AD model with an added world supply curve that captures the effect that globalization can have on an economy.

e. The amount of tradable goods that other countries in the world will supply to the country at a given price level and exchange rate.

f. Homogeneous goods that could be produced in a variety of countries without any special skills and shipped at a low cost.

g. The movement of trade from low-skill manufacturing to more and more complicated goods and services.

h. The combination of stagnation and inflation.

i. The lowest wage that a person needs to receive to accept a job.

PROBLEMS AND APPLICATIONS

1. An economy with output $20 trillion with trend growth of 3 percent enters a recession in which output declines by 2 percent in one year. What are the following values?

    a. The level of output that must be recovered due to the recession.

    b. The level of output that must be recovered to stay on a 3 percent long-run growth trend if the economy returns to its trend within 2 years.

    c. Demonstrate your answer to parts *a* and *b* graphically.

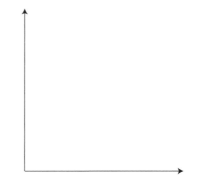

2. Using the graph below, show an economy in domestic equilibrium that does not trade with the world.

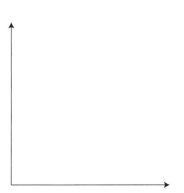

  a. How does your graph change with globalization where the world price level is below the domestic price level? Demonstrate your answer graphically

  b. Label the resulting trade deficit.

  c. Demonstrate the effect on potential output.

  d. Label consumption before and after globalization.

3. What is the effect of the following on the globalized AS/AD model?

  a. The United States discovers natural resources that will largely be exported.

  b. Workers lower their reservation wages.

  c. Government implements contractionary policies.

4. What is the effect of expansionary monetary and fiscal policy in the globalized AS/AD model on the following?

  a. Inflation.

  b. Trade deficit.

  c. Unemployment.

  d. Asset prices.

5. What policies would address the following short-run structural problems?

  a. Housing inventory overhang.

  b. Unwinding expansionary policies.

MULTIPLE CHOICE

Circle the one best answer for each of the following questions:

1. According to the structural stagnation hypothesis, what is the long-run cause of the recent problems facing the United States?
  a. Globalization.
  b. Too low investment.
  c. Inflation.
  d. Unemployment.

2. According to the structural stagnation hypothesis, expansionary macro policy tends to lead to:
  a. goods inflation.
  b. goods deflation.
  c. asset price inflation.
  d. low exchange rates.

3. Suppose an economy's trend growth rate is 3% and current output is $10 trillion. If the economy enters a recession where output declines by 5% in one year, by how much does output have to rise to return the economy back to its trend? Assume it takes two years for the economy to return to its trend.
   a. $0.5 trillion.
   b. $0.6 trillion.
   c. $1.4 trillion.
   d. $1.7 trillion.

4. What is the difference between the structural stagnation hypothesis and secular stagnation theory?
   a. Structural stagnation sees globalization as the cause of a stagnation, while secular stagnation sees too little investment as the cause.
   b. Structural stagnation sees too little investment as the cause of a stagnation, while secular stagnation sees globalization as the cause.
   c. Structural stagnation sees foreign countries moving down the value-added change as the cause of a stagnation, while secular stagnation sees foreign countries moving up the value-added chain as the cause of a stagnation.
   d. There is no difference; they both attribute stagnation to too little investment.

5. Refer to the graph on the top of the next column. According to the globalized AS/AD model, which best represents to the world aggregate supply and trade in the 1970s?
   a. WAS_0 and the United States had a large trade surplus.
   b. WAS_1 and the United States had a large trade deficit.
   c. WAS_2 and the United States had a small trade deficit.
   d. WAS_3 and the United States had a small trade deficit.

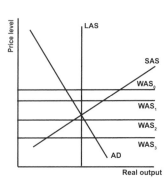

6. Refer to the above graph for Question #5. According to the globalized AS/AD model, which best represents to the world aggregate supply and trade in the 2000s?
   a. WAS_0 and the United States had a large trade surplus.
   b. WAS_1 and the United States had a small trade deficit.
   c. WAS_2 and the United States had a small trade surplus.
   d. WAS_3 and the United States had a large trade deficit.

7. According to the globalized AS/AD model, expansionary monetary policy shifts the AD curve to the right and:
   a. increases goods inflation.
   b. has no effect on goods inflation.
   c. shifts potential output to the right.
   d. shifts potential output to the left.

8. The globalized AS/AD model relates:
   a. to tradable goods only.
   b. directly to both tradable and nontradable goods.
   c. to tradable services only.
   d. directly to tradable and indirectly to nontradable goods.

9. Adding globalization with large trade deficits to the standard AS/AD model shows:
   a. reduced domestic production and consumption.
   b. increased domestic production and consumption.
   c. increased domestic production and reduced consumption.
   d. decreased domestic production and increased consumption.

10. Which of the following would help address structural stagnation problems?
    a. Expansionary macro policy.
    b. Contractionary macro policy.
    c. A decrease in workers' reservation wages.
    d. An increase in workers' reservation wages.

11. According to the structural stagnation hypothesis, if world prices decline and domestic prices do not change:
    a. the AD curve shifts to the left.
    b. the AD curve shifts to the right.
    c. the domestic LAS curve shifts to the left.
    d. the domestic LAS curve shifts to the right.

12. Expansionary government policies during a period of increasing globalization:
    a. increases unemployment in both the nontradeable and tradable sectors.
    b. decreases unemployment in both the nontradeable and tradable sectors.
    c. decreases unemployment in the tradable sector but leaves unemployment in the nontradable sector unchanged.
    d. decreases unemployment in the nontradable sector and leaves unemployment in the tradable sector unchanged.

13. Which group most benefited from globalization?
    a. International traders and those associated with them.
    b. Workers in the "commodities" sector.
    c. Workers in the nontradable goods sector.
    d. No one benefited.

14. Which of the following would help eliminate the trade deficit?
    a. Reduced reservation wages.
    b. A rise in the exchange rate.
    c. Expansionary fiscal policy.
    d. Lower tariffs.

15. Refer to the graph on the top of the next column. The economy:
    a. is experiencing structural stagnation.
    b. is experiencing secular stagnation.
    c. has a trade deficit.
    d. has a trade surplus.

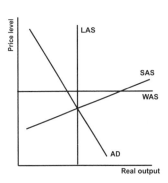

16. Which of the following would make the effects of globalization worse for the United States?
    a. China and India move up the value-added chain.
    b. China and India move down the value-added chain.
    c. China and India raise the value of their currencies.
    d. Wages in China and India rise, leading to more outsourcing.

POTENTIAL ESSAY QUESTIONS

You may also see essay questions similar to the "Problems & Applications" exercises.

1. Why do you suppose secular stagnation theory gained popularity in the 1940s and the structural stagnation hypothesis in the 2000s?

2. Why is the trend growth rate important to policy?

3. If a dynamic economy, according to Joseph Schumpeter, always faces some structural adjustments as an economy evolves, why are structural adjustments today leading to lower growth today compared to its long-term trend?

ANSWERS

SHORT-ANSWER QUESTIONS

1. Structural stagnation is a long-term readjustment of the economy to deal with global competition. It means a much longer recovery with more unemployment than a standard recession and it makes demand-side fiscal policy less effective.

2. The conventional view is that trend growth can continue at a constant level of about 3%. The structural stagnation view is that the rate of growth has slowed to 2.25% and will not recover for several decades.

3. Once structural changes are complete, U.S. growth is expected to return to its long-term growth of 3% a year. By then, however, the U.S. will have a much smaller share of global output than it did before.

4. The world aggregate supply curve must be at a lower price level than the domestic one, in this case domestic prices are P_D and world prices are P_W. The trade deficit is $Y_2 - Y_1$. Without this, there would be no trade deficit.

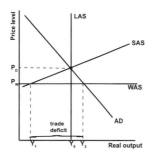

5. Contractionary policy results in a leftward shift of the aggregate demand curve from AD_0 to AD_1. This change reduces domestic consumption from Y_0 to Y_1. The trade deficit falls from $Y_0 - Y_2$ to $Y_1 - Y_2$. It has no effect on domestic tradable production.

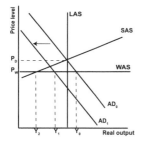

6. Policymakers did not realize that the economy had exceeded potential output because the economy was growing at 3% per year without significant goods inflation. Since economists use goods inflation as an indicator that the economy has exceeded inflation, they did not see the economy as having exceeded potential.

7. The value-added chain is the movement of trade from low-skill manufacturing to more and more complicated goods and services. As countries rise on the chain, they are competitive in a greater number of goods, which may extend the effects of globalization in developed countries if these foreign countries can produce these goods at lower prices than can domestic producers.

8. Three policies is for the exchange rate to depreciate, a cut in unemployment benefits that lowers domestic reservation wages, and a rise in tariffs. A lower exchange rate raises the WAS curve from WAS_0 to WAS_1 as shown in the graph below. Domestic production rises from Y_1 to Y_3 and the trade deficit falls from $(Y_0 - Y_1)$ to $(Y_2 - Y_3)$.

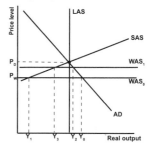

Another possibility is to cut unemployment benefits, which will pressure workers to lower their reservation wages and lower the SAS curve from SAS_0 to SAS_1. This raises domestic production from Y_1 to Y_2, which lowers the trade deficit from $(Y_0 - Y_1)$ to $(Y_0 - Y_2)$. A third policy is to raise tariffs, which like the first policy will shift the WAS curve up.

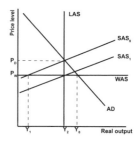

ANSWERS

MATCHING

1-f; 2-c; 3-d; 4-i; 5-b; 6-h; 7-a; 8-g; 9-e.

ANSWERS

PROBLEMS AND APPLICATIONS

1. a. Output fell $0.4 trillion to $19.6 trillion due to the recession ($20 x .98). Output must rise by $0.4 trillion to recover lost output due to the recession.

b. During the one-year recession and two year recovery, trend output rose to $21.9 trillion. So, it must make up $2.3 trillion (0.4 + 1.9) to remain on its growth path.

c. Output must rise by length 1 to make up for lost output and length 2 to make up for the rise in potential output.

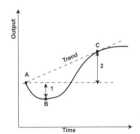

2. See the graph below. A country that does not trade is represented by curves WAS_0, LAS_0, SAS and AD curves that all intersect at the same location.

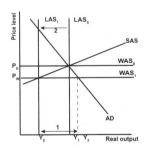

a. Globalization with a world price level below the domestic price level is reflected with a WAS curve below the domestic price, in this graph, WAS_1.

b. The trade deficit is shown by length 1, or $Y_2 - Y_0$.

c. Potential output shifts to the left from LAS_0 to LAS_1.

d. Consumption after globalization increases from Y_1 to Y_2.

3. a. An economy that discovers a significant natural resource that can be exported will push the trade balance toward surplus, which will push the value of its currency up. This raises the costs of its other tradable goods to foreign countries, leading to unemployment in those tradable sectors. To the degree that the resources use fewer workers than those other sectors, it increases unemployment.

b. Lower reservation wages lower the SAS curve, reducing the trade deficit and increasing domestic production.

c. Contractionary policies shift the AD curve to the left, improving the trade deficit but leaving domestic production unchanged.

4. a. Expansionary policies do not affect inflation since the world price level puts a cap on domestic prices.

b. Expansionary policies increase domestic consumption, which is met by increased imports. The trade deficit rises and domestic production does not change.

c. Expansionary policies do not affect unemployment in the tradable sector, even though it increases the trade deficit. The policies may reduce unemployment in the nontradable sector.

d. Expansionary policies may increase asset prices.

5. a. Policies that make it easier for banks to restructure their loans and to temporarily rent houses to "underwater" homeowners.

b. The unwinding of expansionary policies will slow the economy, a situation policy makers will have to accept. One possibility is to unwind the policies slowly.

■■■ ANSWERS ■■■

MULTIPLE CHOICE

1. a Globalization is the cause. Too low investment is the explanation for secular stagnation.

2. c With the structural stagnation hypothesis, goods inflation is held down by the world price level. Inflation due to expansionary policies, tends to show up in asset inflations.

3. c It must make up for the decline in output due to the recession, or $0.5 trillion—($10 x .05). During the one-year recession and 2 years of recovery, trend output rose by $0.9 trillion to $10.9 trillion (10 x 1.03 x 1.03 x 1.03). The total rise in output required is $1.4 trillion (0.5 + 0.9).

4. a Structural stagnation hypothesis focuses on globalization while secular stagnation focuses on investment. While structural stagnation points to the value-added change, foreign countries moving up (not down) the chain contribute to a structural stagnation.

5. c The country had a small deficit, which can only occur if the world price level is below the domestic price level as it is with WAS_2 and WAS_3. c is the right answer because the trade deficit was small in the 1970s. When the WAS curve is above the domestic price level, the country has a trade surplus.

6. d The country had a large deficit, which can only occur if the world price level is below the domestic price level as it is with WAS_3. When the WAS curve is above the domestic price level, the country has a trade surplus.

7. b Because the world price level puts a cap on domestic prices, expansionary policy will not cause inflation. It will only shift the AD curve to the right and make the trade deficit worse. Potential output is unaffected.

8. d Globalization affects the tradable goods market directly and nontradable goods indirectly. The effect on tradable goods is direct because that sector competes directly with imports. Nontradable goods do not compete with imports, but are still affected by globalization, just indirectly.

9. d The lower world price level is represented by a movement down along the AD curve. Consumption increases. Because the price level is lower than the domestic price level, the quantity of aggregate supply falls.

10. c In the globalized AS/AD model, changes in macro policies would not address structural problems because it would not affect the domestic price level and therefore domestic production. Falling reservation wages address structural problems because it makes the economy more competitive.

11. c Lower world prices further reduces the amount of goods domestic producers can sell, essentially shifting the LAS curve to the left. While consumption will increase (movement along the AD curve), a declining world price level does not shift the AD curve.

12. d The answer is d because expansionary policy increases imports while leaving domestic production of tradables un-changed while increasing demand for nontradables since they cannot be imported.

13. a Since global trade increased and the U.S. has a comparative advantage in facilitating trade, globalization has benefited interna-tional traders.

14. a A higher exchange rate makes foreign goods less expensive, which would raise the trade deficit. Lowering tariffs makes foreign goods cheaper, worsening the trade deficit. Reducing reservation wages decreases domestic costs, making domestic goods more competitive.

15. d   Because world prices are higher than domestic prices, domestic producers can sell their goods abroad and fulfill all domestic production. There is a trade surplus.

16. a   When countries move up the value-added chain, they can compete on a wider range of goods, worsening the effect of globalization. A rise in the value of foreign currencies is the same as the domestic currency depreciating, which lowers the relative value of domestic goods.

ANSWERS

POTENTIAL ESSAY QUESTIONS

The following are annotated answers. They indicate the general idea behind the answer.

1. The main reason is that both offered an explanation for contemporary declines in growth that fit global economic conditions at the time. In the 1940s, the U.S. was by a wide margin the wealthiest economy in the world and its weak postwar growth motivated many to find an idea that explained why the wealthiest economy in the world would grow slowly. Secular stagnation, which stated that a lack of productive investment opportunities in an advanced economy would slow growth, fit the conditions and became popular. Similarly, structural stagnation today reflects globalization, the dominant economic force of the past decade. The structural stagnation hypothesis uses the importance of globalization to explain current economic outcomes. Unsurprisingly, the theory will be popular until new evidence contradicts its predictions.

2. The trend growth rate is important to policy because it affects expectations and, by extension, policy choices. If policy makers have assumed an incorrect trend growth rate, then they may take action to move the economy to their assumed path when it could be growing at its trend. If the assumed trend growth rate is higher than actual, then they will use expansionary policies. As we have seen, such policies can divert investment and create asset bubbles when they push the economy above its potential. If the assumed trend is too low, then the government will curtail growth and induce a recession unnecessarily. Therefore, the trend growth rate is immensely important to the formulation of government policy because an incorrect trend can lead to harmful policies.

3. Structural adjustments today are leading to lower growth than before because external conditions require more significant adjustments. Schumpeter's "creative destruction" usually involves the destruction of certain industries, like typewriter manufacturers, as more advanced ones, such as computers, emerge. The typical structural changes were relatively isolated and did not result in major employment outflows from the United States. The changes identified by the structural stagnation hypothesis are different in that they point to international competition as the major problem and a long-term adjustment of wages and prices to correct it. Unlike typical structural adjustments, this involves weak growth and low employment in the United States for a prolonged period of time. Broadly, structural adjustments are usually much less severe. The specific conditions of globalization allow for structural stagnation and its low levels of growth.

MACRO POLICIES IN DEVELOPING COUNTRIES

38

CHAPTER AT A GLANCE

1. Eighty percent of the world's population lives in developing countries, with average per capita income of under $500 per year.

   Be careful in judging a society by its income alone. Some developing countries may have cultures preferable to ours. Ideally, growth would occur without destroying the culture.

2. There are differences in normative goals between developing and developed countries because their wealth differs. Developing countries face basic economic needs whereas developed countries' economic needs are considered by most people to be normatively less pressing.

   The main focus of macro policy in developing countries is on how to increase growth through development to fulfill people's basic needs.

3. Economies at different stages of development have different institutional needs because the problems they face are different. Institutions that can be assumed in developed countries cannot necessarily be assumed to exist in developing countries.

   Developed nations have stable governments and market structures, which are often lacking in developing countries.

4. "The dual economy" refers to the existence of the two sectors in most developing countries: a traditional sector and an internationally-oriented modern market sector.

   Often, the largest percentage of the population participates in the traditional sector. Tradition often resists change.

5. A régime change is a change in the entire atmosphere within which the government and the economy interrelate; a policy change is a change in one aspect of government's actions.

   A régime change and macro institutional policies designed to fit the cultural and social dimensions of developing economics are what developing economies need.

6. Central banks recognize that printing too much money causes inflation, but often feel compelled to do so for political reasons. Debate about inflation in developing countries generally concerns those political reasons, not the relationship between money and inflation.

   Governments in developing economies risk being thrown out of office unless they run deficits and issue too much money.

7. Full convertibility means one can exchange one's currency for whatever legal purpose one wants. Convertibility on the current account limits those exchanges for the purpose of buying goods and services.

   Very few developing countries allow full convertibility.

8. Seven obstacles facing developing countries are:
   1. Political instability.
   2. Corruption.
   3. Lack of appropriate institutions.
   4. Lack of investment.
   5. Inappropriate education.
   6. Overpopulation.
   7. Health and disease

   ✔ *Know why these are problems!*
   ✔ *The opposite constitutes the ingredients for growth. Remember them!*

● SHORT-ANSWER QUESTIONS

1. What percentage of the population of the world lives in developing countries?

2. What is the average per capita income in developing nations?

3. Why is there often a difference in the normative goals of developed and developing countries?

4. Why do economies at different stages of development often have different institutional needs? Explain.

5. What is the dual economy?

6. What is the difference between a régime change and a policy change?

7. "Inflation is simply a problem of central banks in developing countries issuing too much money." Is this true or false? Why?

8. What are two types of convertibility?

9. Economists can't tell developing countries, "Here's what you have to do to grow." But they can identify seven obstacles facing developing countries. What are they?

MATCHING THE TERMS
Match the terms to their definitions

___ **1.** balance of payments constraint	**a.**	A change in one aspect of a government's actions.
	b.	A change in the entire atmosphere within which the government and economy interrelate.
___ **2.** brain drain	**c.**	A stage when the development process becomes self-sustaining.
___ **3.** conditionality		
___ **4.** convertibility on the current account	**d.**	A system that allows people to exchange currencies for whatever legal purpose they want.
___ **5.** credentialism	**e.**	A system that allows people to exchange currencies for the purpose of buying goods and services only.
___ **6.** dual economy	**f.**	A system that places some limitation on people's ability to exchange currencies to buy assets.
___ **7.** economic takeoff	**g.**	Changing the underlying economic institutions.
___ **8.** foreign aid	**h.**	Funds that developed countries lend or give to developing countries.
___ **9.** full convertibility		
___ **10.** inflation tax	**i.**	Investment in the underlying structure of the economy.
___ **11.** infrastructure investment	**j.**	Limitations on expansionary domestic macroeconomic policy due to a shortage of international reserves.
	k.	Method of comparing income by looking at the domestic purchasing power of money in different countries.
___ **12.** limited capital account convertibility	**l.**	Outflow of the best and brightest students from developing countries to developed countries.
___ **13.** policy change	**m.**	The degrees become more important than the knowledge learned.
___ **14.** purchasing power parity		
___ **15.** régime change	**n.**	The existence of two sectors: a traditional sector and an internationally-oriented modern market sector.
___ **16.** restructuring	**o.**	The making of loans that are subject to specific conditions.
	p.	An implicit tax on the holders of cash and the holders of any obligation specified in nominal terms.

● MULTIPLE CHOICE

Circle the one best answer for each of the following questions:

1. Annual GDP per capita is about ____ in developing countries and ____ in the United States.
    a. $50; $20,000.
    b. $500; $60,000.
    c. $50; $10,000.
    d. $4,000; $20,000.

2. Two methods of comparing income among countries are the purchasing power parity method and the exchange rate method. Of these:

    a. the exchange rate method generally gives a higher relative measure of the income in developing countries.
    b. the purchasing power parity method generally gives a higher relative measure of the income in developing countries.
    c. the purchasing power parity and exchange rate methods generally give approximately equal measures of the income in developing countries.
    d. sometimes one gives a higher relative measure of income in developing countries, and sometimes the other gives a higher relative measure.

3. The concept "dual economy" refers to:
    a. the tendency of developed countries to have a traditional sector and an internationally-oriented sector.
    b. the tendency of both developed and developing countries to have a traditional sector and an internationally-oriented sector.
    c. the tendency of developing countries to have a traditional sector and an internationally-oriented sector.
    d. the fight, or dual, between developed and undeveloped countries.

4. If a country changes its entire approach to policy, that is called:
    a. a major policy change.
    b. a policy change.
    c. a régime change.
    d. a constitutional change.

5. The inflation tax is:
    a. a tax on those individuals who cause inflation.
    b. a tax on firms who cause inflation.
    c. a tax on both individuals and firms who cause inflation.
    d. a tax on holders of cash and any obligations specified in nominal terms.

6. The "revenue" of an inflation tax:
    a. goes only to government.
    b. goes only to private individuals.
    c. goes to both private individuals and government.
    d. is a meaningless term because there is no revenue from an inflation tax.

7. If you hold a fixed interest rate debt denominated in domestic currency and inflation rises more than expected, you will:
    a. likely lose.
    b. likely gain.
    c. likely experience no effect from the large inflation.
    d. find that the large inflation could cause you either to gain or to lose.

8. If you hold a fixed interest rate debt denominated in a foreign currency and the exchange rate remains constant, and there is a large domestic inflation, you will:
    a. likely lose some.
    b. likely gain some.
    c. likely lose all your debt.
    d. likely experience little direct effect from the large inflation.

9. Conditionality refers to:
    a. the U.S. government's policy of only making loans to countries who will repay loans.
    b. the IMF's policy of making loans to countries subject to specific conditions.
    c. central banks' policies of making loans to firms only under certain conditions.
    d. the conditions under which inter-firm credit is allowed in transitional economies.

10. Foreign aid is:
    a. the primary source of income of the poorest developing countries.
    b. one of the top three sources of income of the poorest developing countries.
    c. one of the top three sources of income of developing countries who have ties to the United States.
    d. a minor source of income for developing countries.

11. The nickname for economics as "the dismal science" caught on because:
    a. the law of diminishing marginal productivity predicted the population tends to outrun the means of subsistence.
    b. the law of diseconomies of scale predicted the population tends to outrun the means of subsistence.
    c. learning supply and demand economic models is dismal.
    d. it predicted that economic takeoff would seldom be reached.

12. Which of the following best represents the textbook author's view of development?
    a. Optimal strategies for growth are country-specific.
    b. A country's development strategy should include as much education as possible.

c. Countries should focus on infrastructure investment.

d. Countries should follow a policy of laissez-faire.

POTENTIAL ESSAY QUESTIONS

You may also see essay questions similar to the "Problems & Applications" exercises.

1.   What is the difference between economic development and economic growth?

2.   What are some institutional differences between developed and developing countries that make it difficult for developing countries to develop?

3.   Why is it that no developing country allows full convertibility?

ANSWERS

SHORT-ANSWER QUESTIONS

1. 80 percent of the population of the world lives in developing countries.

2. The average per capita income in developing countries is about $500 per year.

3. Developing countries face true economic needs. Their concern is with basic needs such as adequate clothing, food, and shelter. Developed countries' needs are considered less pressing. For example, will everyone have access to a DVD player?

4. Economies at different stages of development have different institutional needs because the problems they face are different. Institutions that can be assumed in developed countries cannot necessarily be assumed to exist in developing countries. For example, developing countries often lack the institutional structure that markets require.

5. Dual economy refers to the existence of the two distinct sectors in most developing countries: a traditional sector and an internationally-oriented modern market sector.

6. A régime change is a change in the entire atmosphere within which the government and the economy interrelate; a policy change is a change in one aspect of government's actions. A régime change affects underlying expectations about what the government will do in the future; a policy change does not.

7. Any simple statement is generally false, and this one is no exception. The reason why this one is false is that while it is true that inflation is closely tied to the developing country's central bank issuing too much money, the underlying problem behind the central bank's actions is often large government deficits that cannot be financed unless the central bank issues debt and then buys the bonds, which requires an increase in the money supply (printing money to pay for the bonds).

8. Two types of convertibility are full convertibility and current account convertibility. Full convertibility means you can change your money into another currency with no restrictions. Current account convertibility allows exchange of currency to buy goods but not to invest outside the country. Many developing countries have current account convertibility, but not full convertibility.

9. Seven problems facing developing countries are (1) governments in developing countries are often unstable, (2) governments in developing countries are often corrupt, (3) developing countries often lack appropriate institutions to promote growth, (4) developing countries often lack the domestic savings to fund investment for growth, (5) developing countries tend to have too much of the wrong education, (6) developing countries are often overpopulated so that raising per capita income is difficult, and (7) people in developing countries have limited access to healthcare and face greater incidence of disease.

ANSWERS

MATCHING

1-j; 2-l; 3-o; 4-e; 5-m; 6-n; 7-c; 8-h; 9-d; 10-p; 11-i; 12-f; 13-a; 14-k; 15-b; 16-g.

ANSWERS

MULTIPLE CHOICE

1. b   As stated in the text, b is the closest.

2. b   The purchasing power parity method of comparing income cuts income differences among countries in half.

3. c   See the text for the definition of dual economy. Choice d was put in to throw you off. When the word means "a fight" it is, of course, spelled "duel."

4. c   See text.

5. d.   The answer has to be d. The individuals and firms who cause the inflation are gaining from the inflation; they pay no inflation tax.

6. c The only answer that makes any sense is c. The "revenue" goes from holders of fixed nominal interest rate debt to those who owe that debt. Those who owe the debt include both private individuals and government.

7. a Unexpected inflation wipes out the value of fixed interest rate debt.

8. d Because the debt is denominated in a foreign currency and exchange rates remain constant, what happens to the domestic price level does not directly affect you. There could be indirect effects, but d specifies direct effects.

9. b See text.

10. d Total foreign aid comes to about $28 per person for developing countries. While this does not preclude b or c, it makes it very difficult for them to be true, and in fact, they are not true.

11. a The nickname "the dismal science" was used by Thomas Carlyle in an attack on economists for their views against slavery. It became a popular description of economics however largely because of the writings of Thomas Malthus, whose model of population focused on the law of diminishing marginal productivity and led to the prediction that society's prospects were dismal because population tends to outrun the means of subsistence.

12. a The author believes the problems of economic development are intertwined with cultural and social issues and hence are country-specific. The other answers do not necessarily fail to reflect the author's viewpoint, but he presented arguments on both sides when discussing them. Thus, a is the best answer.

ANSWERS

POTENTIAL ESSAY QUESTIONS

The following are annotated answers. They indicate the general idea behind the answer.

1. Growth occurs because of an increase in inputs, given a production function. Development occurs through a change in the production function. Development involves more fundamental changes in the institutional structure than does growth.

2. First, developing nations often lack stable, socially-minded governments with which to undertake policy. Second, developing economies often have a dual economy, that is, a traditional and an international sector. This can create some policy dilemmas. A third difference is the way in which fiscal policy is run. Collecting taxes can be very difficult in developing countries. Expenditures are often mandated by political survival.

3. One reason is that they want to force their residents to keep their savings, and to do their investing, in their home country, not abroad. (Remember that saving is necessary for investment, and investment is necessary for growth.) These citizens usually don't want to do this because of the risks of leaving their money in their own countries; a new government takeover could possibly take it all away.

Pretest
Chapters 9-10 and 35-38

Take this test in test conditions, giving yourself a limited amount of time to complete the questions. Ideally, check with your professor to see how much time he or she allows for an average multiple choice question and multiply this by 28. This is the time limit you should set for yourself for this pretest. If you do not know how much time your teacher would allow, we suggest 1 minute per question, or about 28 minutes.

1. Country A's cost of widgets is $4.00 and cost of wadgets is $8.00. Country B's cost of widgets is 8 euros and cost of wadgets is 16 euros. Which of the following would you suggest?
   a. Country A should specialize in widgets and Country B in wadgets.
   b. Trade of widgets for wadgets would not benefit the countries.
   c. Country A should specialize in wadgets and Country B in widgets.
   d. Both countries should produce an equal amount of each.

2. In the United States, globalization has caused workers in the education, healthcare, and government sectors to face:
   a. lower wages.
   b. higher prices on consumer goods.
   c. little or no downward pressure on their wages.
   d. longer hours to compete with the higher production levels abroad.

3. Transferable comparative advantages are:
   a. based on factors that are relatively unchangeable.
   b. based on factors that can change relatively easily.
   c. becoming more like inherent comparative advantages with technological innovations.
   d. rarely eroded over time.

4. In the graph in the following column, the value of the dollar is:

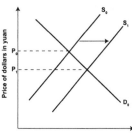

   a. appreciating because the dollar buys more yuan.
   b. depreciating because the dollar buys more yuan.
   c. appreciating because the dollar buys fewer yuan.
   d. depreciating because the dollar buys fewer yuan.

5. Which of the following would raise the world price level facing the United States?
   a. The dollar appreciates.
   b. The dollar depreciates.
   c. The trade deficit rises.
   d. The trade deficit falls.

6. If a country has a trade deficit, it is:
   a. consuming more than it is producing.
   b. lending to foreigners.
   c. buying financial assets.
   d. buying real assets.

7. In the graph below, which area represents the revenue collected by government if it imposes a tariff T?
   a. A.
   b. B.
   c. B and C.
   d. A and B.

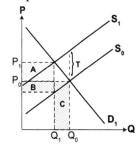

8. Economists generally oppose trade restrictions for all of the following reasons *except:*
   a. from a global perspective, free trade increases total output.
   b. the infant industry argument.
   c. trade restrictions lead to retaliation.
   d. international politics.

9. If a country has perfectly flexible exchange rates and is running a current account deficit, it is running:
   a. a financial and capital account surplus.
   b. a financial and capital account deficit.
   c. a government financial account surplus.
   d. a government financial account deficit.

10. Assuming flexible exchange rates, if the European demand for U.S. imports increases, one would expect the price of euros in terms of dollars to:
    a. rise.
    b. fall.
    c. remain unchanged.
    d. sometimes rise and sometimes fall.

11. If U.S. income increases:

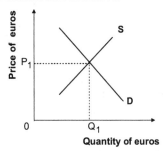

    a. the supply curve will shift out to the right.
    b. the supply curve will shift in to the left.
    c. the demand curve will shift out to the right.
    d. the demand curve will shift in to the left.

12. If a country with flexible exchange rates runs expansionary monetary policy, in the short run one would expect the value of its exchange rate to:
    a. rise.
    b. fall.
    c. be unaffected.
    d. sometimes rise and sometimes fall.

13. Say the Bangladeshi taka is valued at 42 taka to $1. Also say that you can buy the same basket of goods for 10 taka that you can buy for $1. In terms of dollars the purchasing power parity of the taka is:

a. overvalued.
b. undervalued.
c. not distorted.
d. nonconvertible.

14. Suppose inflation in the United States is 3 percent and inflation in Europe is 4 percent. If the U.S. dollar exchange rate falls by 5 percent relative to the euro, the real exchange rate of the dollar relative to the euro has:
    a. risen 2 percent.
    b. risen 6 percent.
    c. fallen 2 percent.
    d. fallen 6 percent.

15. If a country has a flexible exchange rate, the exchange rate:
    a. is determined by flexible government policy.
    b. is determined by market forces.
    c. fluctuates continually, changing by at least 1 percent per year.
    d. fluctuates continually, changing by at least 10 percent per year.

16. Compared to a fixed exchange rate system, a flexible exchange rate system:
    a. allows countries more flexibility in their monetary policies.
    b. allows countries less flexibility in their monetary policies.
    c. has no effect on monetary policies.
    d. allows countries more flexibility in their industrial policies.

17. If a country wants to maintain a fixed exchange rate above equilibrium, but does not have the necessary official reserves, it can:
    a. increase demand for its currency by running contractionary monetary policy.
    b. reduce supply of its currency by running expansionary monetary policy.
    c. increase demand for its currency by running contractionary fiscal policy.
    d. increase supply of its currency by running expansionary fiscal policy.

18. If the trade deficit has gone up, it is most likely that the government ran:
    a. an expansionary monetary policy.
    b. a contractionary monetary policy.
    c. a contractionary fiscal policy.
    d. an expansionary monetary policy and a contractionary fiscal policy.

19. Expansionary monetary policy tends to push income:
    a. down and the trade deficit down.
    b. down and the trade deficit up.
    c. up and the trade deficit down.
    d. up and the trade deficit up.

20. A country has the greatest domestic policy flexibility with:
    a. fixed exchange rates.
    b. flexible exchange rates.
    c. a trade deficit.
    d. a trade surplus.

21. According to the structural stagnation hypothesis, what is the long-run cause of the recent problems facing the United States?
    a. Globalization.
    b. Too low investment.
    c. Inflation.
    d. Unemployment.

22. What is the difference between the structural stagnation hypothesis and secular stagnation theory?
    a. Structural stagnation sees globalization as the cause of a stagnation, while secular stagnation sees too little investment as the cause.
    b. Structural stagnation sees too little investment as the cause of a stagnation, while secular stagnation sees globalization as the cause.
    c. Structural stagnation sees foreign countries moving down the value-added change as the cause of a stagnation, while secular stagnation sees foreign countries moving up the value-added chain as the cause of a stagnation.
    d. There is no difference; they both attribute stagnation to too little investment.

23. According to the globalized AS/AD model, expansionary monetary policy shifts the AD curve to the right and:
    a. increases goods inflation.
    b. has no effect on goods inflation.
    c. shifts potential output to the right.
    d. shifts potential output to the left.

24. Which of the following will help address structural stagnation problems?
    a. Expansionary macro policy.
    b. Contractionary macro policy.
    c. A decrease in workers' reservation wages.
    d. An increase in workers' reservation wages.

25. Which of the following would make the effects of globalization worse for the United States?
    a. China and India move up the value-added chain.
    b. China and India move down the value-added chain.
    c. China and India raise the value of their currencies.
    d. Wages in China and India rise, leading to more outsourcing.

26. The inflation tax is:
    a. a tax on those individuals who cause inflation.
    b. a tax on firms who cause inflation.
    c. a tax on both individuals and firms who cause inflation.
    d. a tax on holders of cash and any obligations specified in nominal terms.

27. Conditionality refers to:
    a. the U.S. government's policy of only making loans to countries who will repay loans.
    b. the IMF's policy of making loans to countries subject to specific conditions.
    c. central banks' policies of making loans to firms only under certain conditions.
    d. the conditions under which inter-firm credit is allowed in transitional economies.

28. The nickname for economics as "the dismal science" caught on because:
    a. the law of diminishing marginal productivity predicted the population tends to outrun the means of subsistence.
    b. the law of diseconomies of scale predicted the population tends to outrun the means of subsistence.
    c. learning supply and demand economic models is dismal.
    d. it predicted that economic takeoff would seldom be reached.

ANSWERS

1.	b	(9:5)	**15.**	b	(35:19)
2.	c	(9:8)	**16.**	a	(35:20)
3.	b	(9:9)	**17.**	a	(36:3)
4.	d	(9:13)	**18.**	a	(36:4)
5.	b	(9:15)	**19.**	d	(36:5)
6.	a	(10:4)	**20.**	b	(36:10)
7.	d	(10:10)	**21.**	a	(37:1)
8.	b	(10:14)	**22.**	a	(37:4)
9.	a	(35:1)	**23.**	b	(37:7)
10.	b	(35:7)	**24.**	c	(37:10)
11.	c	(35:8)	**25.**	a	(37:16)
12.	b	(35:11)	**26.**	d	(38:5)
13.	b	(35:16)	**27.**	b	(38:9)
14.	d	(35:17)	**28.**	a	(38:11)

Key: The figures in parentheses refer to multiple choice question and chapter numbers. For example (1:2) is multiple choice question 2 from chapter 1.